A NEW ACADEMIC COMPACT

A New Academic Compact

Revisioning the Relationship between Faculty and Their Institutions

LINDA A. MCMILLIN
Susquehanna University

JERRY BERBERET
Associated New American Colleges

Editors

Foreword by R. Eugene Rice

ANKER PUBLISHING COMPANY, INC.
Bolton, Massachusetts

A New Academic Compact
Revisioning the Relationship between Faculty and Their Institutions

ISBN 1-882982-44-4

Composition by Nicolazzo Productions
Cover design by Nicolazzo Productions

Anker Publishing Company, Inc.
176 Ballville Road
P. O. Box 249
Bolton, MA 01740-0249

www.ankerpub.com

Contents

About the Editors

About the Contributors

Participants

Foreword

Acknowledgments

Introduction

ABOUT THE EDITORS

LINDA A. MCMILLIN is Associate Professor and Head of the Department of History at Susquehanna University. She was Susquehanna's institutional representative to Phase I of the Associated New American Colleges' (ANAC) Faculty Work Project and served as project manager for Phase II. She is a medieval historian and author of a number of studies on religious women in twelfth and thirteenth century Barcelona. She is currently coediting a collection of essays on the tenth century canoness and playwright, Hrotsvit of Gandersheim.

WILLIAM G. (JERRY) BERBERET is founding Executive Director (1995) of the Associated New American Colleges (ANAC) at The Woodrow Wilson National Fellowship Foundation. He earned tenure as an American historian while active both in institutional governance and the faculty union movement. Later he held senior posts at three comprehensive institutions (SUNY-Plattsburgh, Willamette University, and North Central College) where his community outreach included leadership roles in the arts, humanities, and economic development. Besides American history, he has published articles and edited works on environmental history and policy, international studies, and higher education.

ABOUT THE CONTRIBUTORS

PATRICIA BACON was Vice President for Organizational Development at Butler University during the time of the change initiative about which she writes. During her 20 years with Butler University, she also held various administrative management positions setting goals and objectives for human resources functions and various other administration services. She is now in private practice as a consultant emphasizing strengths in designing organizational structures and processes using principles of organizational development and behavior to maximize alignment of individual potential with organizational goals.

ED BIGLIN is Professor of English at Saint Mary's College of California. A specialist in South African literature, he also directs the January term at the college. He represented St. Mary's in both phases of the Associated New American Colleges' (ANAC) Faculty Work Project.

GARRY BRODHEAD is Associate Provost and Dean of Graduate Studies at Ithaca College. A professor of music theory, his research is in the area of musical time and its perception. He has been active in teaching and learning initiatives at Ithaca College and campus leadership and governance for over two decades. He served as campus project leader for the Associated New American Colleges' (ANAC) Faculty Work Project.

MARY BURGAN is General Secretary of the American Association of University Professors (AAUP). She was professor of English at Indiana University where she served as chair of the English department.

ROBERT M. DIAMOND is President of The National Academy for Academic Leadership. He served for over 20 years as assistant vice chancellor for instructional development at Syracuse University, where he also was professor and director of the Institute for Change in Higher Education. From 1991 to 1999 he directed the National Project on Institutional Priorities and Faculty Rewards.

LAWRY FINSEN is Professor of Philosophy at the University of Redlands, where he has been teaching courses in such areas as Philosophy of Mind, Epistemology, Logic, Critical Thinking, and Ethics for 20 years. He now serves as associate dean of the College of Arts and Sciences at Redlands. Among his publications are two coauthored books: *The Animal Rights Movement in America: From Compassion to Respect* (Twayne, 1994, with Susan Finsen) and *The Persuasive Pen: An Integrated Approach to Reasoning and Writing* (Jones and Bartlett, 1997, with Nancy Carrick).

CHARLES E. GLASSICK is a Senior Scholar with the Carnegie Foundation.

CHRISTINE M. LICATA is a Senior Associate for the American Association for Higher Education (AAHE) and Associate Dean for Academic Affairs at Rochester Institute of Technology/National Technical Institute for the Deaf. Her work for AAHE has focused on post-tenure review.

THOMAS C. LONGIN is Vice President for Programs and Research for the Association of Governing Boards of Universities and Colleges (AGB). Prior to joining AGB in 1997, he served for 12 years as provost of Ithaca College. He also has served as vice president for academic affairs at Seattle University, as dean of the School of Humanities and Sciences at Ithaca College, and as a faculty member at Ithaca College, Virginia Tech, and Carroll College in Montana. He was a charter leader of the Associated New American Colleges (ANAC) and is a frequent presenter at conferences and workshops on issues of institutional governance, the basic responsibilities of governing boards, and board responsibility for governance, institutional planning, and academic affairs.

JACQUELINE A. MINTZ is founding Director of the Princeton University McGraw Center for Teaching and Learning. Previous to this position, she spent ten years as the founding director of the Graduate Student Instructor Teaching and Resource Center at the University of California, Berkeley. She is a Berkeley PhD in comparative literature. A focus of her research and writing in literature and higher education has been shame, values, and conflict and contradiction as they function in literature and impact pedagogy and professional development in the academy. She is a former chair of the Professional Development Committee of the Professional and Organizational Development (POD) Network in Higher Education.

MARION TERENZIO holds a joint academic appointment in the Divisions of Psychology and the Arts at the rank of professor at The Sage Colleges in Troy, New York. Currently, she is serving as Vice President for Campus Life at Sage and has been recently named an American Council on Education 2001–2002 National Fellow.

RIC WEIBL is Director of Programs for the Association of American Colleges and Universities. He also serves as Manager of the Preparing Future Faculty Program (PFF).

C. J. WEISER is Dean Emeritus of the College of Agriculture at Oregon State University.

JON WERGIN is Professor of Educational Studies at Virginia Commonwealth University and Senior Scholar with the American Association for Higher Education (AAHE). He was the founding director of the AAHE Forum on Faculty Roles and Rewards in 1992, and has conducted extensive research on the evaluation of faculty and academic programs. He is the author of *Departmental Assessment,* published by AAHE in 2000.

PARTICIPANTS
**Associated New American College
Faculty Work Project, Phase II**

Project Director
Jerry Berberet
Associated New American Colleges

Working Group Coordinators
Lawry Finsen
University of Redlands

Project Participants
Graeme Auton
University of Redlands
Michael Awalt
Belmont University
Deb Bickford
University of Dayton
Ed Biglin
St. Mary's College of California
Garry Brodhead
Ithaca College
Janet Brown
Valparaiso University
Elizabeth Burt
University of Hartford
Francis C. Dane
Mercer University
Don Davidson
Rollins College
Lynn Franken
Butler University
Jerry M. Greiner
Hamline University
Steve Kaplan
Butler University
Ed Kavanagh
Quinnipiac University
Warren Kosman
Valparaiso University

Project Manager
Linda A. McMillin
Susquehanna University

Marion Terenzio
The Sage Colleges

Jim Malek
Ithaca College
James Marshall
Quinnipiac University
Heather Mayne
University of the Pacific
Robert Morrow
University of the Pacific
Pat O'Connor
The Sage Colleges
Ray Posey
University of the Pacific
Alan Silva
Hamline University
George Sims
Belmont University
Catherine Stevenson
University of Hartford
Barbara Temple-Thurston
Pacific Lutheran University
Susan Traverso
North Central College
Ron Troyer
Drake University
Mark D. Wood
Drury University
R. Dean Wright
Drake University

Project Consultants

Zeddie Bowen
 University of Richmond
Amy Driscoll
 *California State University
 Monterey Bay*
Thomas C. Longin
 Association of Governing Boards
Allison Pingree
 Vanderbilt University

Jack Schuster
 Claremont Graduate School
Mary Deane Sorcinelli
 *University of Massachusetts
 Amherst*
Jon Wergin
 *Virginia Commonwealth
 University*

FOREWORD

The publication of this book could not have been better timed. The disconnection between faculty priorities and institutional purpose has been widely documented and highlighted in one national conference after another. The changes institutions of higher education and their faculties are confronting have been enumerated so frequently their recitation has become something of a litany. What is most needed now are concrete, campus-based solutions to the structural problems we are facing and constructive responses to the monumental changes about which we have been more than adequately warned. This is what you will find—presented in an especially refreshing way—in this call for *A New Academic Compact*. All of higher education is indebted to the Associated New American Colleges (ANAC) for this provocative and timely volume.

There is no better coalition of colleges and universities to undertake the task of "revisioning the relationship between faculty and their institutions" than the Associated New American Colleges. It has been a delight to see the project culminating in this book emerge full blown from the struggle of the ANAC institutions to forge their own special niche in the rich mosaic that makes up American higher education. These private institutions are no longer small, liberal arts colleges— although that identity and mission continues to be important—nor do they aspire to be research universities or want to drift into being nondescript comprehensives. Through their vigorous search for a distinctly articulated mission and a new kind of excellence they kept coming back to the relationship between faculty and their institutions. It soon became apparent that to sustain an educational vision encompassing highly personal faculty-student relationships and an academic community that is both effective and collegial a new academic compact would be required.

The new academic compact between faculty and their institutions being called for here is not a need limited to the Associated New American Colleges. Across the various sectors of American higher education, a growing tension between faculty and their institutions has become immediately apparent and is now widely acknowledged. Particularly troubling is the emerging gulf developing on campus between two dominant cultures—the collegial culture that has historically informed the professional self-understanding of most faculty, and an expanding managerial culture that is pressing for greater accountability, efficiency, and productivity. Exacerbating this strain between faculty and their institutions is a reform strategy that, although well intentioned, has made matters worse. Calls for the improvement of undergraduate teaching, more direct and effective service to external communities, better assessment, and a host of other incrementally imposed enhancements have overwhelmed faculty, making the academic career increasingly unmanageable and less attractive, particularly to new faculty. A new academic compact is needed, and this volume represents a creative, campus-based effort to initiate that quest.

This Faculty Work Project stands out from other similar endeavors in being a genuine collaboration between faculty leaders and academic administrators. When observing the project's working session—which I was privileged to do—I was not aware of whether initiatives were emerging from a faculty member or a dean or provost. In contrast to so many reform initiatives where the faculty is often subjugated to blame—if not bashing—the ANAC quest for a new academic compact is firmly rooted in concerns for both the professional growth and vitality of individual faculty and the good of the institution. They are not viewed as competing priorities. It is the active participation of faculty in the formulation of the initiatives leading to the compact that make it particularly promising.

Even in Chapter Three, "Faculty as Institutional Citizens: Reconceiving Service and Governance Work," the call for more active participation of faculty in institutional building is balanced with the developmental needs of faculty at particular career stages. The recommendation that colleges and universities be more "open" as organizations, with a freer flow of information, and the observation that governance assignments need to build on the diversity of faculty talent and the changes in faculty interests and commitments occurring at different times in a professor's career make a great deal of sense. Throughout this report there is the imperative that reciprocity be sustained in all faculty-institutional relationships and that there is a commitment to community that is different from those operative in the marketplace.

As you read the various chapters of this book, pay particular attention to the notion of the "circle of value." It effectively depicts the reciprocal obligations implied in the compact and the interdependent relationships between faculty at different stages in their careers and their institutions.

Building on the idea of the circle of value, two themes emerge that are central to the viability of the compact: the concept of the differentiated workload and a fresh approach to governance. ANAC is contending that faculty must find ways to share the workload—something that has become an intolerable burden—and that in evaluating what counts in faculty work, the contribution to the success of the unit, department, or program be seen as a central element. This represents a major departure from the way we organize and assess faculty performance now. The academic compact also calls for a reenvisioned approach to governance, inviting faculty into a more collaborative, participatory relationship in the governance of institutions, one that reconceptualizes traditional notions of shared governance.

The Associated New American Colleges' search for a new academic compact stands in a powerful, distinctly American intellectual tradition. The dominant tenets can be traced to the work of Ralph Waldo Emerson—particularly his momentous speech of 1837 "The American Scholar"—and even more directly to Emerson's philosophical heir, John Dewey. Jon Wergin (Chapter Nine) is right in pointing to the striking precedence to be found in Dewey's work on democracy and education. The call is for full collaboration in decision-making, and for reciprocity between the individual and the institution, where the individual takes responsibility for the work of the unit as well as the accomplishments of the mission of the whole. Then, there is the emphasis on the full development of individual talents as a mutual obligation, where, according to the new compact, the growth and learning of faculty, as well as students, is seen as an institutional responsibility.

I was privileged to be involved with the Associated New American Colleges when they were first coming together. Many of the key leaders, early on, are still active participants in the life of the organization, even though they have changed their institutions and positions. Some are among the contributors to this volume. It is that kind of persistence and faithfulness that gives vitality to a collaborative endeavor of this sort, and generates the imagination and audacity to call for a new academic compact. It has been the steadfast leadership and enormous energy of Jerry Berberet, however, that gave life to the organization and the Faculty Work Project. Reflecting the collaborative intent of the new academic compact, it was a faculty member who stepped forward to manage the project, Linda McMillin. Because of the intelligent leadership, dedication, and hard work of these two people the new academic compact has the potential for being more that just another good idea.

R. Eugene Rice
American Association for Higher Education

ACKNOWLEDGMENTS

This volume has roots in the mid-1990s origins of the Associated New American Colleges (ANAC), when faculty and administrative leaders first envisioned a project that would align emerging notions of integrative institutional and faculty professional models in service of higher education's mission. What became ANAC's Faculty Work Project began with extensive 1997–1998 assessments of faculty perceptions that laid the foundation for the year-long think tank of ANAC faculty and academic administrators whose insights and hard work have resulted in this volume. We appreciate the opportunity to collaborate with The Carnegie Foundation for the Advancement of Teaching and the special contributions of Charles E. Glassick, Mary Taylor Huber, and Mary Jean Whitelaw. Our deep thanks to Mara Winick of the University of Redlands, who analyzed and presented the data before ANAC and other audiences.

We gratefully acknowledge the generosity of The Pew Charitable Trusts for both funding support and intellectual engagement that began with the earlier assessment phase of the project and continued with this current work. We are especially thankful to Ellen Wert, our program officer at The Trusts, for her steadfast involvement, ideas, and encouragement, all of which have made our work better. Of course, the opinions expressed in this volume are those of ANAC and do not necessarily reflect the views of The Pew Charitable Trusts. ANAC and this project have also benefited from the support of The Woodrow Wilson National Fellowship Foundation, especially Vice President Judith Pinch, who has nurtured ANAC in a variety of ways great and small.

The 30 project participants from 19 ANAC member institutions met five times during 1999–2000. We are grateful for the hospitality of our member hosts, St. Mary's College of California (also host to ANAC's Woodrow Wilson Summer Institute in 1997–1998), Belmont University, Pacific Lutheran University, and Ithaca College. Our two-day gatherings were marked by hard work, critical exchanges, frequent laughter, growing friendships, and steady progress—hallmarks perhaps of collegial professional community in the best sense. Certainly, an early marker of the project was its demonstration that faculty and administrators can come together in a collaborative partnership to address the pressing questions that confront our institutions in the twenty-first century. We can attest together that we have experienced the kind of academic community our proposed compact advocates.

The project consultants who advised us and facilitated our efforts at different points in the project have added a richness of perspectives that we believe significantly enhances the usefulness of this volume. To Amy Driscoll, Jack Schuster, Mary Deane Sorcinelli, Allison Pingree, and Zeddie Bowen we express our deep thanks. One consultant, Jon Wergin, has "been there" for the project from start to finish and we can't thank him enough for his critical insights, unfailing encouragement, and great good humor. Another, Thomas C. Longin, a former ANAC member provost, has been an invaluable advisor to the project on an ongoing basis at meetings and from afar. In contributing guest essays on the three major compact areas where our work has focused, Jon and Tom, along with Jacqueline Mintz, have earned our continuing gratitude. Finally, we appreciate Eugene Rice, who served as project consultant during the assessment phase, for continuing to advise us, as his foreword to this volume so visibly testifies.

ANAC's June 2000 and 2001 Woodrow Wilson Summer Institutes at Ithaca College have been seminal project events. These gatherings have brought teams of ANAC member faculty and administrators into conversations with national association representatives and experts in faculty work from across higher education. The 2000 Institute discussions and feedback on our preliminary report greatly enriched what appears here in chapters one through four, and led to the volume's "responses from the field" section. Our thanks to Mary Burgan, Robert Diamond, John Hammang, Christine Licata, James Slevin, Marilla Svinicki, Cathy Trower, Ric Weibl, and Conrad J. Weiser for their presentations on faculty work and comments on the preliminary report at the Institute, several also providing responses that are included in this volume. Although the outcomes are beyond the scope of this work, the 2001 Summer Institute was devoted to ANAC member efforts to implement elements of the compact.

This manuscript has been a truly collaborative effort. Many individuals have read and commented on drafts. We wish especially to acknowledge Catherine Stevenson, whose kind and insightful editing at a key moment provided much needed perspective and encouragement. Marion Terenzio and Lawry Finsen have worked tirelessly on this project as chapter authors and members of the project management team. Ultimately, our responsibility has been to draw the many elements of the volume together; we have done that, acknowledging our responsibility for the volume's content, with the goal in mind that ANAC's work should benefit higher education in general.

Linda A. McMillin
Project Manager
Susquehanna University

Jerry Berberet
Project Director
Associated New American Colleges

June 2001

INTRODUCTION
A Primer on the Associated New American Colleges

Jerry Berberet

The Associated New American Colleges (ANAC) is a national consortium of 21 midsize, private comprehensive colleges and universities located in all regions of the United States. ANAC members possess trademark features of both larger research universities (e.g., a diversity of undergraduate, graduate, and professional programs serving residential, commuter, and older adult students) and smaller liberal arts colleges (e.g., a highly personalized residential campus environment with small classes and a faculty whose primary commitment is to educating traditional age undergraduates "one student at a time"). Their enrollment (typically 3,000–6,000 students) and organization (separate undergraduate, graduate, and professional schools and colleges) introduce the complexity of larger universities, but within a context of manageable size where institution-wide solutions are possible and expected and a community ethos is fundamental.

ANAC members articulate institutional missions that make student learning primary within a traditional higher education commitment to teaching, research, and service. Most express dedication to education that is value-centered (often reflecting the church-related heritage many ANAC members have in common). Beyond such expressions of private higher education mission, however, ANAC members acknowledge their comprehensive character and qualities of practice, integration, and application that reflect their identification with the new American college paradigm. These include the mission of educating diverse graduate and professional, as well as liberal arts, students; the commitment to service in their surrounding region; and the goal of developing applied competence focused on performance outcomes, as well as theoretical knowledge and reflective capacities. ANAC members pursue their missions within well-integrated institutional frameworks that emphasize knowledge, problem solving, and career/professional preparation; faculty-staff cooperation in meeting student needs; and connections between academic and student life.

ANAC institutions are philosophically attuned to Alexander Astin's (1994) measure of institutional excellence based on talent development with an outcomes standard rather than one based on the size of resource inputs such as student selectivity, endowment growth, and low teaching loads. They resonate with the late Ernest Boyer's (1990) strategy of institutional integration that creates connections to better focus resources on student needs. As a consequence, they encourage curricula that integrate liberal and professional studies and pedagogies that blend theory and practice. Their pragmatic bent owes in part to their responsiveness to needs of the regional communities around them with which they often share a recent history of rapid growth and development. Because of these characteristics, ANAC member colleges and universities represent a national laboratory for experimentation with models designed to integrate flexible and personalized approaches for meeting diverse student, faculty, and community needs within complex and technologically sophisticated higher education institutional environments.

Creation of the Associated New American Colleges resulted from an intense period of study and self-discovery among academic leaders (presidents, provosts, deans, and faculty) that culminated in the identity affirming Wingspread Conference on the New American College in 1994. ANAC was founded in 1995, as a national consortium of small to midsize private comprehensive colleges and universities that would use strategies involving integration to develop generative institutional and faculty professional models. In articulating this integrative vision, the late Frank Wong (1994) was fond of citing Robert Pirsig's classic, *Zen and the Art of Motorcycle Maintenance* (1974), to illustrate the problem of disconnected specialization in higher education, whether a separation between reductionist science and general education, or between faculty scholarship and service (one might add between faculty and administrators). In the book, Pirsig was continually frustrated at his inability to find a mechanic who would tune up his motorcycle so that it would run smoothly. He encountered mechanics with expert knowledge of motorcycles and experienced mechanics who had fixed motorcycles for years, but he was unable to find a knowledgeable and experienced mechanic who really cared about repairing motorcycles. Pirsig concluded that knowing and doing are not enough; fixing motorcycles and getting an education both require caring. For Wong, the motorcycle was a metaphor for the college or university, and the mechanic represented the faculty who must care about the institution for it to function well. In a prophetic analogy with the health care industry, Wong used the metaphor of the "primary care professor" to depict a faculty professional model that would maintain an educational ideal rooted in collegial academic community and personalized faculty-student relationships.

The four-year Faculty Work Project of the Associated New American Colleges, supported by two grants from The Pew Charitable Trusts, has been engaged in rethinking historic relationships between faculty members and their institutions. On grounds that alignment between faculty work and institutional mission is critical to effective fulfillment of mission, the project has developed principles of mutuality designed to provide a strong foundation for the self-conscious renewal of the faculty-institutional compact in American higher education. At its core this compact serves mission best, ANAC has concluded, when institution and faculty alike nurture the effectiveness of the other, or, in the current parlance, to "add value." A healthy institution is best able to support a vibrant learning environment and encourage faculty professional development when faculty members value institutional citizenship responsibilities, as well as their teaching and research roles. The project has focused on the articulation of principles and policies designed to advance healthy institutions and faculty professionalism, especially in student-centered institutions such as the members of the Associated New American Colleges where personalized teaching and learning and academic community are core values.

REFERENCES

Astin, A. W. (1994). Higher education reform and citizenship: A question of values. *Perspectives: The New American College, 24* (2), 79-91.

Boyer, E. (1990). *Scholarship reconsidered: Priorities of the professoriate.* Princeton, NJ: The Carnegie Foundation for the Advancement of Teaching.

Pirsig, R. M. (1974). *Zen and the art of motorcycle maintenance: An inquiry into values.* New York, NY: William Morrow.

Wong, F. F. (1994). Primary care education: A new American college model. *Perspectives: The New American College, 24* (2), 13-26.

The Compact

1

A NEW ACADEMIC COMPACT

Jerry Berberet

The economic, social, and technological effects of the information revolution have forced a profound rethinking of higher education's traditional campus-based, faculty-intensive, and personalized-learning structures. For more than a decade, as part of this rethinking, the roles, workload, and productivity of faculty have come under intense public scrutiny. The results have run the gamut from calls for greater educational accountability to largely unfair criticisms of faculty workload reflecting ill-defined and poorly understood measures such as class contact hours and stereotypes of research university scholars who do not teach. In a society undergoing such transformation, it is critical to figure out what is fundamental to an effective student learning process in order that higher education might experience constructive change. Such an analysis requires an understanding of faculty values and perceptions, how faculty members contribute to the core learning mission, and how these contributions might be reconfigured in addressing the challenges of changing times. It also calls for new insights about how the traditional college or university, itself under intense scrutiny and facing growing competition from new educational providers, nurtures the effectiveness of its primary resource for learning—its faculty.

The Associated New American Colleges (ANAC) launched the Faculty Work Project in 1996 as an undertaking to adapt the faculty professional model to an educational landscape where the pace of change is accelerating and new demands call for redefinition of faculty roles and institutional relationships. The project was also founded to advance the student-centered mission of ANAC member colleges and universities, on the assumption that to serve students successfully institutions must invest in faculty professional development. Consequently, the overriding goal of the project has been to lay the conceptual groundwork for bringing the institution's faculty policies and practices and the actual work patterns of faculty into optimal alignment with the institutional mission. In rethinking the faculty professional model, the project assumes that preservation of academic core values such as open inquiry, academic freedom, and professional community are both central to the advancement of knowledge in a democratic society and a primary justification for faculty engagement with institutional planning and decision-making. This line of reasoning helps to explain why an academic professional community requires an organizational structure that will serve its core mission and values, inescapably one reflecting a faculty-institutional reciprocity that enables each to thrive in its essential roles.

THE URGENCY BEHIND ANAC'S FACULTY WORK PROJECT

The host of internal and external pressures that face higher education reflect the rapid change occurring in many sectors of society as people adapt to the information age. Transformation from a society based on mechanical industry to one based on electronic intelligence has unleashed competitive forces and consumer demands that force goods producers and service providers to increase efficiency, improve quality, and customize goods and services simultaneously, all the while cutting costs and lowering prices. To cope (indeed, to survive), goods producers and service providers alike have sought to become learning organizations, capable of engaging the full intellectual capacities of their work forces. In the main, organizations that thrive in the wake of these influences have adopted strategies which employ open communications and collaboration and dismantle hierarchy. The ultimate learning organization, higher education, is also being required to respond to these forces reshaping the globe—sometimes enthusiastically, sometimes kicking and screaming. Indeed, no sector of higher education, even its most elite, has proven to be exempt from these influences, although interpretations and response times for what is happening vary widely. Ultimately, this is the larger context that frames ANAC's Faculty Work Project. This volume is a lens designed to bring the perceptions and behavior of higher education and its faculty into clearer focus in order to better serve education's societal mission.

These relatively recent information revolution pressures on higher education have exacerbated longstanding differences that have bedeviled faculty-institutional relationships. Perhaps more than most care to contemplate, people in higher education tend to think in terms of dualisms that put them at odds with the other—whether with other people, the institutions where they work, or the larger society. Yet, paradoxically, people wish for connection and community, and have a desire to contribute to something larger than themselves that in return validates their work and provides meaning in their personal and professional lives. Undoubtedly, the academy's signature dualism is a historic divide between faculty and administration, an offshoot of labor-management dualism in the larger society, certainly, but a separation, as well, that has its own philosophical, cultural, and political traditions more misunderstood than understood when characterized simply in terms of employee-employer relationships. In fact, the daily lives of faculty members and others on campus—students, administrators, staff—are all about the comings and goings within an interdependent community, flawed in many ways due to the academy's fragmented institutional culture. This fragmentation reflects not only the tensions that faculty concerns about autonomy pose when institutional functions and relationships are described solely in the language of community, but, as well, the impact of external pressures and the academy's subcultural disciplinary differences that can make all campus constituencies feel defensive and relatively powerless.

William H. Bergquist (1992) has written as clearly as anyone about the internal divisions within higher education institutional culture. In *The Four Cultures of the Academy*, he argued that faculty and administrators operate from different cultural frameworks that almost inevitably lead to misunderstanding and conflict. According to Bergquist, the corporate managerial culture of administrators is student and institutionally centered and looks ultimately to a hierarchy beginning with the president and board of trustees for its power base. Rather than being institutional in its focus, faculty culture is based on the assumption that faculty occupy a special status in society due to the larger intellectual purposes they serve which, ultimately, transcend the local institution. As a result of this identification with autonomy, the primary loyalties of many faculty are to academic freedom and to their particular discipline and students. Small wonder, then, that faculty members may feel estranged from institutional structures, especially if they perceive that the institution lacks an ethos of reciprocity. In such a context the agendas of faculty meetings and committees may seem to have the practical urgency of issues in a debating society.

The price to be paid for such internal fragmentation, although painful and frustrating, may have been acceptable in years gone by. It seems less acceptable now in an era of growing competition among educational providers for the attentions of a consumer-conscious public demanding greater educational responsiveness and cost-effectiveness. James Carlin, former chairman of the Massachusetts Board of Higher Education, blamed this dualistic faculty-administration paradigm and catered to external critics in painting faculty and institutions across higher education with the same brush in *The Chronicle of Higher Education*: "Faculty members do ever more meaningless research while spending fewer hours in the classroom . . . Never have I observed anything as unfocused or mismanaged as higher education . . . Trustees and administrators must provide bold, innovative solutions in spite of faculty members' objections" (1999, p. A76). Allegations of division and mismanagement, such as Carlin's, expose higher education's vulnerability in a complex, information-driven society that does, indeed, require ever more from colleges and universities in order to function effectively. The nation has moved from an era 50 years ago when the high school diploma was the standard credential to current educational needs that have made the bachelor's degree the standard and accelerated pursuit of advanced degrees.

For those who believe that personalized teacher-student relationships in residential campus communities—hallmarks of a major sector of American higher education since colonial times—are among the values at stake in today's educational environment, the issue of faculty-institutional mutuality has taken on new gravity. Few may argue, in the United States at least, that there is a more effective educational model than a faculty-intensive one, but many are pursuing the cost advantages they believe technology-intensive education will ultimately hold, possibly at the expense of education with a personal touch. Writing in the *New York Times*, Arthur Levine, President of Columbia Teachers College, noting Henry Adams's lament (in *The Education of Henry Adams*, 1918) that Adams had received an eighteenth-century education in a world on the verge of the twentieth century, quoted a corporate executive who called higher education "the next health care: a poorly managed nonprofit industry which was overtaken by the profit-making sector." Levine warned that colleges and universities are "knowledge-producing organizations . . . not in the campus business but the education business" (2000, p. A21). Educators must address the reality of online instruction in the home and workplace, Levine asserted, or risk going the way of railroads, which made the mistake of thinking that they were in the railroad, rather than the transportation, business, and were nearly put out of business by airplanes. For higher education, the message may be that faculties and administrations must learn to collaborate better around primary mission, if traditional higher education is to be sustained, not solely that faculty- and technology-intensive education should reach an accommodation that advances learning.

These daunting environmental pressures—quality, cost effectiveness, accountability, and internal fragmentation—that institutions and their faculties face during today's changing times have intensified a host of immediate challenges, making it timely to review traditional relationships and perceptions and to consider professional and organizational innovations. Like never before faculty feel the crunch of new institutional expectations, as new programs and services are being offered to ever more diverse student audiences, a phenomenon Burton Clark (2000) has characterized as demand overload. This is happening just as faculty are struggling to develop and maintain currency with technology, keep pace with the explosion of new knowledge in their fields, adapt their pedagogies to diverse student learning styles, and meet expectations regarding their scholarly output that seem to be ratcheting up. Time has become an ever more precious resource in this responsibility-laden environment. For their part, institutions are struggling to provide educational services in a rapid response environment that places a premium on strategic planning and timely decision-making, while facing both escalating costs related to technology, institutional student aid, physical facilities, and equipment and limited revenue-enhancing opportunities. A shared governance faculty-administrative relationship that has many of the constitutional features of an executive-congressional separation of powers is more likely to produce gridlock on many campuses than effective collaboration through strategic partnership for the benefit of all.

THE FACULTY WORK PROJECT: PHASE I

ANAC began Phase I of the Faculty Work Project in the midst of calls for a rethinking of the research and discipline-centered faculty professional model set in the 1960s. Ernest Boyer, in his widely acclaimed *Scholarship Reconsidered* (1990), announced the advent of a new paradigm in arguing that the traditional scholarship of discovery is really only one of several forms of scholarship—that faculty members are doing scholarship in synthesizing and interpreting knowledge across disciplines (scholarship of integration), in performing their role as teachers (scholarship of teaching), and in using knowledge for problem solving (scholarship of application). Significantly, late in his life Boyer characterized the latter as the scholarship of service, and his successor, as President of the Carnegie Foundation for the Advancement of Teaching, Lee Shulman, argues persuasively that Boyer considered the scholarship of teaching to be the ultimate form of scholarship due to the teacher's critical societal responsibility to interpret and communicate findings of the scholarly tradition—in a very real sense a passing on of the culture's understanding of itself.

Boyer's elevation of teaching and service as forms of scholarship paved the way for Eugene Rice (1996), who, in *Making a Place for the New American Scholar*, advocated a student-centered and institutionally collaborative "new American scholar" faculty professional model that would enable faculty to create various mixes of teaching, research, and service at different stages of their careers. Rice proposed a flexible career path that would facilitate faculty evolution toward the goal of what he called "the complete scholar"—a mature career stage where the faculty member has achieved significant professional integration (knowledge, values, and performance) of accomplishments in teaching, research, and institutional citizenship. In advocating a single scholarly standard for evaluating research, teaching, and service, Boyer in his last work, *Scholarship Assessed* (completed by colleagues and published posthumously in 1997), completed the articulation of a new faculty professional paradigm—namely, that all faculty work should be susceptible to evaluation as a form of scholarship.

In The Pew Charitable Trusts' *Higher Education White Paper* (1997), Russell Edgerton added new weight to what is at stake in thinking about faculty work by connecting the quest for a more appropriate faculty professional model to higher education's larger social purpose, arguing that colleges and universities should pursue more ambitious missions in meeting societal needs. Declaring, "American expectations for higher education and higher education's expectations for itself are simply too low" (p. 62), he asserted that "the faculty holds the keys to progress on every item" of an agenda for putting students first, refocusing the professoriate, and revitalizing higher education's role in society (p. 64). By highlighting the professions as "inherently public and communal," Shulman has prodded faculty to recognize that society has conferred on them a privileged status that brings not only public accountability regarding individual practice, but also responsibilities as members of a professional community (1997, p. 155). Ernest A. Lynton was even more explicit regarding faculty communal responsibility. In calling for unit evaluation of faculty work, he observed, "If universities are to have the resilience and adaptability they will need in the decades to come, they must find better ways to make individual faculty member's work contribute to common organizational needs, priorities, and goals" (1998, pp. 8–9).

Given this powerful argument in the literature for holding the feet of both faculty and institution to the accountability fire, ANAC's goal in the project's 1997–1998 initial phase was to examine the current state of the profession on our member campuses with the lens clearly focused on relationships between faculty and their institution. We wanted to assess the alignment among the missions of our institutions, the expectations institutions have for faculty work, what faculty actually do, and how faculty are rewarded. Ideally, in an institution committed to Rice's complete scholar model, mission should shape expectations that guide actions which lead congruently to rewards. Our assessment was accomplished in several ways. First, an audit of current institutional mission and policy statements was conducted. Second, in collaboration with the Carnegie Foundation for the Advancement of Teaching (CFAT), 1,400 ANAC faculty were surveyed using the CFAT standard survey instrument supplemented by an instrument designed specifically for the project. In addition, ANAC conducted a number of time motion studies of faculty work on selective campuses. Finally, each ANAC institution discussed faculty work issues in a series of faculty focus groups and faculty town meetings. The results of these assessments document significant faculty satisfaction with students, teaching, and scholarly activities (Table 1.1).

TABLE 1.1 Faculty Individual Satisfaction Responses

(% Strongly or Somewhat Agree)

My students	94%
Courses I teach	93%
The teacher/scholar model	85%
My colleagues	82%
The opportunity to pursue my own ideas	81%
My personal job situation	80%
I have collaborated with colleagues in the last three years	79%
Now is an especially creative/productive time in my field	78%
I began new research in the last three years	78%
I published or presented in the last three years	77%
I am fairly evaluated	74%

On average, faculty report working 50-55 hours per week, spending approximately 30 hours on teaching and nearly ten hours each week in both research and service. Faculty subscribe to the mission of their institution, value collegial community, and believe that their work practices match institutional expectations, at least insofar as mission and institutional expectations are expressed in policy. The rub occurs in moving from policy to practice, both in prescribing an appropriate level of practice in policy documents and in developing habits of practice that enable the educational outcomes implied by the institutional mission to be achieved and the institutional community to function well on an ongoing basis. In moving from policy to practice, Phase I uncovered substantial faculty dissatisfaction with institutional rewards and support for faculty development. The willingness of institutions to acknowledge faculty contributions in ways that provide incentives appears to be a key element in improving the functioning of institutional community.

The CFAT/ANAC survey results are especially revealing. They show both the very high degree to which individual ANAC faculty support their institution's mission (76% approve) (Table 1.2) and, seemingly paradoxically, the much lower number (43%) who believe that faculty as a whole have a shared understanding of the mission and work (51%) to support that mission (Table 1.3).

TABLE 1.2   Faculty Institutional Support Responses

(% Strongly or Somewhat Agree)

I support my institution's mission	76%
Faculty have an obligation to serve society	75%
My interests have become more interdisciplinary	72%
Faculty have an obligation to serve community	68%
Service is important in faculty evaluation	61%

This suggestion of a disconnect between individual faculty and the faculty community parallels significant disconnects the assessments exposed between faculty and their institution. In contrast with the relatively low faculty perception of the degree that faculty work in general supports the institutional mission, the survey reveals close alignment in nearly every work dimension (e.g., teaching preparation, research, advising, student tutorials, institutional service, etc.) between what faculty perceive institutional expectations to be and how they say they allocate their individual work time. The widest deviation between perceptions of serving mission and actual work practice is only 4%; specifically, faculty indicate that they actually allocate 14% of their time to scholarly/artistic pursuits, while perceiving that their institution expects 18% (Figure 1.1)!

This perceived alignment of individual faculty work patterns with mission helps to explain another set of assessment results—the substantial dissatisfaction faculty members express regarding institutional rewards, governance, and management, and their belief (69%) that overall faculty morale is fair to poor. Nearly half complained of work-related stress, and 70% complained of insufficient time to focus on a

FIGURE 1.1   Work Allocation and Institutional Expectations

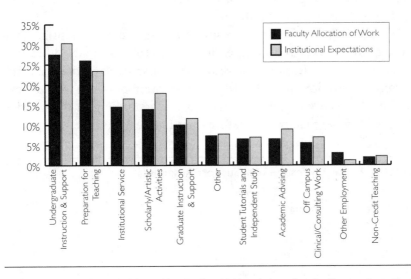

"piece of work" (Table 1.3). Only 40% of faculty believe that their institution's system of faculty rewards supports the mission, and even fewer (37%) rate institutional support for scholarship and other professional growth as good or excellent. Faculty also gave low marks to the effectiveness of evaluation and feedback on their professional work (Table 1.4). The CFAT/ANAC survey appears to capture a faculty frustration that they are "doing for the institution," but their institution is not "doing for them," perhaps an inevitable tension in the best of times, but certainly one that their conflicting views exacerbate. The response tables illustrate the dichotomy in faculty perceptions of

TABLE 1.3 Faculty Satisfaction with Institutional Community Responses

(% Strongly or Somewhat Agree)

I have insufficient time to focus on a "piece of work"	70%
Faculty work practices support the mission	51%
Effectiveness of institutional management	45%
I experience work-related stress	43%
Faculty have "shared understanding" of mission	43%
Sense of community on my campus	37%
Positive faculty/administration relationships	32%
Effectiveness of faculty governance	31%

their satisfaction with "my" work and sense of personal commitment to their institution and the larger community, on the one hand, and their dissatisfaction with their institution's faculty policies, professional support, faculty work environment, and community functioning, on the other. Given the project's core proposition regarding the importance of faculty and institutional alignment with mission, the need to lay groundwork for more effective and satisfying faculty-institutional relationships emerged as the focus for continuation of the Faculty Work Project in Phase II.

TABLE 1.4 Faculty Satisfaction with Institutional Policies Responses

(% Strongly or Somewhat Agree)

Need better ways to evaluate teaching	71%
Need better ways to evaluate faculty scholarship	64%
Effectiveness of new faculty orientation	51%
Effectiveness of tenure-track feedback	46%
Faculty rewards support the mission	40%
Institutional support for professional growth	37%
Service is evaluated effectively	37%
Faculty reward system provides incentives	30%
Effectiveness of post-tenure review	25%

When the ANAC data are placed in the context of the cross-sector CFAT survey data, the results make clear that ANAC faculty perceptions mirror those of faculty at other types of institutions. Although perceptions vary somewhat in individual areas, the "double disconnect"—individual faculty being satisfied with their work but feeling estranged from both formal institutional structures and the faculty community as a whole—seems to hold. Indeed, the data suggest that ANAC faculty members are more satisfied with most aspects of their work than faculty members in other types of four-year institutions, including other Carnegie Masters classification schools, with the possible exception of their relationship with students (Table 1.5). [The ANAC faculty satisfaction level with students increases to 94% when the "somewhat" satisfied responses are included (Table 1.1)].

The presence of a hardworking faculty seems to cut across all institutional types as well, with a variance of less than three hours per week in number of hours faculty report working.

TABLE 1.5 Comparisons of Faculty Satisfaction Across Institution Type

(% Responding "Very Satisfied)

	Research	Masters	Bachelors	ANAC
Relationship with students	70%	78%	74%	60%
Courses taught	41%	50%	55%	54%
Opportunity to pursue own ideas	29%	34%	48%	50%
Job security	50%	43%	42%	44%
Relationship with colleagues	33%	40%	45%	42%
Department management	22%	27%	32%	36%
Job situation as a whole	31%	25%	31%	30%
Institutional management	5%	7%	11%	12%
Faculty reward system	8%	5%	5%	6%

In documenting a pattern of faculty-faculty as well as faculty-institutional misalignment, the findings underscore the importance of institutional and faculty community-building activities. Presumably, because the project methodology was so comprehensive, full faculty gatherings to digest project results seem imperative to replace divisions and uncertainty with consensus and corrective institutional initiatives. The positive response to project findings on the part of the faculty community at several ANAC institutions, in fact, has been nothing short of breathtaking. At North Central College, for example, the faculty not only broke a ten-year logjam in approving a new general education curriculum, but also increased class contact hours with students within the existing faculty teaching load and participated actively in institutional strategic planning. The Rollins College faculty community responded to widespread dissatisfaction with faculty governance and incivility within the faculty by suspending governance and declaring a "community day" to heal relationships and begin to create a better governance system. As part of an institutional agreement to bring the Saint Mary's College of California teaching load more in line with that of other ANAC members, the faculty community dedicated itself to renewal of a historically close and intellectually intense relationship with students outside the formal classroom that many faculty felt had declined in recent years. And, at Quinnipiac University, ANAC's only collective bargaining member where faculty-administrative tensions had delayed agreement on the most recent contract for more than a year, faculty discussions of Phase I findings brought support to improve orientation of new faculty and evaluative feedback faculty receive, including that during the post-tenure years.

The credibility that Phase I generated among ANAC faculty owes much to a combination of gathering convincing empirical data and engaging in open deliberations of the faculty community. In effect, the project methodology modeled canons of scholarly inquiry and peer review within the community of scholars that faculty most respect. Such a process is essential for institutions to respond effectively to the reform calls of Rice, Edgerton, Shulman, Lynton, and others. ANAC's Faculty Work Project Phase I dissemination conference at Saint Mary's College of California in June 1998 distilled a clear focus from findings of the assessment process, assisted by reports from institutional project coordinators and faculty-administrator institutional teams who brought institution-specific faculty work issues. Invited speakers such as Alan Guskin, Eugene Rice, Mary Huber, Jerry Gaff, Michelle Gilliard, David Pollick, and Jacqueline Mintz added a range of insights. To illustrate, in calling for faculty and institutions to recognize that their's is a holistic and interdependent relationship, Mintz expressed powerfully the project's underlying integrative assumption:

> Our institutions must not just rationalize but integrate, in human intellectual and emotional terms, the issues of workload, control, community, rewards, fairness and respect in our workplace. This requires participation in all levels and endeavors of our campus life. If we as faculty are going to be able to respond to the myriad demands made upon us, then we need to work together to grow within and be nurtured by our institutions. (1999, p. 33)

The Saint Mary's conference identified several focal points that guided design of the project's second phase.

Career path. Nurturing professional vitality at different stages of the faculty career is essential whether achieved through effective socialization of new faculty to New American College priorities or institutional support for professional development.

Clarifying service/streamlining governance. Strategic and effective faculty/institutional collaborations in service and governance must be developed.

Unit accountability. Evaluating and rewarding the performance of departments, programs, and schools, as well as individual faculty, is needed to build institutional accountability.

Flexible workload. The one-size-fits-all model regarding expectations of faculty must be replaced by alternatives that better serve faculty and their institutions.

PHASE II: A PROCESS FOR REVISIONING FACULTY-INSTITUTIONAL RELATIONSHIPS

In the months following the June 1998 conference at Saint Mary's College, ANAC designed a second phase of the Faculty Work Project in order to rethink the faculty-institutional relationship and develop the intellectual underpinnings for more holistic and integrative faculty work models and institutional policies and practices. This second phase was designed to build on faculty members' demonstrated work ethic and to extend the high degree of satisfaction they experience with their teaching and research to their work and relationships in the larger institutional community. Eugene Rice (1996) has noted this division in calling for an attitude shift from "my" work to "our" work—from faculty work as "private" to faculty work as "public"—as a way for faculty to conceptualize the integration of their work with the full functioning of their institution. This new project, supported by a second grant from The Pew Charitable Trusts, took the form of a think tank of faculty and academic administrators that held the first of five two-day meetings in June 1999. The goals of the think tank were to articulate the rationale and design principles for new models in self-evident ways and to provide guidance for ANAC members and other institutions that seek to improve the alignment of faculty policies and practices with mission. Taking its cue from the consensus reached at the 1998 Saint Mary's conference, the new project think tank organized itself into three working groups, one to focus on each of the three project objectives which had emerged in the design phase of the project. Each of these groups articulated a set of assumptions and identified areas for further exploration and discussion as follows.

1) *To initiate institutional policies, practices, and rewards that treat the faculty career as an integrated whole, responsive to faculty needs and potential from the point of hiring to post-tenure and late career, for the purposes of sustaining career-long professional growth, effectiveness, and satisfaction.*

Project assessments reveal significant disconnects between faculty and their institutions at all stages of the faculty career whose address appears essential for faculty and institutional well being. The project has found adult development theory and flexible approaches to faculty work priorities and rewards to be significant in maintaining career-long faculty vitality. More than with the next two objectives, progress on this one shapes faculty willingness to embrace a broad professional vision that encompasses the institution, that in fact causes faculty to view themselves as institutional citizens engaged in career-long professional growth and development, as well as members of a larger professional academic community. As the tenure track is the norm in full-time appointments at ANAC member institutions, the project envisions a long-term faculty-institutional compact developed around tenure. Moreover, as a norm, full-time faculty teach 70–90% of the courses, depending on the particular ANAC member. Thus, ANAC members neither experience on the whole the types of issues associated with excessive reliance on part-time faculty, nor the presence of significant numbers of full-time contract rather than tenure-track faculty.

2) *To define clearly institutional service expectations within the framework of all faculty professional responsibilities (e.g., teaching and research), including faculty roles in governance and quasiadministrative functions at the nexus of institutional life.*

The need to rationalize, evaluate, and reward institutional service has emerged as a linchpin in investing the faculty-institutional relationship with new purpose and vitality. Much is at stake in achieving this objective, including a meaningful definition of faculty professional responsibility to the institution, that is, a faculty civic ethic, and a strategic rethinking of the purposes and structure of governance. Unless collaborative relationships are institutionalized, movement toward a more generative institutional community capable of renewing the faculty-institutional compact seems problematic. Our assumption bears underscoring: The special professional knowledge that faculty possess is mission-critical to effective institutional decision-making.

3) *To develop differentiated faculty workload policies and unit planning and evaluation models (at the department,*

program, or school level) in order to use faculty resources
most effectively in serving the institutional mission.

The project assumed that achievement of this objective requires
individual faculty and unit collaborative planning and negotiation to
best match individual expertise, interests, and goals with strategies for
fulfillment of unit mission. Such strategies include individual and unit
short- and long-range work planning, performance evaluation, and
rewards connected with service to the unit and institutional missions.
Parallel and administratively integrated academic unit and individual
faculty member policies, criteria, and procedures are key in achieving
workload reciprocity and alignment of work with mission.

At the 1999 Saint Mary's Phase II project kickoff gathering, working group outcomes were discussed in plenary sessions to assure
project unity and integration. A resource person from outside ANAC
(typically a faculty work scholar or faculty development specialist)
participated in the deliberations of each working group—at Saint
Mary's, Amy Driscoll of California State University Monterey Bay,
Jack Schuster of the Claremont Graduate School, and Jon Wergin of
Virginia Commonwealth University fulfilled this role. An online
threaded conversation forum was initiated at the ANAC web site
(http://anac.vir.org) in order that working group conversations
might be ongoing. In addition to this online conversation, a comprehensive bibliography of existing scholarship in all three areas was
developed during the 1999 summer and posted to the web site to provide a grounding in the scholarly literature about faculty work issues
across higher education. Thus, a basic process was put in place that
resulted not only in a continuous drafting and refining of text but an
ongoing infusion of new ideas from these diverse sources that made
each of the four remaining two-day project meetings extraordinarily
rich.

The second project meeting was held November 5–6, at Belmont
University in Nashville, where Jon Wergin, Thomas Longin of the
Association of Governing Boards, and Allison Pingree of Vanderbilt
University helped the project to frame a series of propositions and
tentative conclusions. At Belmont, the differentiated workload group
conceived of a "circle of value" notion in ascribing a value-adding
interdependency to the relationships among faculty, academic units,
and institution. At the third meeting, February 2–3, in New Orleans,

where a preliminary outline for the project report was presented at the AAHE Faculty Roles and Rewards Conference, the governance and institutional service group settled on the term "institutional citizenship" to depict faculty obligations to the institution and the faculty development group formalized the reciprocity in faculty-institutional relationships as a compact. At this meeting, in addition to Wergin, Mary Deane Sorcinelli of the University of Massachusetts-Amherst, and Zeddie Bowen of the University of Richmond, served as resource persons. With fundamental principles identified and project report writing underway, the fourth project meeting convened April 5–6, in Tacoma, Washington, to complete and critique preliminary working group drafts and to begin integration in a comprehensive way of the range of reciprocal obligations important in a healthy institution with fully engaged faculty professionals. Some 20 project faculty and administrators contributed text in this report development process, which resulted in a preliminary report prepared after the Tacoma meeting. This report became the central text for deliberations at the ANAC Woodrow Wilson Summer Institute, held June 14–17, 2000, at Ithaca College.

In addition to the more than 90 faculty and academic administrators from ANAC member institutions who participated at the Summer Institute, the project invited faculty work specialists from across the spectrum of higher education to critique the draft report. Those who participated as respondents and panelists at the Institute included Tom Longin and Jon Wergin; Mary Burgan, American Association of University Professors; Charles Glassick, Carnegie Foundation for the Advancement of Teaching; Christine Licata, American Association of Higher Education; Ric Weibl, Association of American Colleges and Universities; Conrad J. Weiser, Oregon State University; Cathy Trower, Harvard University; James Slevin, Georgetown University; Marilla Svinicki, University of Texas; Robert Diamond, National Academy for Academic Leadership; and John Hammang, American Association of State Colleges and Universities. Not only did the panelists make suggestions to improve the report, but they joined with the ANAC participants in institute working group discussions that further scrutinized project conclusions and recommendations. Following the institute, the report was circulated among other scholars who also provided comments. A number of these invited responses have found their way into this volume as a means both to facilitate a continuing conversation about faculty work and to make this document as accessible as possible to stakeholders in all sectors of higher education.

REAFFIRMING THE TIES THAT BIND: TOWARD A NEW FACULTY-INSTITUTIONAL COMPACT

As the project think tank contemplated first principles around which to ground our evolving convictions regarding the interdependence of faculty and institution, it grappled with the seemingly paradoxical core values of intellectual autonomy and collegial community that undergird the academy. The project members concluded not only that autonomy and community are essential to the vitality of higher education but that a faculty-institutional relationship based on reciprocity must be established to balance the obligations implied by these seemingly competing core values. Elsewhere in this volume, Jon Wergin identifies academic freedom and autonomy as the primary wellspring of faculty motivation, followed closely by deep faculty desires to be members of a community of scholars and to have impact on their academic environment. Our review of the literature on faculty professionalism confirms that a community of practice and an ethic of collegial criticism are critical in fostering what Donald Schön (1987) has called "the reflective practitioner"—the faculty member who is keenly self-conscious both regarding the practice of one's professional craft and how to make positive the impact of one's interaction with students and one's professional community.

Understanding what is fundamental about faculty professional practice is essential in prioritizing faculty institutional roles, providing institutional support for faculty professional development, and responding to external calls for higher education accountability. What is it that faculty are professionally prepared to do and how do they do it? How can faculty members and their institutions work together to focus faculty roles most effectively among a myriad of competing demands on faculty time that appear to be growing with the accelerating pace of change institutions are experiencing? Regarding the first question, Glassick, Huber, and Maeroff argued in *Scholarship Assessed* (1997) that all faculty professional work—whether teaching, research, or service—is a form of scholarship that might be defined, evaluated, and rewarded according to scholarly standards. Such a view serves as a basis for developing an integrative faculty work model linking teaching, research, and service responsibilities in a way that enables a faculty member to formulate a coherent professional self-concept, including service to the institution. Oregon State University formalized the implications for institutional partnership of defining all faculty work as scholarship through a "living job description," an annual work plan that allows individual faculty responsibilities to be adjusted according to changing institutional and faculty needs and opportunities.

Higher education has always felt uncomfortable with external criticisms that suggest things would be much better if colleges and universities would only operate like businesses. This unease arises both from obvious differences between manufacturing widgets and educating students and from an intuitive recognition that the academic enterprise requires a different organization than business. The recent literature on entrepreneurism and collaboration, in fact, suggests not only that higher education's reluctance to adopt business models may be well founded, but that some of the most successful Fortune 500 companies have cultivated qualities commonly found in higher education. According to Robert C. Allen (2000), these include a focus on core values beyond making money that unify and inspire a workforce around a larger shared vision and the nurturing of unconventional intellectual entrepreneurism. Moreover, the emergence of collaboration in interdisciplinary teams in industry as a means to accomplish a variety of project tasks imitates a longtime practice in colleges and universities. Such experiences invoke confidence that we in higher education can take hold of our destiny to create a faculty-institutional framework more productive and responsive in serving mission, one more purposeful and satisfying for faculty and other constituencies.

Two leading higher education voices for restructuring, as a means of preserving traditional higher education values, lend support to observers of business such as Allen. Peter Ewell (1999) advises proceeding from core values and established organizational structures to achieve change in higher education that will attract faculty and staff ownership of it. Bill Tierney (1999) identifies community and academic freedom as two such core values in an institutional restructuring that he feels must come to higher education. Tierney quotes

Michael Katz (1987) in defining what differentiates academic community, at least as an ideal, and makes it worthy of preservation:

> A community of persons united by collective understanding, by common and communal goals, by bonds of reciprocal obligation, and by a flow of sentiment which makes the preservation of the community an object of desire, not merely a matter of prudence or a command of duty. Community implies a form of social obligation governed by principles different from those operative in the marketplace and the state. (Qtd. in Tierney, 1999, p. 11)

THE COMPACT

In its emphasis on reciprocal obligation, preservation of the community, and social obligation, the Katz definition frames ANAC's call for a renewal of the compact between faculty and institution, as a formalized set of reciprocal understandings embracing the faculty career at the institution. ANAC has self-consciously chosen the term "compact" to define its vision of a restructured faculty-institutional relationship. The external threats and challenges higher education faces and the impacts internally of the current pace of change expose higher education's present vulnerability. These are hazards of sufficient gravity to call for rededication to a mission held in common and to reciprocal obligations enacted in a covenant for the well being of a traditional higher education community that deserves to survive and thrive. In fashioning the notion of the compact, historic images and metaphors come freely to mind—the Enlightenment idealism that inspired Locke's social contract, the adversity that elicited the Mayflower Compact, the recognition of strength through union in the framing of the American Constitution, and the affirmation of individual autonomy within inclusive community that is the dominant theme of the Bill of Rights. The meaning of compact implies that the well being of the whole, as well as that of each partner to the compact, depends on faculty and institution fulfilling essential obligations to the other related to the mission that defines their reason to exist. The mission strategic nature of the compact suggests that these obligations are ongoing and organic, responsive to changing needs and opportunities as they affect the institutional community.

The reach of the compact is intended to be comprehensive—

extending from workload responsibilities to faculty development, from institutional service to governance, from self and unit evaluation to parallel recognition and rewards. For many faculty the compact timeline may be career-long—from hiring and orientation to socialization and evaluation on the tenure track, from tenure and promotion to post-tenure review, from mid- and late-career work options and professional development support to options at retirement age. The compact is intended to nurture the professional maturation of Rice's aforementioned complete scholar and the ability of the institution to fulfill its mission with distinction. It embraces part-time faculty as well as full-time faculty, in part to assure one class of faculty citizenship; in part because, as a member of one project working group observed, "In the eyes of students the faculty member standing in front of them represents the institution, whether full-time, tenured, or adjunct."

THE CIRCLE OF VALUE AND INSTITUTIONAL CITIZENSHIP

Implementation of the bonds of compact, that is, operationalizing the interdependent relationships within academic community, led the think tank to coin the term "circle of value" to depict the reciprocal obligations within the compact. In fulfilling their workload obligations, individual faculty members add value to their academic unit (e.g., department or school) which in turn adds value in contributing to the mission of the institution as a whole. The institution in turn adds value to individual faculty, notably through professional development support that enhances the value of faculty contributions to unit and institution. In advocating workload differentiation and parallel individual faculty and unit work plans, evaluations, and rewards, the think tank proposes a mechanism for optimizing, on the one hand, faculty and unit productivity and satisfaction and, on the other, accountability and reciprocity.

To incorporate systematically and equitably the obligation of faculty service to the institution, the think tank developed the core value of institutional citizenship as a means to define faculty responsibilities for maintenance of the institutional community, obligations that are frequently poorly defined, inequitably distributed, and haphazardly evaluated and rewarded. As a core value, institutional citizenship occupies a place at the table with teaching and research in an integrated faculty professional work model. ANAC envisions principles of governance that place faculty in a more collaborative and strategic relationship with institutional functioning than is currently typical of faculty involvement in governance, even where shared governance is embraced. Emphatically, we are not proposing that faculty shadow the work of administrators, nor that they spend more time than is necessary in governance activities. Such a reading of the proposed new compact would grossly misrepresent the project's intent. Rather, in serving the strategic priorities of the institution, the well being of both institution and faculty requires that the academic expertise and professional judgment of faculty play a central role in addressing the challenging times higher education is facing. Moreover, as their comprehensive institutions respond to an increasingly diverse range of demands and opportunities, faculty will assume ever-growing leadership roles in addressing strategic institutional priorities.

In many ways the compact is about revisioning the interdependent relationships between faculty and their institutions over the life stages of the faculty career, especially since many faculty spend their entire career at a single institution. The project has focused on identifying values, structures, and resources that faculty and institutions must bring to the relationship to be worthy partners, that is, to establish a mutuality that enables the institution to prosper in its educational mission and faculty to achieve their professional potential. To ensure their success, institutions must nourish a faculty entrepreneurial spirit, creating an institutional ethos of true partnership that enables what Burton Clark (2000) calls faculty collegial entrepreneurialism to flourish as a force for institutional advancement. New technologies and other innovations will challenge these collaborative and collegial assumptions. New modes of teaching, learning, research, and service will create new roles for faculty, new forms of governance and institutional relationships, and new demands for faculty professional development. But they will not change fundamentally what is at the heart of an educational model rooted in notions of integrating personal relationships and sophisticated tools in a setting of interdependent community.

Insights from adult development theory can undergird enlightened institutional faculty development policies based on a recognition that human priorities, as well as professional priorities, change over a lifetime. Perhaps the most important are those that pay particular attention to the lifelong spectrum of faculty needs from the imprinting effects of doctoral training to faculty renewal and personal inclinations at the late career stage. The former may require intensive mentoring and evaluative feedback regarding teaching and institutional citizenship; the latter an understanding that faculty in the late career often seek new roles, especially in campus and community service, that enable them to pursue more focused interests. Institutional policies that make such options possible may encourage work contributions that constitute a legacy of lasting significance to the institution. As Jon Wergin (1999) notes, institutions attentive to faculty intrinsic needs, as well as extrinsic rewards, create organizational motivation by recognizing and rewarding faculty identification with the institution.

Ultimately, the ANAC Faculty Work Project envisions the faculty-institutional relationship being defined by a civic professionalism that nurtures the qualities that are both unique to higher education and essential to its mission. Foremost are policies and practices borne of the recognition that the vitality of the academic enterprise requires a healthy tension between the faculty autonomy necessary for open inquiry and meaningful academic freedom, on the one hand, and the faculty citizenship necessary for institutional community building on the other. Faculty yearn for an institutional community that will help to balance this tension, one that supports and recognizes their work and professional development while visibly welcoming and benefiting from their contributions. Such an institution would act as an enabler for a faculty member to become over a career, in the words of Eugene Rice, the complete scholar—a mature professional who not only adds significant value in teaching, research, and service, but has integrated these roles in ways that yield superior student learning, distinguished scholarship, and consequential institutional leadership.

REFERENCES

Adams, H. B. (1918). *The education of Henry Adams: An autobiography.* Boston, MA: Houghton Mifflin.

Allen, R. C. (2000, July 21). Why can't universities be more like businesses? *The Chronicle of Higher Education,* pp. B4–5.

Astin, A. W. (1994). Higher education reform and citizenship: A question of values. *Perspectives: The New American College, 24* (2), 79–91.

Bergquist, W. H. (1992). *The four cultures of the academy.* San Francisco, CA: Jossey-Bass.

Boyer, E. (1990). *Scholarship reconsidered: Priorities of the professoriate.* Princeton, NJ: The Carnegie Foundation for the Advancement of Teaching.

Boyer, E. (1994). The new American college. *Perspectives: The New American College, 24* (2), 6–12.

Carlin, J. (1999, November 5). Restoring sanity to an academic world gone mad. *Chronicle of Higher Education,* p. A76.

The Carnegie Foundation for the Advancement of Teaching. *The national survey of faculty 1997.* Unpublished survey results cited with permission of Mary Taylor Huber. See also, Huber, M. T. (1998). *Community college faculty: Attitudes and trends 1997.* Stanford, CA: National Center for Postsecondary Improvement.

Clark, B. R. (2000). Collegial entrepreneurialism in proactive universities: Lessons from Europe. *Change, 32,* 10-19.

Edgerton, R. (1997). *Higher education white paper.* Philadelphia, PA: The Pew Charitable Trusts.

Ewell, P. T. (1999). Imitation as art: Borrowed management techniques in higher education. *Change, 31,* 10-15.

Glassick, C. E., Huber, M. T., & Maeroff, G. I. (1997). *Scholarship assessed: Evaluation of the professoriate.* Princeton, NJ: The Carnegie Foundation for the Advancement of Teaching.

Katz, M. (1987). *Restructuring American education.* Cambridge, MA: Harvard University Press.

Levine, A. (2000, March 13). The soul of a new university. *New York Times,* p. A21.

Lynton, E. A. (1998, March). Reversing the telescope: Fitting individual tasks to common organizational ends. *American Association for Higher Education Bulletin,* 8-10.

Mintz, J. (1999, Spring). Faculty development and teaching: A holistic approach. *Liberal Education,* 32-37.

Rice, E. (1996). *Making a place for the new American scholar.* American Association for Higher Education New Pathways Working Paper Series. Washington, DC: American Association for Higher Education.

Schön, D. A. (1987). *Educating the reflective practitioner: Toward a new design for teaching and learning in the professions.* San Francisco, CA: Jossey-Bass.

Senge, P. M. (1990). *The fifth discipline: The art and practice of the learning organization.* New York, NY: Doubleday Currency.

Shulman, L. (1997). Professing the liberal arts. In R. Orrill (Ed.), *Education and democracy: Re-imagining liberal learning in America* (pp. 151-175). New York, NY: The College Board.

Tierney, W. G. (1999). *Building the responsive campus: Creating high performance colleges and universities.* Thousand Oaks, CA: Sage.

Wergin, J. F. (1999, December). Evaluating department achievements: Consequences for the work of the faculty. *American Association for Higher Education Bulletin,* 3-6.

2

PROFESSIONAL DEVELOPMENT ACROSS THE FACULTY CAREER: AN ENGINE FOR IMPLEMENTING A NEW FACULTY-INSTITUTIONAL COMPACT

Faculty Development/Career Stages Working Group
Marion Terenzio, Group Coordinator

A comprehensive institutional approach to faculty professional development over the lifetime of the faculty career is a cornerstone to successful implementation of a new compact in faculty-institutional relationships. Such an approach must be rooted in institutional behavior which demonstrates that faculty are the institution's indispensable human resource in achieving its primary mission of student learning and that the academic enterprise requires an environment nourishing to scholarly processes at the core of teaching and learning and the practice of faculty professionalism. The former suggests that institutional support for faculty human and professional needs as they evolve and change over time is indispensable to protect the institution's most critical human investment. The latter acknowledges the special mission entrusted to higher education to foster human development and democratic values—a stewardship requiring a central faculty role in institutional life. The principle of reciprocity fundamental to the compact calls, on the one hand, for institutions to create conditions that enable faculty to work effectively and develop professionally over the stages of the faculty career. On the other, it calls on faculty members to align their work with the priorities of the institutional mission and to contribute their special knowledge in enabling the institutional community to function effectively. The Associated New American Colleges (ANAC) has labeled the compact's symbiotic faculty-institutional relationship a "circle of value" in which each partner's actions are mutually enhancing and reinforcing.

The Associated New American Colleges' and The Carnegie Foundation for the Advancement of Teaching's (CFAT) survey and related Phase I activities reveal that many faculty members perceive that their institutions have not lived up entirely to their part of the compact. Faculty members commonly feel that they are doing the work their institutions expect of them, but that professional development support and faculty recognition and rewards are inadequate. They are highly satisfied in their individual work, but often feel frustrated and alienated in their relationships with the institutional community. Although the need to improve monetary rewards has received widespread attention, ANAC's assessments suggest, as well, that enabling faculty to experience the intrinsic satisfaction in the community interactions they gain from their individual work would go far in revitalizing faculty and institutional life. As with their students and their scholarship, faculty must believe that their efforts have impact on their institutional community if they are to value such service contributions.

FACULTY DEVELOPMENT FOR A NEW AGE

Historically, the primary focus of faculty development efforts has been on the individual faculty member and his or her ability to be productive. Faculty members and academic administrators alike often perceive faculty development as having just two purposes: to assist junior faculty in achieving tenure and to improve teaching skills. Almost all institutions have formal or informal programs that are designed to orient and support junior faculty during their probationary years. Faculty often view these programs with mixed feelings. On the one hand, there is a desire to help young faculty members during a stressful period. On the other, the pretenure trial period can be viewed as a harsh, but necessary process of natural selection. Consequently, according to this view, a probationary faculty member that needs too much assistance may not be a good risk for tenure. Many faculty development programs, of course, focus on improving the teaching skills of faculty members regardless of rank or longevity. These programs are often innovative and staffed by dedicated individuals who keep abreast of the latest developments in pedagogy and instructional technology. Still, such programs may have a limited impact because, understandably, they are not mandatory and their clients may be innovative teachers who are already "members of the choir." Indeed, when perceiving faculty development in terms limited primarily to teaching, it is understandable that many faculty members feel no need for development beyond the personal efforts they expend on their own scholarship and in the classroom. The needs of faculty members who may be disengaged from their institution for a variety of reasons appear not to be addressed in most faculty development programs.

Faculty professional development needs to be cast in a new role with a more far-reaching and strategic impact, one that acknowledges both the developmental nature of faculty careers and the evolution of institutional priorities. Such a rethinking of faculty development is essential in order to elevate its contribution to the total vitality of the institution. At the core of such a redefinition must be the recognition that faculty work is the fundamental technology of higher education and that faculty knowledge, skills, and attitudes must be fully engaged to help institutions find creative and feasible solutions to the challenges facing higher education. The capacity of faculty development programs to enhance faculty work through a natural and sustainable transformation process related to meaningful and rewarding faculty engagement with the institutional enterprise is essential for higher education to become more effective in educating students, to be more responsive and resilient in the face of rapid change, and to provide leadership in shaping our future society.

The need for colleges and universities to better anticipate and respond to societal trends in order to remain viable has been repeatedly addressed in the literature (Angelo, 1994; Finkelstein, Seal, & Schuster, 1998; Zahorski, 1993). Such commentators argue that changes in student and faculty demographics, the proliferation of technology in all domains of society, and increased public skepticism regarding faculty worth, will have a profound impact on current institutional practices and cultures. If ignored, the argument goes, the effects will severely hamper institutional success and, as a result, jeopardize students' ability to learn. Consequently, a persuasive connection is being made between faculty professional development and institutional readiness to accommodate change (Baiocco & DeWaters, 1998). Moreover, institutional culture and its impact on faculty represent an influential backdrop to the faculty development paradigm and its relationship to the faculty-institutional compact ANAC proposes.

Bland and Bergquist (1997) have provided a comprehensive review of institutional characteristics that contribute to a positive climate for faculty development and high levels of faculty satisfaction. They identify a number of institutional prerequisites shared by productive colleges and universities with vital faculties.

- Clear and consistent institutional goals and a distinctive organizational culture
- An uplifting and reinforcing campus climate characterized by collaborative governance, decentralized institutional structures, and effective communication networks
- Adequate resources in the form of time, space, equipment, supplies, and research and project funds
- Systems of rewards that convey the message that the members of the institutional community are valued
- Opportunities for members of the community to rejuvenate their careers
- Effective leadership

The governance culture that develops from such institutional characteristics is one in which administrators enable faculty leadership to flourish and to focus on strategic priorities critical to institutional well being.

The enhancement of faculty careers is dependent on the alignment between institutional culture and faculty work, on the alignment of both with institutional mission, and on faculty roles that go beyond teaching and research. This alignment should occur within an environment that recognizes and values the developmental nature of faculty lives and careers and allows for differentiation of work according to individual abilities, career phases, and institutional priorities. Faculty development, as envisioned through enactment of the faculty-institutional compact, is an indispensable vehicle in bringing faculty career planning and institutional mission together. The principle of reciprocity of the compact informs faculty roles and validates interdependent relationships among individual faculty members, faculty and their academic units, faculty and other members of the institution, and between higher education and the larger community.

The faculty development paradigm proposed here is responsive to contemporary issues and contexts that affect institutional health, encompasses individual and institutional development phases, and fosters collaborative relationships among faculty and between faculty and the institution. At many institutions this approach will require a fundamental shift in thinking about the faculty role, about the community work and governance associated with that role, and about the broader role of professional development in all domains of the institution. Such a rethinking would both empower faculty members and increase their sense of institutional accountability, while strengthening bonds of connectedness for all members of the institution. This process would encourage faculty to develop their sense of professionalism not only in their discipline but also in their larger institutional roles, as the institution strives to remain resilient and strategic while accommodating changing student learning patterns and contemporary professional work sector needs. In such a framework faculty will use their collective talents to further the institutional mission, and the institution will nurture faculty professional development patterns that assist faculty members to realize their full potential through differentiated work that is valued, recognized, and rewarded in its multiple dimensions. The ultimate outcome is a partnership where individual and institutional goals are aligned, one that advances effective instruction, responds to societal issues, and is prepared to accommodate change.

In short, the new compact requires a definition of faculty development actualized in an institutional environment where faculty members and administrators are able to collaborate in negotiating a "good fit" in advancing the professionalism of faculty work, addressing faculty needs at each career stage, and assuring institutional responsiveness to the demands of internal and external communities. This model of faculty professional development will increase institutional efficacy in meeting the evolving challenges of higher education, provide opportunities for faculty growth in the broadest sense, and promote quality in the educational experiences of students.

A DEFINITION OF FACULTY DEVELOPMENT

Faculty development is the process of nurturing the continuous learning, growth, and vitality of the faculty person (in all his or her roles) as a key community member in meeting the aims/goals of the organization, including long-lasting student learning and institutional agility in responding to internal and external forces.

Holistic definitions of faculty development have been advanced (Baiocco & DeWaters, 1998; Millis, 1994; Mintz, 1999) that acknowledge connections between faculty developmental and career stage issues and institutional mission, but which focus insufficiently on relationships between faculty roles and the institution's educational and community service missions and between faculty investment in the organization and the organization's ability to reward and support faculty work. The ANAC notion of faculty development encompasses two important characteristics: 1) that faculty work and institutional purpose shape each other, and 2) that there is a developmental /evolutionary quality of faculty, of their work, and of institutional functioning. These characteristics are at the center of a definition of faculty professionalism that calls for the highest expression of faculty expertise as a citizen of the institutional community, as well as a highly trained scholarly practitioner of teaching and research.

Both of these characteristics help to frame faculty roles that go beyond teaching, research, and service and an environment (Angelo, 1994; Krahenbuhl, 1998) that allows for change. Faculty development can provide the means through which faculty help to sustain institutional and individual flexibility. Such development can yield a type of professionalism that transcends discipline-based boundaries such as what Rice (1996) envisages in the evolution of "the complete scholar." This type of professionalism is an integral part of the fundamental process of discovery that is associated with the core scholarly role of faculty and long-lasting student learning. The professional challenge is to balance the need to be entrepreneurial with canons of scholarly professionalism associated with the pursuit of discovery. Put another way, faculty professionalism operationally requires accountability to codes of ethics and competence in scholarly practice, whether in determination of what is important to know or the design of learning experiences for students.

FACULTY DEVELOPMENT AND THE COMPACT: PRINCIPLES AND PROCESSES

ANAC proposes a faculty development paradigm based on five principles. In combination with the faculty development definition and faculty assessment findings, these principles are also an attempt to address faculty frustration widely identified in the literature regarding unmet professional expectations, dissatisfaction with salary, distrust of administrative motives, and stagnation in teaching and scholarship (Baiocco & DeWaters, 1998). Given such diverse sources of faculty dissatisfaction, a one-size-fits-all standard in teaching, research, and service seems archaic and no more relevant for faculty today than the assembly line in business. It jeopardizes, as well, the institution's ability to fulfill its mission and thrive. Rather, faculty development should be conceived of as a career-long process undertaken in the context of the institutional circle of value, where the needs and responsibilities of faculty as individuals are recognized and addressed within academic units and faculty roles are aligned with institutional mission and strategic plans.

The compact ANAC proposes validates these principles and processes, becoming the ethical and strategic equivalent of a covenant rooted in the interdependence of faculty and institution. Fundamental to the compact is a recognition of the centrality of the faculty role and the primacy of an appropriate and adequate investment in the continuing professional vitality of the faculty. This first principle of the compact seems never more critical than in the present when the majority of the tenured professors in this country are age 50 or older (Finkelstein et al., 1998) and when the advent of large numbers of new faculty is at hand.

> 1) *Faculty development occurs most effectively within the context of a healthy institution.*

A healthy academic institution has a vibrant intellectual culture and an ethos that fosters creativity, cultivates a sense of entrepreneurship, promotes risk taking, and has student learning and well being as its central outcome. The university, as defined through its structure, relationships, and key community members, takes a strategic stance in anticipating and responding to external opportunities and challenges and aligns mission, policies, practices, and rewards.

Governance is designed to focus the expertise of faculty and staff on the strategic priorities of the institution through processes that build institutional loyalty and community. Core values such as openness, consistency, flexibility, integrity, and fairness are critical to the institution's success. Faculty are understood to be the institution's mission critical human resource and the institution is committed to career-long faculty professional development and satisfaction. Equally important, the institution promotes the differentiation of faculty work as a strategy for negotiating the complex internal and external forces that impact not only the institution itself, but the processes and outcomes of education. Finally, the institution recognizes faculty and staff achievements and institutional contributions in ways that produce intrinsic human satisfaction.

INSTITUTIONAL EXAMPLE

FACULTY IMPROVEMENT GROUPS AT BELMONT UNIVERSITY

At Belmont University, Faculty Improvement Groups (FIGs) provide a powerful, yet informal method of continuing professional development for members of the university faculty. Similar to the teaching circles that are found at other institutions, Belmont's FIGs combine the advantages of collegial conversation, the exchange of new ideas, peer problem solving, and mutual support to produce a steady stream of innovative practices for both individual classes and university-wide processes. A Faculty Improvement Group forms whenever a group of faculty colleagues agree to meet regularly to talk about teaching and classroom experiences. Usually, the members of a FIG are faculty members in different academic disciplines. The optimum size of a group seems to be about six or seven, but groups with as few as five members and as many as ten have been successful. Most FIGs meet about once a month for an hour and a half to two hours. Depending on the preferences of the members, the FIG may set an agenda for its discussions and designate a discussion leader, but this is the group's choice. The effectiveness of the group depends on the group's ability to engage in authentic conversation about teaching.

The first Faculty Improvement Group began meeting during the 1990–1991 academic year. The members of that first group (four men and two women from five different academic disciplines) found the experience to be so beneficial that they shared their simple model with colleagues who formed additional groups. With the encouragement of the university's provost and, later, the active support of the teaching center, Belmont faculty members have formed more than 12 FIGs since the first group began meeting. In addition to stimulating the continuing professional development of individual members, FIGs have influenced the whole university in numerous ways.

- Members of Belmont's initial FIG championed the creation of a university-wide teaching center during Belmont's 1992–1993 strategic planning cycle. The teaching center was established at the beginning of the 1993–1994 academic year and has become the focal point for the institution's professional development of faculty as teachers.

- Members of Belmont's only all-female FIG recognized the need to connect students' learning experiences in classes with campus celebrations and observances outside of class. This group championed the campus-wide celebration of the Martin Luther King, Jr. national holiday and its members have sponsored special programs to engage students in reflection and action related to issues such as hunger and homelessness and cultural diversity.

- During the spring of 1998, members of one FIG enrolled as students in courses taught by other members. Each member took one class in a discipline other than his or her own. Throughout the semester, each member completed all assignments, received grades, and kept a journal of experiences as a learner. Their experiences served as the basis for discussion in FIG meetings as the members reflected on how their experiences can help them become more effective teachers. This FIG has also presented the results of its experiences at the Lilly Conference on Teaching (April and November 1999) and at the Association of American Colleges and Universities (January 2000).

At Belmont University, Faculty Improvement Groups have become an essential component of a collegial conversation about teaching that supports and advances the institutional vision to become a premier teaching university. They continue as a self-initiating means of professional development for faculty members that contribute incalculable benefits for the entire institution.

2) The institution is strategic and anticipatory in identifying faculty roles and in allocating resources in ways critical to mission fulfillment in changing times.

Higher education's ability to survive and thrive in today's fiercely competitive environment, where colleges and universities must simultaneously increase their cost-effectiveness and quality, requires acute responsiveness to the educational marketplace and the pressures of changing societal goals and perceptions. This has not always been the case. Indeed, a perceived lack of responsiveness resulting in a disconnection between educational outcomes and employment needs expressed by the professional world of work contributed to widespread criticism of faculty and institutional accountability throughout the decade of the nineties (Licklider, Schnelker, & Fulton, 1997–1998; Rice, 1996). Another type of public criticism comes from those who believe higher education has provided inadequate access and inappropriate learning environments for underrepresented and at-risk students (Mintz, 1999). Such inattentiveness to external pressures and expectations may well be symptomatic internally of the inability of higher education to develop a strategic connection between faculty roles and institutional needs. One essential component in this process is an expansion of faculty roles that transcend traditional tripartite boundaries of teaching, scholarship, and service. Mintz (1999) refers to this as a holistic approach that requires all levels of the institution to be engaged in developing the attitude and infrastructure of colleges and universities.

At times, faculty development needs to be daring by asking faculty members to explore new skills that may not seem immediately important to the institution. Consider a possible corporate analogy. Christensen (1997) has studied a succession of firms that made disk drives for the computer industry in recent decades. Almost all of the firms involved in the manufacture of disk drives were run by individuals who viewed themselves as forward-looking and who paid close attention to the concerns of their current customers. Yet each new wave of technology (each new generation of increasingly smaller disks) caused the demise of or severe hardships in most disk manufacturing firms. Only those firms that were daring enough to develop new skills for emerging technologies and practices enjoyed continued success. Almost always these new technologies and practices were not in demand by current clients and in their initial stages they were usually not as effective as the then current technologies and practices. Yet, those with the daring to invest in developing skills in areas that might, in the future, be applied to the firm's main field of attention achieved success. Similarly, academic institutions need to develop faculty and institutional expertise that may not yet be desired by our current students or which may not yet be as effective as our traditional methods.

INSTITUTIONAL EXAMPLE

THE ELON INITIATIVE ON THE SCHOLARSHIP OF TEACHING AND LEARNING

The Elon initiative on the scholarship of teaching and learning focuses on the course as its unit of study. Elon faculty wished to increase intellectual engagement in courses 1) by bringing fresh insights to bear, 2) applying learning to life, and 3) creating space for reflective integration. The college committed to fund four creative proposals a year for three years—proposals for designing, enacting, and studying courses meeting such goals. Thus, at the end of the academic year 2001–2002, 12 projects will have been completed and the results harvested. The Elon leadership team, noting that learning is best seen as a faculty-student partnership, required that all proposals be studied by faculty-student teams. This aspect proved crucial.

Elon's stance is to see student and teacher as a partnership in service of goals larger than either and to center on the conditions of learning such that learning occurs for both student and teacher. Elon's most recent work deepens and expands faculty-student partnerships by seeing how such partnerships can be strengthened in courses and how courses can be best studied by faculty-student research teams.

---

3) *The institution actively prepares and adequately recognizes and rewards faculty for flexible roles, including those that go beyond teaching and scholarship.*

This call to action is not new. Boyer (1990), in differentiating scholarship, and Rice (1996), in articulating the career path of the complete scholar, envision the emergence of a "new American scholar," a paradigm in which faculty work is differentiated. Mintz (1999) discusses the need to utilize faculty development to help foster the values of the community. Palmer (1996) identifies the need to counter a faculty independent contractor mentality and to remove the sense of isolation that many faculty report. Krahenbuhl (1998) advocates that faculty workload be configured in ways that both maintain faculty vitality and contribute to discovery within the community of learning. According to Krahenbuhl, the discovery process takes different forms and requires a mutually collaborative partnership between faculty and the institution. Denham et al. (1996) propose that faculty work should be assessed in terms of quality, significance, and impact rather than in terms of work categories. Such assessment must include artic-ulation of the roles and responsibilities of the academic unit and the relationship between the unit and the faculty member and the unit and the institution.

The ability to reconfigure roles, be they at the individual faculty, the academic unit, or the broader institutional level serves a dual pur-pose. The first is to accommodate natural and evolutionary changes in each domain, for example, individual faculty career paths, acquisition of new knowledge and techniques of discovery in academic disci-plines, and mission-focused service to the greater community. The second purpose, dependent on accomplishment of the first, is the abil-ity of the institution to remain agile. This attribute is necessary in a cli-mate of continuous pressures to improve the quality of education, of fierce and constant competition for funding, and of increasingly diverse student and faculty demographics.

Higher education has been notably conservative about developing new forms of faculty recognition and rewards appropriate to the grow-ing institutional expectations of faculty in changing times. Indeed, CFAT and ANAC faculty assessments reveal that gaining tenure and promotion are still far and away the most effective incentives that high-er education offers, but, at best, these occur only three times in an entire faculty career! The surveys show further that faculty dissatisfaction with institutional performance in all types of institutions is nowhere more pronounced than in regard to institutional rewards. Although merit salary increases rank third among reward incentives for faculty and one-time bonuses attract some support, the widespread practice of awarding faculty standard percentage or dollar salary increases attracts almost no support as a faculty incentive. Two-thirds of faculty believe salaries are inadequate, understandable in comparison to compensation in other professions, but, unfortunately, perhaps reflective of the value society places on education and the need for bold new approaches to higher education cost-effectiveness. Interestingly, the surveys demonstrate significant faculty interest in testing the reward value of innovative nonmonetary forms of recognition.

INSTITUTIONAL EXAMPLE

PROVOST'S SEMINAR AT MERCER UNIVERSITY

The provost's office at Mercer University initiated a 2000–2001 seminar and workshop program for faculty interested in careers in academic administration. Entitled the "Provost's Seminar," this 15-month faculty and administrative staff leadership and professional development program attracted 20 participants. Participants used as a text the 1997 work by James Martin, James E. Sammels, and Associates, *First Among Equals: The Role of the Chief Academic Officer,* and read and discussed a variety of articles from higher education periodicals such as *Change, The Journal of Higher Education,* and *About Campus.* In addition to its two-hour monthly sessions, the Provost's Seminar included intensive two-day workshops during the 2000 and 2001 summers.

Seminar sessions included presentations from senior administrators at Mercer University and elsewhere on topics ranging from administrative roles and challenges in areas such as planning, budgeting, governance, curriculum development, personnel administration, learning assessment, enrollment management, accreditation, distance education, and community engagement. In addition to seminar and workshop activities, each participant used the seminar as a framework to complete a project related to some aspect of the participant's college or division that would improve student welfare. In this way the Provost's Seminar both modeled the integration of theory and practice that is a central ANAC learning tenet and enabled participants to gain practical experience in testing their interest in academic administration.

> 4) *Faculty work and institutional mission are aligned, and faculty members fulfill the responsibility of active professional development.*

While the institution has an obligation to provide a supportive environment for faculty to perform their critical roles in achieving higher education's mission, faculty, for their part, must engage themselves continuously with the institution, as well as their own discipline. As Krahenbuhl (1998) has observed, faculty work must not only encompass a broad range of responsibilities, but the focus of such work should be on the collective efforts and accomplishments of the faculty, and not on individual member contributions. This type of orientation allows faculty the freedom and ability to shape their work in a variety of ways in collaboration with the institution, to concentrate on learning outcomes, and to fulfill important faculty roles beyond the classroom. Rice (1996) contends that such an arrangement would require faculty to give up what he characterizes as the "assumptive world" of the academic professional where many faculty have viewed themselves as independent agents, a stance that has created a disconnect between faculty and their institutions and between faculty and society. Such a change in self-perception, and thus in perceived status and identity, means expanding the notion of faculty professionalism beyond the discipline and broadening and differentiating concepts of teaching, research, and service (Denham et al., 1996; Krahenbuhl, 1998; Zahorski, 1993).

Too often members of academic communities view the future through the perspective of what has always been. An important new role for faculty development will be to provide strategic perspectives and tools that assist faculty to assess critically alternative futures for higher education and for their institution. Colleges and universities could benefit greatly from faculty critical analysis and scholarship regarding internal and external forces that frame strategic decisions shaping institutional futures. Developing effective faculty participation in the scholarly assessment of the institution's future could help, as well, to identify additional capacities that faculty members might develop for institutional and professional benefit.

INSTITUTIONAL EXAMPLE

FACULTY DEVELOPMENT AT DRURY UNIVERSITY

Drury University recognizes the necessity of being responsive to rapid changes in higher education, but there must be a set of common purposes that transcend passing fads and technological innovations. These goals, which give distinctive purpose to an institution, must become an integral component of the campus culture. The Drury University board of directors, faculty, staff, administration, and alumni worked in unison to define a vision for the next ten years. The result was a strategic plan that established five clear goals, and was strongly endorsed by all constituencies of the university. A primary goal of the strategic plan was to strengthen academic programs, and a significant part of the strategy to accomplish this objective was to establish a center for faculty excellence.

The Center for Faculty Excellence (CFE) at Drury University was established in the summer of 2000, with the purpose to enhance all areas of faculty life. Like many teaching/learning centers across the nation, the CFE will provide assistance for faculty seeking to enhance their teaching. What sets the Drury program apart is a recognition of faculty life as a rich, complex interaction between teaching, scholarship, and service. The Association of New American Colleges made a significant impact on Drury's expectations for the responsibilities and citizenship of the university professor. Faculty development must enhance scholarship and service as well as teaching. For example, the CFE sponsored a public lecture by Christopher Lucas on striking an appropriate institutional balance between effective teaching and rigorous faculty scholarship. The lecture gave rise to a roundtable discussion among faculty, staff, and administration that has reshaped institutional policies for faculty evaluation.

The Center for Faculty Excellence has strategic goals of enhancing interdisciplinary work between faculty that leads to active scholarship and publication. For example, the CFE has taken the lead in designing Drury Interest Groups (DIGs), interdisciplinary learning communities built around a shared research agenda. Other goals include facilitating the changes that occur across the trajectories of faculty careers, including the change from young scholar to being the mentor of a young scholar. New faculty orientation sessions throughout the 2000–2001 academic year have been built around this general theme.

5) *Faculty development is most effective within a broad context of human, career, and organizational development perspectives and is forward looking.*

It is not enough for institutions to recognize the need to differentiate faculty work; faculty work must also be placed in a developmental context. Increased attention in the professional literature is being
paid to the progressive nature of faculty careers, shifts in demands
and responsibilities that accompany evolutionary career changes, and
the need to address this progression (Baiocco & DeWaters, 1998; Rice,
1996). As we have noted, this discussion needs to take place within
the context of the institutional mission (Millis, 1994). Additionally, the
progressive nature of faculty careers should be understood within the
framework of what is known about adult development. While theo-
ries vary regarding adult capacity to develop over time, a common
element in all is the human need for differentiation—whether of
interests, abilities, domains of expertise, or life tasks (Bland &
Bergquist, 1997). The implications of adult development theory for
higher education also center on the institution's ability to be sensitive
to the human need for intrinsic rewards. For faculty members such
rewards arise from opportunities to pursue the passions of their intellectual curiosity, their abiding interest in improving student learning,
their desire to disseminate their discoveries—whether from research,
teaching, or a combination of both—and their wish to have an impact
in bettering their institution (Angelo, 1994).

INSTITUTIONAL EXAMPLE

THE LEARNING-TEACHING CENTER AT UNIVERSITY OF DAYTON

The University of Dayton recently created a Learning-Teaching
Center (LTC) designed to serve as a laboratory for innovation in learning and teaching. The center, which serves both students and faculty
in their development needs, brings together the work of several complementary areas, including learning assistance, academic technology,
faculty development, service-learning, and students with disabilities.
Located in the ground floor of the university's library, it houses many
offices and centers, including learning assistance, groupware labs,
students with disabilities, service-learning, media services, the web
mentors, academic technology, and faculty development, initiatives
united in their pursuit of excellence in learning processes. In addition
to offices for these groups, the LTC contains an experimental classroom, a seminar room, a growing collection of print materials, cozy

spaces (including a fireplace area) for meetings or study, small group meeting rooms, and a student-run coffee and espresso bar (The Blend) which demonstrates the power of learning by doing.

Faculty development at the University of Dayton is viewed as a process of continuous growth and renewal regardless of career stage. The center's design reflects that. The coffee bar attracts faculty from across campus to the space, and the furnishings and ambiance of the space invite people to attend seminars, meet with others or enjoy some quiet time with a book or a laptop, to linger, and to browse through a collection of print materials or interact with center staff. An experimental classroom (the "Studio") promotes a community of practice around teaching. Faculty submit an application to teach an entire course in the space, so that they are doing their work within the center. While teaching in the Studio, the usual student evaluation forms are not used, in favor of more developmental feedback. The room is designed to facilitate the active engagement of students, with movable whiteboards and flexible furniture and technology support, and the class size is limited to 24. Faculty teaching in the space agree to meet every three weeks in a community of practice, to talk about teaching issues and challenges and to share ideas with each other. Faculty research on learning and decision-making processes is strongly encouraged.

With interesting and inviting architecture, high-quality furnishings, and hospitality, as well as good coffee, the Learning-Teaching Center has positioned itself as a space where people can build community, find hospitality, and connect with other teacher-scholars on campus. Early indications are that the combination is an appealing and sustaining one.

THE COMPACT THROUGH TIME

If faculty development is to be a process for preparing faculty for increasingly valuable roles, opportunities for faculty to invest in and feel part of their institutional community must be essential elements in the development program. In this sense, the compact operates at two levels. On the macro level is the set of relationships that define and bind the faculty body and institution as a professional community. Equally important, the compact requires a micro-level negotiation of the professional relationship between individual faculty and the institution over time. To this point this chapter has focused largely on the compact at the macro level. The analysis now turns to where the two levels intersect in shaping the faculty career path, in the process enabling the compact to act as a gyro or rudder in guiding relationships over time that will shape the destiny of both individual faculty members and their institution.

ANAC views the key intersection in the micro-compact to be the individual faculty member plan of work, a formalized set of understandings that articulate faculty and institutional agreement on work responsibilities and performance expectations (primarily, although certainly not entirely through the academic unit), the criteria and process by which the faculty member's work will be professionally evaluated, and the faculty member's plan of professional development. Critical to the work plan is a process of faculty member self-assessment and a clear understanding of the role of self-assessment in shaping work responsibilities, evaluation of professional performance, and the focus of the plan of professional development. At minimum, general understandings regarding faculty recognition and rewards must also be incorporated to seal the compact as a true faculty-institutional partnership and to underscore faculty obligations to institutional mission and expectations, and institutional obligations to support faculty roles and to invest appropriately in career-long faculty professional development.

ANAC's Faculty Work Project has been predicated on the assumption that a faculty-institutional compact is especially important in defining relationships within a professional community where individual membership is expected to be long term. Elements central in a macro-level compact providing career-long employment commitments to faculty, through tenure or other long-term appointment policies, might include the following.

- A hiring and institutional orientation process that articulates clearly institutional mission and expectations and faculty status, responsibilities, and rewards
- A tenure/promotion/post-tenure review process that recognizes faculty contributions in their differentiated academic unit and institution-wide roles and promotes long-lasting learning and professional development

- An institutional ethos and procedures that fosters meaningful intrinsic and extrinsic faculty rewards
- An institutional mission that commits to meeting the needs of society while providing a work environment that inspires engagement
- A campus culture that encourages building connections among colleagues, students, and staff
- An institutional strategic plan that acknowledges faculty personal and professional growth as a key institutional development strategy

A compact environment with these institutional characteristics has the capacity both to implement ANAC's model of faculty development and to foster a circle of value among faculty, academic units, and the institution as a whole.

There are at least five major phases in the stages of the faculty career when the micro and macro dimensions of the compact intersect in ways critical in negotiating fulfillment of institutional mission and faculty personal and professional well being. The table which follows serves as a template for conceptualizing the reciprocal policies and behavior designed to nurture faculty-institutional mutuality over a faculty career. Listed in each phase are the roles and responsibilities of the institution, in its broadest policy and practice sense, and those of the individual faculty member. Although the micro-level compact is negotiated between individual faculty members and the academic administration, it is predicated on clearly articulated macro-level compact features, for example, the role of the academic unit, the inventory of faculty work in that unit, and the mission of the institution. The process of enacting the compact involves the identification of faculty workload expectations within the service context of the college or university's mission, and as mediated by the academic unit during each compact phase.

The Pre-Hire Phase

During the initial pre-hire phase, the institution, represented by the academic administration, is responsible for assuring that policies reflect the interactive partnership between faculty and their academic unit, and that the respective faculty and institutional roles are clearly articulated, internally consistent, and aligned with mission prior to

TABLE 2.1 The Compact (The Work Plan)

Compact Phases and Career Stages	Institution *(General institutional and specific academic unit policies and practices)*	Individual *(Education background, talents, skills, expectations, and understanding of higher education)*
Pre-Hire Phase	Tenure to the institution; faculty positions institutionally approved and reflect unit and institutional priorities. Institution provides in writing: • The mission statement and institutional profile (including student profile) • Professional rank requirements • Workload policies and professional development • Evaluation, reward, and governance policies	Candidate: • Understands and selects ANAC institutional model as career calling • Is prepared to demonstrate qualifications and commitments specific hiring institution has articulated • Understands and is prepared to enter a compact relationship with hiring institutions.
Hiring Phase	Institution and individual candidate approach hiring process, especially interview, as a full exchange of compact understandings (see above) and expectations in search of a good "fit" for candidate and institution: • Participation of key stakeholders (faculty, students, administrators, possibly others) • Candidate demonstration of research, teaching, and service qualifications, and capacity for flexible roles • Exploration of potential for long-term mutuality, including ability to negotiate terms of mutuality • Agreement on mutual expectations essential	
Early Career: Probationary Compact (Normally, tenure track)	• Extended orientation and mentoring • Workload assignments that test full range of institutional expectations • Succession of term appointments • Regular evaluation and feedback with appropriate recognition and rewards • Support for professional development • Opportunities mutually to refine compact regarding roles and workload expectations to meet institutional and individual needs	• Periodic self-assessment and active alignment of work patterns and professional development with institutional mission and evaluative feed back • Planning and seeking of institutional feedback on short- and long-term professional goals • Assessment of satisfaction with institutional mutuality

Long-Term Compact	(Normally, lifetime tenure with mid- and late-career stages)	
Mid-Career Phase (Longest career phase for most faculty)	• Periodic assessment of institutional and individual priorities re new roles and professional development • Effective periodic post-tenure review; appropriate recognition, rewards, and professional advancement • Support for evolution of the complete scholar	• Work priorities and professional development reflect institutional negotiation with specific mutual long-term objectives • Planning for professional advancement regarding the complete scholar • Maturation of research and teaching • Assumption of major institutional service roles
Sage/Legacy Compact (Approximately the final decade of career)	• Prepare opportunities to use faculty interests and accumulated expertise flexibly for institutional priorities • Institute flexible phased retirement and unit faculty replacement plans • Provide special professional development and career recognition for senior faculty	• Assess institutional roles that most reflect interests, expertise, and capacity for contributions that represent an institutional legacy and negotiate terms of implementation • Partner with institution on mutually beneficial retirement plans • Establish rewarding lifetime relationship with institution

the actual hiring process. This includes anticipated workload assignments, tenure and promotion processes, and professional development support and expectations that will lead to successful faculty career paths at the institution. The responsibility of the faculty candidate during this phase is to determine whether there appears to be a reasonable "fit" between individual interests and abilities and institutional needs and policies. Concluding that such a fit exists should be based on the potential candidate's understanding and preference for the institutional type, as well as an ability to articulate potential work contributions and how that work would add value to the academic unit and serve the larger institutional mission.

The potential for a disconnect between a new faculty member and the institutional type is high due to the acculturation of prospective faculty to a "research first" faculty professional model during their research university doctoral training. The overwhelming majority of new faculty are hired at institutions whose primary mission is teaching, who are "students first" in their focus, and where there are strong expectations regarding institutional service as a fundamental workload responsibility. Hiring faculty candidates who see themselves launching research careers that involve minimal investment in teaching and little sense of obligation or interest in engaging in building the institution may be a recipe for disaster. This hazard is sometimes exacerbated in cases where faculty or academic administrators at the hiring institution become overly enamored with the seeming promise of high-powered research a candidate might bring to create a stronger research climate at the institution. As the difficulties many institutions have in rewarding adequately superior teaching and service indicate, the institution itself may become an intentional or unintentional co-conspirator in wooing such a candidate, while inadequately recognizing other candidates' potential contributions to pedagogical innovations more central to fulfillment of the unit's or institution's particular mission. If the institution is clear about its mission and related work priorities of its faculty, its representatives are less likely to fall into this trap and are better able to provide prospective faculty members with realistic expectations prior to hiring that will contribute to a good fit in filling the position.

The Hiring Phase

A successful hiring phase occurs when the candidate and institution complete an interview process in which a full disclosure of institutional policies and expectations, and a full demonstration of the candidate's abilities and commitments, produce a match validated through a contractual agreement that initiates the compact. The successful candidate and the institution have agreed to enter into a collaboration in which role expectations for the new faculty member and his or her career path aspirations are mutually understood and in alignment with unit and institutional mission, resources necessary to sustain the compact are identified, and the institution's new faculty orientation, mentoring, and tenure track evaluation, feedback, and socialization processes are in place.

INSTITUTIONAL EXAMPLE

ORIENTING NEW FACULTY AT THE UNIVERSITY OF THE PACIFIC

In the late 1990s a New Faculty Orientation Program was developed at the University of the Pacific which aims to acculturate new faculty more fully into the institutional culture. During a period characterized by a large exodus of retiring faculty, the institution found it necessary to provide more than the obligatory day and a half of orientation activities previously provided by the university. The new process, then, actually begins with the on-campus interview process experienced by all finalists in faculty searches. During the on-campus interview all candidates meet with the assistant provost for a 30-minute session. This session focuses on the university's mission, vision and priorities statements, and how the candidate's strengths and experiences can help to augment the university's ability to achieve its mission. Once a hire has been made, the traditional day and a half orientation schedule is expanded into a year-long series of monthly luncheons which focus on topics relevant to the first-year faculty experience such as "Designing and Teaching a Course" and "The Nature and Sources of Faculty Stress." Gerald Gibson's excellent text, *Good Start* (1992), serves as the faculty development workbook throughout the year. At the end of this rather comprehensive orientation program, new faculty receive a certificate of completion, as well as a sense of community with other new faculty across the campus that would have been impossible to achieve without this type of regular interaction.

Early Career: Probationary Compact

Critical to successful completion of the early career probationary compact, normally the tenure track, is a mutual recognition that faculty member and institutional patterns and relationships that are developed during this period have long-term, even career-long, implications. Consequently, faculty member and institution alike must have their eyes on the ultimate prize—the professional evolution of a complete scholar—not only the near-term achievement of a tenure decision or long-term contract favorable to each. To accomplish this goal, institution and faculty member alike must engage in ongoing assessment of workload, performance, and professional development. Perhaps the most telling indicators of a probationary faculty member's potential are a capacity for self-evaluation that leads to increasingly productive and effective work patterns and related professional development planning that identifies activities to address areas for potential improvement in the short term, as well as charting longer-term professional accomplishments. Too often, and perhaps inevitably, faculty who are going up for tenure and faculty who mentor those going up for tenure focus almost solely on tenure as the prize, neglecting the larger career path and preparations for contingencies that the institution may face that could affect faculty roles in the future. The intent in expressing the compact and stages of the faculty career as a continuum is to post a reminder that there is life after tenure and to assist the institution in providing an environment where faculty invest productively in the institution at each career phase.

For its part, the institution must create a work environment that nurtures faculty professional satisfaction, that engages faculty in a ongoing review of faculty and institutional effectiveness, that provides professional evaluation and feedback focused on institutional expectations expressed in compact agreements, that provides guidance and resources for professional development, and recognizes and rewards faculty achievements in ways that further compact understandings and relationships. Such conditions extend to involving faculty in meaningful institutional service work that engages their interests and expertise as much as possible, and governance relationships connecting individual faculty with the larger faculty and institutional community. A logical axiom for relationships established during the probationary compact might be that what happens will have imprinting effects as powerful and long lasting, or more so, than the imprinting regarding the faculty career that occurs in doctoral programs.

INSTITUTIONAL EXAMPLE

PROBATIONARY FACULTY REVIEWS AT DRAKE UNIVERSITY

At Drake University, new tenure-track faculty members in the College of Arts and Sciences receive the following documents at the fall orientation: the college handbook that contains the statements or criteria for promotion and tenure, the department of appointment's elaboration of the college criteria, and the promotion and tenure committee guidelines for preparing credentials for promotion and tenure. These documents are critical to each year's review. During the annual review, the tenure-track faculty member presents credentials following the guidelines in these documents. The tenured department faculty review the materials and evaluate the performance in light of the college and department statements. The chair of the department then prepares a statement that discusses the candidate's performance with reference to teaching, scholarship, and service. The statement is circulated among all tenured faculty members. When all have agreed, the final draft is prepared and each tenured faculty member signs the document. Before the letter goes to the dean, the candidate under review is given a copy of the document with the opportunity to prepare a response. The signed letter and the candidate's response, if there is one, are then submitted to the dean. The dean reviews the document and prepares a letter to the candidate noting significant accomplishments and areas that need attention. All documents become a part of the file presented to the promotion and tenure committee when the candidate presents credentials for consideration at the end of the probationary period. The advantage of the procedures is that a written record exists, all parties concerned are aware of the contents, and there are no surprises at the time of the tenure decision.

Mid-Career Phase

Historically, colleges and universities have largely ignored (with the exception of promotion to full professor) the fourth phase of the compact, the post-tenure mid-career years, with unfortunate consequences for both faculty member and institution. Although many liberal arts colleges and smaller comprehensive institutions have had periodic post-tenure faculty evaluation processes in place for some time, performance evaluation in higher education as a whole frequently ended with the tenure decision until the advent of the post-tenure review movement of the past decade. The results of this neglect have been debilitating for the faculty member who may experience professional isolation, career drift, declining competence, and scholarly atrophy, effects extremely costly to the institution as well. Virtually every institution has experienced the mid-career faculty member who, instead of actively achieving professional maturation and promotion to full professor, seems increasingly out of touch and embittered, setting the stage for a ten-to-15 year late career stage as a senior faculty member who can be a powerful, expensive, and predominantly negative influence difficult to reckon with. Such a sorry outcome and its consequences for students, junior faculty looking for role models, and institutional effectiveness—not to mention the human and career toll for such faculty members themselves—seem as unnecessary as they are unfortunate.

Having just laid the groundwork resulting in a tenure decision to engage in a career-long compact, faculty member and institution must now implement essential processes that will enable both partners to flourish in a reciprocal relationship that, properly attended to, could last for the remainder of the faculty member's career—perhaps several decades. Joined at the hip, faculty member and institution must attend to the post-tenure years as a time for periodic review and revitalization of work and professional development plans with reciprocity foremost. In some sense, the immediate post-tenure years are an opportunity for the faculty career to move into a higher gear than was possible during the tenure probationary years. Although it may be a hard-sell to faculty due to the career securing "up or out" importance that has been placed on the tenure decision, the argument can be made that the stakes are higher for institution and faculty member during the post-tenure compact.

INSTITUTIONAL EXAMPLE

NORTH CENTRAL COLLEGE AND POST-TENURE REVIEW

At North Central College, tenured faculty members are reviewed every five years to assess their professional competence and to assist in their continued professional development. As in reviews for tenure and promotion, faculty members present a self-evaluation, along with documentation and peer and student evaluations, to the faculty personnel committee. Based on this review, faculty performance is measured as "commendable," "acceptable," or "unacceptable." In the case of an "unacceptable" ranking, the faculty would have ample opportunity to improve his or her performance with care for due process, but termination is possible if, after the next five-year review, the faculty member's performance is still unacceptable. Post-tenure review at North Central is both a formative and summative evaluation.

For faculty members, the post-tenure years are what earning a doctorate and gaining a faculty position are all about—the opportunity to pursue a meaningful professional career that allows for deep intrinsic personal satisfaction, membership in a community, public recognition, and service to society in a fundamental way. For the institution, these are the years when the investment in faculty potential really pays off—in master teaching, mature scholarship, experienced institutional leadership, and enhanced institutional reputation—in ways that serve the mission with quality and distinction and secure the institution's future. Therefore, the tenure probationary cycle of institutional review, evaluation, rewards, and professional development investments and faculty self-assessment, professional development planning, and institutional service must continue, if anything, with a heightened flexibility as the partners seek roles, relationships, and investments in each other that will yield maximum mutual return.

The Sage/Legacy Phase

If the mid-career stage of the faculty career following tenure has suffered historically from neglect, the last decade or so prior to retirement may be the most misunderstood and problematical. This occurs at the very time when faculty salaries are at a career high point and faculty members, at least in an ideal world, are poised to contribute a career's worth of accumulated wisdom and expertise for institutional benefit. This fifth and final phase of the compact, representing the last five to ten years of a faculty member's career at an institution, is referred to as the sage/legacy phase. This is a time when a faculty member might be afforded the opportunity and appropriate flexible workload arrangements to impart his or her wisdom to the communities within and without the institution in ways congruent with his or her career path and the institutional mission. The primary responsibility of faculty at this career stage is to engage in self-reflection regarding appropriate legacy service as a culmination of the faculty member's term compact with the institution. Ways in which faculty at this stage might impart their accumulated wisdom include conducting an important institutional study, serving as a special institutional advancement ambassador, mentoring junior faculty, leading a key institutional project, or applying discipline expertise to a myriad of analytical needs such as technology planning, financial analysis, or campus physical enhancement. The point is to allow senior faculty to reach closure, to complete their careers feeling that their contributions had an impact and their work was highly valued. What better way for institutions to benefit from senior faculty than from such legacy service?

Yet, this is also the career stage when many senior faculty are stigmatized as "old guard," "deadwood," and other appellations, and become marginalized as a force for good in the institution. Of course, many other senior faculty become lionized as "Mr. Chips" or with other superstar labels that suggest the much more positive senior faculty professional model that every college and university also experiences. The point is that the faculty-institutional compact can make the latter alternative much more prevalent than it is today on most campuses.

We have chosen the latter model in characterizing the late career as the sage/legacy stage, mindful that the compact must address the negative former condition. In their fascinating study, *The Vitality of Senior Faculty Members* (1997), Bland and Bergquist combine adult and development theory in arguing that older faculty are probably not deadwood at all, but may have lost contact with the institutional community (become "stuck") and are expressing their interests and energies elsewhere, perhaps away from the institution entirely. They contend further that senior faculty have entered a life stage when they become increasingly motivated to leave legacies that benefit what they care about most, that provide meaning to their lives, and that validate their life's work. If Bland and Bergquist are right, and ANAC's assessments suggest that they are, the critical importance of nurturing the faculty-institutional relationship during the mid- and late-career can hardly be overstated. Finally, in addition to meeting institutional and faculty needs during the late career, a relationship based on continuing reciprocity sets the stage for a lifetime compact, extending into the emeritus years a mutuality that has significant human overtones and underscoring community values which help to ennoble higher education's special role in society.

ANAC advocates that institutions adopt even more flexible and individualized approaches to faculty needs and opportunities during the late career stage than at other stages, in part because individual differences vary more widely at this stage and in part because the relative payoff for the institution may be much greater during the late career. Institutions should review workload options, evaluate faculty developmental needs and interests, consider special status recognition and senior faculty awards, develop less than full-time appointment options, and plan collaboratively for early and phased retirement to assure that the needs of faculty, students, and academic units are all met. In one case, a faculty member may have special expertise from which the institution can benefit more significantly on a special institutional project than through the usual faculty workload. In another case, a leave of absence to pursue a special interest may be a renewing experience of tremendous professional development value. Yet another case might involve consideration of special and unusual circumstances in applying the criteria for promotion to full professor. And in still another, a faculty member who is a strong teacher may really want a reduced workload until age 70, calling for an unusual institutional action that enables a department to make a smooth transition in replacing several retiring faculty. Finally, another case may be that of the outstanding senior faculty member who wants simply to continue his or her excellent contributions of the past 30 years.

INSTITUTIONAL EXAMPLE

WORK PLANS AND CAREER STAGES AT ITHACA COLLEGE

The differential work model at Ithaca College encourages faculty to pursue a career path in which change is valued and rewarded. As the academic unit carries out its planning, the faculty member has the opportunity to renegotiate individual goals and objectives periodically with consultation and agreement among colleagues in the academic unit. The reasoning behind this aspect of the model at Ithaca is that the needs of the faculty member at the beginning of a career focus on developing teaching and research experience and expertise while those in the succeeding phase of the career focus on developing greater sophistication in teaching and scholarly or creative activity with hopes of being promoted to full professor. In the next phase of the career, the period between promotion to professor and the preretirement phase, the faculty member begins to focus on particular interests which have evolved earlier and works to establish some notable position in the discipline, a reputation as a notably exceptional teacher, or a faculty member who excels in leadership and service, or some combination of the above. It is during this period that the faculty member often reaches the highest point of attainment. In the preretirement phase many faculty, having achieved a reputation of some distinction and seeing the end of a career ahead, become reflective. The reward system at this point in the faculty member's career must recognize the value, experience, and contribution of the faculty member and provide opportunities for the faculty member to "give back" to the institution and receive public recognition for that work. At Ithaca, this often takes the form of receipt of one of the faculty excellence awards which are given at a special luncheon prior to commencement, with recognition at the commencement ceremony. Other reward possibilities include designation as a distinguished teacher-scholar.

CONCLUSION

ANAC's faculty development paradigm revitalizes institutions of higher education by refocusing commitment on faculty as the institution's preeminent resource. While other strategies should be implemented to assure institutional agility and viability, a focus on faculty development that allows for more flexible and effective faculty roles is paramount for colleges and universities to establish a new compact with faculty in meeting the challenges facing higher education. The new compact calls for reciprocity in relationships between faculty and institution, a recognition that fostering institutional community is both consistent with educational values and a sound strategy for creating mutuality, and a dedication on the part of both institution and faculty to developmental processes at each stage of the faculty career that are critical to the compact's long-term effectiveness.

ACKNOWLEDGMENTS

The Faculty Development/Career Stages Working Group included Deb Bickford (University of Dayton), Francis Dane (Mercer University), Jerry Greiner (Hamline University), Ed Kavanagh (Quinnipiac University), Marion Terenzio (The Sage Colleges), Ron Troyer (Drake University), and Mark Woods (Drury University).

REFERENCES

Angelo, T. A. (1994, June). From faculty development to academic development. *American Association for Higher Education Bulletin*, 3-7.

Baiocco, S. A., & DeWaters, J. N. (1998). Futuristic faculty development: Toward a comprehensive program. In *Successful college teaching: Problem solving strategies of distinguished professors* (pp. 248-277). Boston, MA: Allyn & Bacon.

Bland, C. J., & Bergquist, W. H. (1997). *The vitality of senior faculty members: Snow on the roof—fire in the furnace.* (ASHE-ERIC Higher Education Report, Vol. 25, No. 7). Washington, DC: ERIC Clearinghouse on Higher Education.

Boyer, E. (1990). *Scholarship reconsidered: Priorities of the professoriate.* Princeton, NJ: The Carnegie Foundation for the Advancement of Teaching.

Christensen, C. M. (1997). *The innovator's dilemma: When new technologies cause great firms to fail.* Cambridge, MA: Harvard Business School Press.

Denham, R., Kramsch, C., Phelps, L., Rassias, J., Slevin, J., & Swaffar, J. (1996). Making faculty work visible: Reinterpreting professional service, teaching, and research in the fields of Language and Literature. [Modern Language Association Commission on Professional Service Report.] *Profession*, 161-216.

Finkelstein, M., Seal, R., & Schuster, J. (1998). *The new academic generation: A profession in transformation.* Baltimore, MD: The Johns Hopkins University Press.

Krahenbuhl, G. S. (1998). Faculty work: Integrating responsibility and institutional needs. *Change*, 30, 18-25.

Licklider, B. L., Schnelker, D. L, & Fulton, C. (1997-1998). Revisioning faculty development for changing times: The foundation and framework. *Journal of Staff, Program and Organizational Development*, 15, 121-133.

Martin, J., Sammels, J. E., & Associates. (1997). *First among equals: The role of the chief academic officer.* Baltimore, MD: The Johns Hopkins University Press.

Millis, B. J. (1994). Faculty development in the 1990s: What it is and why we can't wait. *Journal of Counseling and Development*, 72, 454-464.

Mintz, J. A. (1999, Spring). Faculty development and teaching: A holistic approach. *Liberal Education*, 32-37.

Palmer, P. (1996). Divided no more: A movement approach to educational reform. *Higher Education Exchange*, 5-16.

Rice, E. (1996). *Making a place for the new American scholar.* American Association for Higher Education New Pathways Working Paper Series. Washington, DC: American Association for Higher Education.

Zahorski, Kenneth J. (1993). Taking the lead: Faculty development as institutional change agent. *To Improve the Academy*, 12, 227-245.

3

FACULTY AS INSTITUTIONAL CITIZENS: RECONCEIVING SERVICE AND GOVERNANCE WORK

Service/Governance Working Group
Lawry Finsen, Group Coordinator

Phase I of the Associated New American Colleges' (ANAC) Faculty Work Project showed that faculty are often satisfied with their own work, but dissatisfied with their connection to their university or college. In particular, many faculty see their service roles as problematic. Indeed, expectations concerning service are often less clear than expectations about other aspects of faculty work. Faculty wonder how much and what kind of service work they should be doing, and how this work relates to expectations for scholarship and teaching. Is there a service load expectation, which parallels the standard expectations for faculty teaching loads? How is this part of faculty work evaluated (or is it evaluated)? In addition, some faculty wonder to what extent service really matters—to them personally as well as to their university. Certain kinds of service—such as some faculty governance—appear to make little progress toward significant outcomes and the significance of the outcome also seems unrelated to the amount of effort required. Many feel that even though they are expected to perform service, it—unlike teaching and scholarship—is insufficiently rewarded, recognized, or valued. Little wonder that it may seem an unreasonable burden to be avoided rather than an opportunity for fuller participation in the life of one's community.

Nevertheless, there is much to be said on behalf of service. Universities cannot achieve their educational missions without serious faculty engagement in a variety of activities that take them beyond the classroom, library, or laboratory, but that nonetheless have a substantial impact on student learning. At the center of this service engagement is the intense relationship between students and faculty which actualizes educational missions in myriad ways. That relationship is manifested very clearly in the kind of advising that helps students begin to connect their aspirations to a larger societal context to be engaged with understanding. Less immediate than the student-faculty relationship, but as important, is faculty leadership on such things as new and existing program review and revision; creation and oversight of majors and general education; selection of new faculty colleagues; review of faculty for contract, tenure, and promotion; and much more. Finally, faculty need to be a part of the larger processes which determine the strategic direction of their institutions. Their expertise is essential not only to carry out institutional mission, but also to help shape the articulation of that mission and make sure that institutional priorities and decision-making align with it. The need for such faculty involvement is one of the many reasons that our universities cannot effectively achieve their educational missions primarily through the use of a part-time teaching force. Clearly, the service work of fully engaged faculty is crucial to the health of our universities.

MEANINGFUL SERVICE: THE WORK OF FACULTY CITIZENS

Rethinking the faculty-institutional relationship in terms of a "circle of value" and faculty development in terms of a compact provides a context for understanding service more clearly. These new frameworks obviate what can be invisible: that service provides opportunities to engage more fully as citizens of a university community—as individuals who, unlike mere employees, actively engage in academic oversight, planning, and decision-making concerning the overall direction of their university.

Much of what has traditionally constituted service is more frequently a matter of collective responsibility than other kinds of faculty work. Although decisions about what courses to teach and some aspects of teaching can be team efforts, and scholarship rarely exists in a truly individualistic vacuum, nevertheless, the bulk of faculty activity in the arenas of teaching and scholarship results from individual effort and autonomous decision. Most service, however, cannot be completed without the joint effort of many. Therefore, much of what constitutes service is the collective work needed to ensure the health of an educational institution. Such work is done in a context that affirms the mutual responsibility for the well being of the whole, where each of us bears a responsibility to shoulder a fair portion of the work that is needed to make the university function well.

Cultivating a healthy culture of citizenship will be easier if the current categories of research, teaching, and service are revisioned. As recent discussions on faculty work have highlighted (Berberet, 1999; Denham et al., 1996), the current categories carry with them tacit equations of value with research activities assigned greatest worth, teaching identified as of secondary value, and service given the least importance, if credited as valuable at all. Efforts of Ernest Boyer and others to acknowledge a scholarship based on teaching have called into question the secondary ranking of teaching and have forced a recognition—long understood at ANAC schools—that teaching can and usually does engender intellectual inquiry and discovery for faculty as well as students. Service remains unrecognized even in Boyer's schema, however, and continues to be conceived as merely functionary and, therefore, not meriting significant value. Service activities can be, in fact, integral to creating and maintaining knowledge and learning on college campuses. As such, service can represent a vital aspect of faculty work and development, and, therefore, a faculty responsibility that fulfills the educational mission of the institution.

A new approach to revisioning service is suggested in the report of the Modern Language Association (MLA) Commission on Professional Service (Denham et al., 1996). The authors of that report propose that the traditional classification of scholarship, teaching, and service (with its attendant hierarchy of value) is misleading as to the real nature of faculty work, since that classification confuses the site at which various kinds of work are performed with the value that such work might manifest. Instead, they propose a classification in terms of the values exemplified by different kinds of work, specifically identifying two broad kinds of value: intellectual work and academic and professional citizenship. Work that manifests the qualities typical of intellectual work can be found at all three of the sites (teaching, scholarship, and service), as can work called academic or professional citizenship. From the point of view of evaluating the range of faculty work, this makes a good deal of sense, as characteristics that make intellectual work what it is, for example, suggest standards of excellence that lend it to thoughtful evaluation. So, too, distinctive standards for professional work can be developed. Noting that it is committee work or service (i.e., the site at which that kind of work is performed) does not clarify the situation in anything like an analogous sense. Seeing service in these terms helps to answer the question why faculty in particular should be doing these things, as opposed to assigning them to someone else (e.g., administrators or staff). If it does not matter that the work is done, and that faculty in particular do it, then faculty should be left to the kinds of work for which their skills and training make a difference.

EVALUATING SERVICE

EVALUATING SERVICE WITH MLA COMMISSION STANDARDS

Intellectual work is identified as such not because it is performed in scholarship or teaching, but because of the nature of the skill, knowledge, expertise, and judgment that it involves. Intellectual work emerges from profession expertise that "explicitly invokes ideas and explores their consequences" with a sufficiently "public dimension amenable to assessment, evaluation, and modification by a critically informed group of peers" (Denham et al., 1996, p. 3). When intellectual work is excellent, it "is characterized by such qualities as rigor, skill, care, intellectual honesty, heuristic passion for knowledge, originality, relevance, aptness, coherence, and consistency" (p. 17).

"Academic and professional citizenship," on the other hand, "encompasses the activities required to create, maintain, and improve the infrastructure that sustains the academy as a societal institution" (p. 19). These may not involve the kinds of expert or intellectual skills that distinguish intellectual work, but are nonetheless important faculty work. When faculty work is more a matter of academic and professional citizenship, a different set of standards would apply than when intellectual work is considered:

We expect the citizen to be responsible and dedicated; we regard faculty members as having obligation in this regard that they meet more or less thoroughly, collegially, productively, and skillfully. The following may distinguish respected academic and professional citizenship in any category of faculty effort: care and commitment, honesty, punctuality and reliability, knowledge of the institution and of professional organizations; interpersonal skills; thoroughness and perseverance; availability; willingness to inform oneself about educational policy and practices and to keep abreast of changes; organization skills. (p. 19)

By recognizing professional citizenship, the MLA report creates a context for acknowledging and valuing a whole category of faculty work that cannot easily be construed as scholarship. However, this approach is not without its own difficulties. While the MLA Commission urges that both intellectual and professional work are necessary components of faculty work, the way the distinction is drawn may implicitly privilege intellectual work—and thus reproduce the bias against service work as inferior in a new form. Even if this were not a concern, significant doubt would remain about the ability to parse out intellectual work from the context in which it occurs and the infrastructure that supports it. Naming both the types and the sites of faculty work is useful for understanding its complexity and valuing its many components. But the daily experience of faculty work is much more integrated. The work of citizenship, like scholarship and teaching, includes a variety of activities. Although faculty may find most meaningful those citizenship (and teaching and scholarship) roles that challenge them intellectually, some more routine duties will also remain a part of faculty work. Revisioning faculty work, and specifically citizenship, will help faculty and institutions recognize the value of all faculty work to fostering knowledge and learning on their campuses. In addition, it will foreground the opportunity for intellectual endeavor in all areas of faculty work.

RESPONSIBILITIES OF INSTITUTIONAL CITIZENSHIP

As citizens of the university community, faculty bring special talents, expertise, and understanding of the institution's mission. They thus bear a special (though not the sole) responsibility for the well being of the institution. The work of institutional citizenship will vary considerably from context to context and individual to individual. Nonetheless, it is helpful to schematize institutional citizenship as falling into four broad categories, with correspondingly varying degrees of responsibility for faculty as a whole (Table 3.1).

TABLE 3.1 Institutional Citizenship

Type of Faculty Work	Extent of Faculty Involvement
Academic oversight	Primary responsibility
Institutional governance	Significant voice and participation
Institutional support	Strategic contributions
External service	Variable

What follows is a brief listing of examples of the kinds of activities that typically fall within each of these categories. The list is intended to be representative, not exhaustive.

Academic Oversight

Faculty bear primary responsibility for oversight of the standards and quality of academic programs. If there is any area of citizenship that faculty can most reasonably claim as their purview above all other constituencies, it is here. Much of the work here mentioned occurs through one's home unit (e.g., departmental or program committees) and the connection points for such units (e.g., school, college, and university curriculum committees), but it is certainly not limited to those contexts.

The components of academic oversight
- Setting and enforcing academic standards
- General education
- Degree criteria and major, minor, and interdisciplinary program requirements
- Academic program review
- Academic advising
- Faculty hiring, tenure, promotion, and review

INSTITUTIONAL EXAMPLE

*SERVICE IN THE CREATION OF CURRICULUM: INTEGRATED LEARNING OBJEC-
TIVES AT PACIFIC LUTHERAN UNIVERSITY*

After years of a variety of work on assessment by particular departments and schools, the faculty of Pacific Lutheran University in 1999 adopted a common understanding of the primary aims of an undergraduate education throughout the university. This understanding both supplemented and made more substantive the faculty's long-standing assumption that students should achieve both broad knowledge in the liberal arts and more specialized knowledge in the major. The faculty selected five fundamental objectives of teaching and learning, which have come to be called the Integrative Learning Objectives (ILOs): the capacities of critical reflection, expression, interaction with others, valuing, and understanding multiple cultural frameworks. Achieving this common understanding of undergraduate education at the university was itself a time-consuming and at times difficult process. But the largest challenge for the ILOs still lay ahead: using them to focus the work of a student's education in both the general university requirements (core) and the major. For one thing, this requires that assessment efforts be aimed not only at the more specific skills or bodies of knowledge in the major but at these five more ubiquitous, integrative objectives. Sometimes called "core follow-through" in the major, this is one of the largest challenges in accomplishing curricular cohesion and assessing it.

Finding the challenge utterly daunting, faculty in many specific disciplines are prone to resist being asked to share responsibility for all of these broader objectives. Mathematics and computer science, for example, might be expected to resist taking responsibility, in their own assessment efforts, for their majors' abilities in writing, speaking, and perceptive and critical valuing. But in fact a number of departments at the university, including computer science and mathematics, have begun to incorporate the ILOs into the assessment of their majors and curricula. The computer science department, for example, was lauded by a recent accreditation site visit team for the written and oral skills of their majors and the broad presence of ethical considerations in their curriculum.

In the process of developing and implementing the ILOs, faculty come to see their work more clearly as addressed to the whole student and the entire, interrelated curriculum. The impact on faculty initially, of course, was time spent in the discussions that generated the ILOs that might have been spent on something else. As they begin to implement the ILOs, it will be critically important that clearer attention to the entire education of students be seen, not as added work, but as the incorporation of a broader perspective into the work that they already do. To be sure, for faculty to approach the curricula of their majors in this more inclusive way is bigger and different work. Hopefully, though, it is not more work—just transformed work.

Institutional Governance

Faculty, along with other stakeholders in the institution, should have a significant voice in the decisions that articulate the mission and goals of the institution, including the larger strategic budgetary decisions that give life to that mission. To perform this function well, those who will have a responsible voice must have information about the institutional situation, and must understand that this is a shared responsibility.

The components of institutional governance
- Articulating mission and goals
- Long- and short-range strategic planning
- Budget
- Campus policy review
- Administrative hiring and evaluation

INSTITUTIONAL EXAMPLE

STRATEGIC PLANNING AT HAMLINE UNIVERSITY: A VISION FOR A NEW AMERICAN UNIVERSITY

Since 1996, Hamline University has been engaged in a discussion and process designed to develop a shared vision for its future. Early involvement over ten years ago in discussions with a group of similar universities (later to be called the Associated New American Colleges) greatly influenced the focus of the discussion and planning. Despite a predictable number of bumps on the road, Hamline has emerged from this recent strategic planning journey with a unified and university-wide focus on a vision of Hamline University as a New American University. The university council—which is composed of students, faculty, staff, and senior administrators from across the university—served as the discussion group for the development of the strategic plan. Members of the council engaged their constituent groups in the various electronic and face-to-face discussions during the process of developing the strategic plan, with multiple drafts of the plan reviewed by the entire university community at stages along the way. The board of trustees also played a key role by reviewing and questioning the plan during its development.

All university budget planning and resource allocation now occurs within the context of the university strategic plan. The schools and other administrative units of the University also have developed strategic plans which are connected to the overall New American university vision. Resources follow projects designed to enhance or extend the vision, so the various parts of the university have quickly learned that it makes sense to think in terms of the overall vision, rather than from a narrow discipline- or profession-based self-interest. Using the New American University vision as an organizing focus is energizing many segments of the university community and providing a strong framework for thinking about Hamline's mission for students in today's society.

Institutional Support

These are various ways in which faculty assist in the building up and maintenance of institutional life that go beyond governance and academic oversight.

The components of institutional support
- Accreditation activities
- Participation in student recruitment and alumni relations
- Fundraising, in particular writing proposals, suggesting donor contacts
- Extracurricular support, for example, cultural arts committee, advising student organizations

External Service

Whether in a professional organization or a local community within which the university is situated, many faculty also serve wider communities in ways that reflect on their citizenship within the university community.

The components of external service

- Community outreach programs
- Coordinating internships, service-learning projects, and other experiential learning opportunities
- Service in professional organizations

One may question certain placements in this schema. For example, academic advising surely has some affinity with teaching and on some campuses is considered part of the teaching role of faculty. Regardless of schematization, however, the key issue in determining the worth of service is that what is being asked of faculty must be significant in sustaining the university as a viable and respected place where knowledge is generated, challenged, and mastered. Thus, faculty are the primary overseers of academic matters. Faculty must have a significant voice in institutional governance so as to inform and influence the important decisions affecting both the health and academic life of the institution. Additionally, because of their public stature and influence, faculty can and should make significant contributions to institutional support by helping to attract students, donations, and good will in the larger community. Finally, knowledge is enhanced when it is applied and shared externally with the immediate local community and the broader communities of learned societies.

INSTITUTIONAL EXAMPLE

DEFINING SERVICE WORK AT DRAKE UNIVERSITY

The Drake University College of Arts and Sciences began a discussion about the importance of advising and mentoring of students in 1996. The conclusion was that advising and mentoring were critical to the educational mission of the college. At the same time, annual reviews and promotion and tenure procedures relied primarily upon the standard categories of teaching, research, and service. Advising and mentoring were grouped, along with a variety of other activities, under teaching. Faculty concluded that the evaluation system did not sufficiently acknowledge the importance of the activity. Therefore, the faculty voted to establish advising and mentoring as a fourth category to be used in evaluating performance. Now the activity is explicitly considered during annual reviews and salary decisions.

INSTITUTIONAL GOVERNANCE: SEEKING A NEW PARADIGM

The role of faculty in institutional governance deserves a more extended discussion here, as it highlights some of the ideas we are proposing. There is a common perception that governance is in trouble at many American universities. When asked "what is broken" about institutional governance (and what needs fixing) at smaller universities such as those in ANAC, responses ultimately focus on two dynamics: 1) the increasing corporatization of the university, and 2) the increasing autonomy of faculty members and "atomization" of the faculty. These are symbiotic developments that together create both a top-down and a bottom-up challenge. In effect, there is de facto collusion between presidents, administrators, and governing boards at one end and faculty at the other end to hobble effective, enlightened, and open institutional governance.

Presidents and governing boards are under sustained pressure to make their universities more efficient, and to respond to the demands of the marketplace in ways that can be in tension with the mandate of institutional missions. The faculty decision-making system is seen by many as cumbersome, slow, lacking in accountability, and ultimately inconsistent with the corporate paradigm on which the institution's survival allegedly depends. As more responsibilities are assumed and more decisions are made by administrators, presidents, and boards, faculty become increasingly disenfranchised and are often treated as employees rather than as vested stakeholders (or, as many faculty like to see themselves, as the embodiment of the university itself).

At the same time, many individual faculty members are less committed to their institutions than in the past and are more inclined to see themselves as self-promoting free agents. Younger faculty in particular are disinclined to see themselves as having responsibility for overall institutional welfare. While some become actively involved in faculty service, others shun service as a waste of time and a distraction from teaching and scholarship. The increasing emphasis on scholarship in faculty evaluation has reinforced faculty members' commitment to discipline first, institution second. Additionally, the increasing corporatization of institutions has led faculty to expect that critical institutional responsibilities will be assumed by administrators and to see themselves as merely employees. On one hand, faculty see their service contributions as not ultimately making much difference, since final decisions will be made by administrators, the president, or the board. On the other hand, many faculty see the increasing centralization of institutional governance in the administration as liberating, absolving them of responsibility for something they really did not want to do in the first place.

In essence, corporatization has encouraged poor faculty citizenship and poor faculty citizenship has encouraged corporatization—creating a downward spiral that has crippled effective collaborative governance. There are some interesting paradoxes in all of this. Presidents and senior administrators sometimes complain about lack of faculty involvement, yet they are instrumental in a dynamic that is ultimately responsible for that lack of involvement. Presidents and senior administrators want more faculty commitment to institutional welfare, but they are often unwilling to cede the access and shared influence (dare we say power?) that ought to accompany such commitment. Faculty, on the other hand, complain that their voices are not heard, that they are disenfranchised, while they at the same time enjoy the freedom that comes with leaving institutional responsibilities to others. In many cases they are only an occasional presence in the university community, and they see responsibility as a one-way street: The university's responsibility to them is set in concrete for the rest of their lives, while their own responsibility to the institution is constantly negotiable. The malaise that often describes overall institutional governance is a two-pronged problem, both top down and bottom up, and requires solutions that depend on a willingness by all institutional stakeholders to let their guard down.

Such intractable problems are not easily solved and we are not offering here any comprehensive model. Rather, we suggest three characteristics that should be a part of any institutional governance structure.

1) Institutional governance must be open. As a general principle of basic organizational theory, an open organization in which information flows freely between its components is healthier and more adaptable than a closed, steeply hierarchical organization in which the flow of information is highly formalized and tightly controlled. In higher education (especially at smaller comprehensive universities such as those in ANAC) openness and the unfettered flow of information is particularly important among the three institutional stakeholders most directly responsible for governance and management: the governing board, the administration, and the faculty. Of course, there are other stakeholders as well: students, nonacademic staff, and alumni. But the most direct responsibility for institutional governance falls most centrally on faculty, administration, and governing boards.

2) Institutional governance must be collaborative. Existing shared governance models are often set up as a series of separate silos—one for faculty, one for administrators, and one for governing boards—that act as a series of checks and balances and can only exercise veto power over one another. In order for true collaboration to occur, faculty, administrators, and governing board members should have more direct access to each other in bodies that allow for some consensus building and collaborative decision- making. However, this in turn requires that administrators (and particularly presidents) abdicate some of their gatekeeper role with respect to the governing board. As Tom Longin argued at ANAC's June 1999 St. Mary's meeting, it takes a very self-assured president to do this, because—given the current climate of higher education—the president's control over access to board members is an important survival mechanism. The message is clear: Certain kinds of presidents must learn alternative strategies for addressing their insecurities, however valid those insecurities might at times be. While the gatekeeper role is probably inevitable, there is a wide range of models for fulfilling that role.

3) Institutional governance requires mutual trust. Reform of overall institutional governance also requires that all the stakeholders learn to work together as part of the same team. Richard Chait's (2000) recent observation that faculty and governing boards have more in common than either might think is useful here—though he contends that such similarities as organizational conservatism and inconsistency lead to greater frustration than mutuality. Board members need to abandon the stereotypes they sometimes hold about faculty and be sensitized to the differences between governing an academic institution and managing a business (which is not to downplay the board's responsibility for ensuring the long-term financial health of an institution in a competitive higher education marketplace). Administrators must let go of tired views of faculty as brilliant but unruly children to be managed and recognize faculty instead as capable professional partners. Faculty members, too, need to dispense with stereotypes about administrators and trustees. How often have professors reduced the faculty-administration relationship to the outdated "us-them" industrial relations paradigm of workers and managers or talked dismissively of board members as merely a bunch of business people? Faculties are inclined to see themselves as being the institution, rather than as constituting one of several stakeholders. This notion does not reflect the reality of contemporary institutions and is incompatible with the approach to shared governance that is necessary if what is broken is going to be fixed. The best way to address such stereotypes is for faculty, administrators, and trustees to work together in a sustained way. Administrators, governing boards, and faculty need to devote themselves to overall institutional governance in the same spirit.

In the long run, faculty, administrators, and trustees must be encouraged to see themselves and each other as vested partners in a collective professional enterprise—not unlike the way in which partners in a large law firm would see themselves. This means that they must share in the institution's successes, but also in its failures. At all universities, of necessity, there is a threshold where collegial governance leaves off and the institution's corporate character takes over. The trend in recent decades has been for less decision-making to take place at the collegial end and more to take place at the corporate end. The question is not simply whether this trend can be reversed in some ways, but also whether faculty have a contribution to make to the corporate aspects of institutional management. Clearly they do, but this in turn requires the development of a more innovative paradigm for shared governance. It also requires faculty to understand that shared governance is exactly that—shared—and that governance is by necessity a team effort.

INSTITUTIONAL EXAMPLE

MOVING TOWARD COLLABORATIVE GOVERNANCE AT ANAC INSTITUTIONS

VALPARAISO UNIVERSITY

At Valparaiso University there is a Budget Advisory Committee (BAC) reporting to the president. The BAC consists of ten members including the provost, associate provost, vice president for administration and finance, two of the five academic deans, and five faculty. The faculty members are appointed by the president upon the recommendations of the deans. The BAC recommends adjustments to tuition, fees and salaries, and prepares a draft budget for submission to the board of directors. This Budget Advisory Committee was instituted by the president in an effort to develop a growing level of expertise in balancing budgetary possibilities with budget realities. Members of BAC are also on the strategic planning committee. This dual membership allows for cross-sharing of information between these committees. The strategic planning committee is thus aware of fiscal realities and the BAC is aware of long-range planning. This structure assures that the budget making process reflects the mission and vision of the university.

SUSQUEHANNA UNIVERSITY

The university council at Susquehanna is a key instrument in promoting and sustaining shared governance. The 16-member group serves as the principal internal advisory body to the president of the university on broad planning and policy issues, including annual budget priorities, tuition and fee levels, and the framework for salary increases and benefit policies for all employees. The council also contributes to the periodic development and revision of the university's strategic priorities. The president of the university chairs the council in a nonvoting capacity. Seven voting faculty members are elected to staggered, three-year terms, five from school constituencies and two at large. Seven administrators serve ex-officio with vote (three deans of schools, the dean of student life, the dean of academic services, the vice president for finance, and the vice president for university relations). The vice president for academic affairs is also a member of the council but votes only in the event of a tie. In practice, the council tends to work toward a consensus. The results of council deliberations

usually are the basis for the president's annual budget planning recommendations to the board of directors. In recent years, in addition to
these annual responsibilities, the council has deliberated about a
number of strategic policy and budget issues such as administrative
structure, university size and growth, information technology priorities, and employee benefits.

QUINNIPIAC UNIVERSITY

Strategic planning at Quinnipiac University has evolved into a vital,
ongoing process which serves to focus both administrative and faculty attention on external challenges and opportunities as they develop.
Planning meetings take place three times per year (two days each in
January and June with a single day meeting in August) at an off-campus location removed from everyday distractions. In addition to the
university deans and senior administrative officers, every meeting is
attended by at least two faculty leaders (the chair of the faculty senate
and the chair of the senate's aims, objectives, and future plans committee). All meetings involve not only the discussion of internal plans
but also the analysis of external reports, market developments, and
advances in technology. Frequently, external consultants are brought
in to brief the planning group on a specific topic and lead discussion
regarding the impact of this topic for the future of the university. We
have found the great strength of these regular planning sessions is
that they give the faculty and administration a common framework
with which to view the future so that our creative efforts are indeed
anticipatory rather than reactionary. (See also the Butler case study
which appears later in this volume.)

EVALUATION OF CITIZENSHIP

If universities are to create and sustain healthy cultures that implement the kind of institutional citizenship we are proposing, a good
deal of thought must be given to how to make those expectations
clear and how to act on them. To this end, evaluation of service should
be taken seriously for a number of reasons. First, the varieties of service that faculty perform include many kinds of work for which faculty have little or no training. In teaching and scholarship, individuals
learn through the guidance of others and by observing models of performance. Where service is concerned, aspiring professionals are typ-

ically less aware of the service roles that their teachers play. And while some graduate programs have begun to take more notice of the need to help develop strong teachers, there is little preparation for service roles. For an institution to commit to a serious evaluation of citizenship means committing to helping individuals recognize what kind of work they should be doing, what kinds of choices are available to them, and where and how they can improve in the work they are doing. Second, systematic evaluation can encourage all to claim their fair share of collective work. If work is left unevaluated, some will consider it unimportant, a nuisance to be avoided. While some faculty will relish the opportunity to participate in the public life of their community, others will seek to reduce their contribution to what is only minimally necessary. This is unacceptable. Those who pitch in voluntarily because there is work that needs to be done should not have to shoulder an unreasonably large share of that work. Third, and probably most important, it matters whether this work is done well. If it does not, if faculty are being asked to serve in roles for which "seat time" is sufficient, then we ought to question whether faculty are needed for those roles. Faculty should be asked to participate because their participation is crucial—so crucial that the quality of that performance should be assessed and rewarded.

Individual universities would, of course, need to develop their own comprehensive systems for evaluating faculty service. As a start in that direction, the following are several issues that need to be addressed in any evaluation of institutional citizenship.

Expectations for Institutional Citizenship Must Be Clear

The meaning and relative importance of citizenship within a university should be articulated to prospective faculty members in the recruitment process and again in new faculty orientation programming. Chapter Two discusses the "probationary compact" in which the individual and the institution arrive at a negotiated set of performance goals, which would include goals for university citizenship. Mentoring is another opportunity to help faculty understand the importance of citizenship within their new academic community. Perhaps the clearest source of information about what is valued are examples of those around them—what they do and do not do and what kinds of institutional response those actions elicit. If participation in governance, or serving as chair of a department are said to be valued, but faculty and administrators do not act as if they are, that message will be clear to new faculty. Thus, institutional leaders need to promote practices that value citizenship—including it in evaluating faculty for tenure and promotion, supporting it with release time or even sabbatical consideration, and making sure that it garners recognition and reward. Analogously, if senior faculty do not assume leadership responsibilities, but instead allow a disproportionate share of the burden of citizenship to fall to junior colleagues, the implicit message will be clear.

Standards and Criteria for Evaluation Must Be Well Articulated

Evaluating citizenship in a meaningful way means that it is assessed both in terms of its quantity and its quality. The quantitative question is more straightforward, though this should not be made mechanical and simplistic. Institutional leadership must differentiate among types of service assignments. Some activities will entail much greater time commitment and responsibility than others. Additionally, differentiation of faculty work will produce service responsibilities that are heavy at certain times, lighter at others. Sometimes, citizenship might constitute a rather minimal part of one's work, while at others it might play a larger role. In addition, as a faculty member enters senior ranks, he or she may be asked to assume positions of greater responsibility. The individual and the institution should work to ensure that the faculty member's overall career trajectory has coherence and that faculty have opportunities to acquire the kind of knowledge and experience of an area that make increasingly responsible roles possible. Thus, opportunities for flexibility and for reapportioning service load should be provided to allow for the ebb and flow of faculty careers. These and other such differences in amount should be negotiated within the unit and recognized by the evaluation process.

Defining the standards that should be employed in evaluating citizenship will vary from campus to campus as a result of mission and traditions. However, the standards articulated in *Scholarship Assessed* (Glassick, Huber, & Maeroff, 1997) may be helpful for the evaluation of citizenship and provide a framework of questions to ask about how effectively someone has served. In many cases, these standards will be more appropriately applied to the collective action of a group, for example, a faculty governance committee. An individual's goals as a member of a committee may not be relevant to considering his or her performance. But it makes perfect sense to ask whether the committee as a whole has developed an agenda that identifies the most important current and future curricular needs of the college. One might then ask what contribution any individual made to that agenda-building process. Analogously, one can see how the other standards could be applied profitably to such work. Such a list of standards is useful in assessing whether one's service made a substantial contribution, but it should not be used mechanically—it would be pointless to insist that in each area of evaluation one addressed all of these standards. And it is important that the evaluation process be simple and straightforward enough that it encourages people to reflect thoughtfully on their contribution while not becoming onerous.

EVALUATING SERVICE

EVALUATING SERVICE WITH SCHOLARSHIP ASSESSED

The authors of *Scholarship Assessed* identified six standards that could be applied to scholarly work of any kind, regardless of discipline and the kind of scholarship involved: discovery, integration, application, or teaching. (Glassick et al., 1997)

1) Goals (clarity, realism, importance)

2) Adequate preparation (understanding of what has gone before, use of appropriate skills and resources)

3) Appropriate methods (relation to goals, effective use, modification in response to changing circumstances)

4) Significant results (achievement of goals, results that matter, opening new possibilities and questions)

5) Effective presentation (clear, well-organized communication to appropriate audiences in appropriate forums)

6) Reflective critique (results subjected to evaluation, with appropriate breadth of questions; suggestions for improvement of future work)

Of course, the potential dangers in poor systems of evaluation of citizenship need to recognized. Whatever approach and standards a university adopts should manifest good sense: Every little task faculty do should not be evaluated, nor should the evaluation system become so draconian that the joy of serving one's community as a citizen is eliminated. As is the case with the evaluation of scholarship or teaching, the point is to balance the need for sufficient information and useful feedback with the values of not overworking everyone in the act of evaluation and not interfering with valuable activities by constantly evaluating them.

Finally, worthy contributions to the processes that make a community thrive are not always uncontroversial. Good citizens are sometimes gadflies who point out mistakes or needle people to reconsider the direction the institution is taking. One advantage of stating a clear set of standards is that, if well conceived, they would help avoid the dangers (pointed out in the recent report of the AAUP's Committee A on Academic Freedom and Tenure) of substituting the vagaries of collegiality (e.g., the expectation that a faculty member exhibit enthusiasm, dedication, a constructive attitude, and a willingness to defer to the judgments of superiors) for the ability to engage constructively in collaborative work (AAUP, 1999). But there is a danger in failing to distinguish between someone who is a gadfly and someone who merely adopts a gadfly style—someone who refuses to work collaboratively and constructively with the give and take that this requires. Contentiousness for its own sake can be as destructive to the community as suppression of genuine criticism. Both need to be avoided in whatever standards are applied.

Evaluation Should Occur on Multiple Levels

There are three groups that need to be centrally involved in evaluating service work: the individual faculty member, those who work most closely with the faculty member in doing the work, and those involved in the faculty review process. Those close to the work (e.g., the chair of a committee) should have an important contribution to the evaluation of service. For example, an annual evaluation of all members of a committee in relation to the work of that committee by a chair would be appropriate. Some schools do this presently. Clearly, such an evaluation would constitute important evidence to be included in consideration of one's performance over a period of time by the appropriate faculty governance committee charged with reviewing faculty for tenure, promotion, or the like. Additional sources of important evaluative information are administrators who have frequently worked closely with faculty on committees or special projects and can compare the performances of many faculty in such roles. Committees themselves can also engage in self-evaluation on an annual basis as an exercise to take stock of goals and directions and to make recommendations to the next committee.

Perhaps the most important way in which a faculty member's citizenship should be evaluated is in the context of periodic reflective self-evaluations as part of a periodic review for recontracting, promotion, tenure, or senior review. Unfortunately, many do not go beyond a mere listing of such things as memberships on committees in evaluating their own service. Such a list does not address the most basic questions that a reflective self-evaluation should consider, such as whether one regularly attended meetings of committees and, once there, could be counted on to contribute in any significant way to the work of that group. A self-evaluation would go far beyond these simple questions. While such evaluation should not simply be limited to self-evaluation, the very fact of having to assess one's own performance can be enormously helpful to many faculty in focusing attention on ways to grow in the roles they play. Self-evaluation first and foremost involves articulating what it is one is doing and why. It should include reflection on what has been accomplished and what has not yet succeeded, on reasons for strategic choices made, and on future plans. This reflection is made clearer as one begins to articulate a coherent overall direction in one's service work. Addressing such questions as these would constitute a significant advance in thinking about one's contribution to the collective work of one's college or university.

REWARDS

If institutions are to move to an academic culture that promotes a healthy university citizenship, they must create incentives for this desired citizenship and reward it. Most of the traditional forms of incentives and rewards are heavily geared toward research. There are some that speak to the area of teaching, but there are few, if any, that specifically address the area of service.

In a 2000 National Center for Postsecondary Improvement study of faculty incentives, William Massy and Andrea Wilger conducted 378 interviews with faculty from research universities, doctoral-granting universities, comprehensive universities, and liberal arts colleges. They sought to discover what incentives and rewards faculty consider as important. The list they developed from their faculty interviews includes tenure/promotion, salary and merit increases, release time/sabbatical, start-up funds, facilities/equipment, travel/conferences, summer funds, working with students, curricular freedom, graduate assistants, decreased teaching load, internal grants, and professional autonomy. ANAC institutions fall into the comprehensive university category and stress a blend of citizenship that values teaching and service. In the survey, comprehensive institutions place a higher emphasis than research institutions on rewards specifically related to teaching: curricular freedom, decreased teaching load, facilities/equipment, travel/conferences, summer funds, internal grants, and working with students. What is of particular interest in this list of rewards is the lack of incentives and rewards directly aimed at faculty citizenship in general and faculty service in particular. While it is possible that salary merit increases, released time/sabbatical, and decreased teaching load could be applied to service, it appears that they are usually directly tied to research and/or teaching.

While rewards are seldom incentives for institutional service, they can be significant acknowledgment of work well done. Institutions should stress that all areas of faculty service have a value in the tenure, promotion, leave, and post-tenure review processes. Institutions should establish means of making exemplary institutional and community service visible to the campus and even the broader community. For example, universities can acknowledge outstanding achievements and commitment through awards for faculty service, both within the university and in wider communities. If universities offer annual bonuses, they could be given for meritorious institutional service. Service awards can also be given in the form of travel, professional development, or book funds for the faculty member. Finally, institutions that choose to use a merit salary system should include institutional service as one of the considerations in such decisions.

The work of institutional citizenship can also carry intrinsic rewards, especially when faculty see that work is productive, meaningful, and timely. In addition to spelling out the nature of faculty service and creating service opportunities with clearly stated goals and procedures, institutions must incorporate the results of these efforts into the life of the university. Faculty also need to experience considerable autonomy in determining how they will contribute to the collective work of the institution. This will happen in a collaborative environment in which individuals have a say in the types of service they perform and in the ways they want to be involved in the life of the university. This means that our colleges move away from the appointments and representation mentalities and seek to involve faculty in areas of their interest and expertise. Faculty must also be able to recognize that the work they are asked to do is appropriate, necessary for the collective well being of the institution, and a collaborative enterprise fairly distributed among constituencies. At too many institutions, a few faculty do most of the work and their names frequent numerous standing and ad hoc committees. We should strive to limit the amount of faculty work to places where it really does make a difference, thereby encouraging more intense involvement in the area of service chosen. Finally, faculty must be truly involved in the shared governance of the institution: in long-range strategic planning, in budget planning and decision-making, and in the development, interpretation, and implementation of the mission of the institution.

INSTITUTIONAL EXAMPLE

STRENGTHENING FACULTY COMMUNITY AT ROLLINS COLLEGE

During the first phase of the ANAC Faculty Work Project at Rollins College, assessment information gathered through survey research indicated that faculty morale was much lower than expected. Despite high levels of job satisfaction, only 15.7% of faculty rated faculty morale as good or excellent. Further analysis of the data indicated that ratings of faculty moral were not associated with years at Rollins, academic rank, or gender. These findings suggested that perceptions of low morale were not linked to a cohort effect (more negative ratings by senior faculty) or gender differences. In addition, faculty also gave low ratings to campus life (17.4%) and sense of community (17.1%).

In response to these and other concerns about faculty community, several initiatives were introduced by members of the faculty. First, to increase the effectiveness of the faculty governance system, faculty voted to suspend and then eliminate the faculty senate. This resulted in greater reliance on standing committees and more frequent faculty meetings to conduct college business. Since 1998, both the number of faculty meetings and the faculty attendance at these gatherings have increased. Through timely postings of minutes from previous meetings and committee reports on a governance web page, faculty are kept up to date on issues ranging from general education requirements to proposed new minors.

To address concerns about a sense of community, a special ad hoc committee made up of faculty, staff, and students was created to plan and coordinate a community building day. Endorsed by a unanimous faculty vote, a day was set aside for a mandatory campus-wide community building effort. The acronym C.A.R.E. was developed to represent the four major goals of the community building day: 1) Celebrate unity and diversity by linking fragmented campus communities, 2) Actively engage in constructive dialogue by maintaining open lines of communication, 3) Reinforce a shared vision of Rollins in which we cultivate responsibility and develop mutual trust so we can take pride in our community, and 4) Evaluate progress toward these goals through follow-up activities. Community Building Day began with an invited speaker addressing faculty, staff, and the entire student body. Next, participants were randomly clustered into mixed groups of 20 and assigned to locations around campus for small group activities. After lunch, larger group discussions were held focusing on community topics identified during previous assessment work. Each large discussion group was facilitated by a team of faculty, staff, and students who recorded goals and promising ideas. Finally, participants reassembled for a closure event facilitated by the invited speaker. The goals and action plans generated during the community building day were then published in the college newspaper and posted on a special web page. All goals were categorized by theme and distributed to appropriate decision makers across campus. Over the following six months, a series of updated reports were published in the college newspaper to document follow-up efforts.

Although it is difficult to measure the impact of these interventions with precision, a follow-up faculty survey conducted two years after the initial assessment survey indicated substantial increases in positive responses to sense of community (from 14% to 30%), faculty morale (from 16% to 27%), and overall quality of campus life (from 17% to 44%). While a sizeable portion of faculty gave neutral or fair ratings to these items, the positive shifts in faculty attitudes appear to be sustainable and gaining momentum.

CONCLUSION

If our universities are to flourish, faculty work will appropriately include much beyond teaching and scholarship. Faculty citizens will be involved in varying ways in the lives of their universities, from advising and mentoring in their own units to playing key roles in larger decisions about the overall direction of their universities, to greater interaction with the larger community. They will have a range of choice and flexibility in the kind and timing of their contributions to their academic communities, and their choices will be negotiated as members of departments or other relevant units, and not merely as individuals. If such work is to be a meaningful part of faculty life, it must be thoughtfully designed—expectations need to be clear, the work faculty are requested to do needs to be efficiently conceived, and faculty should be engaged in ways appropriate to the skills and knowledge they especially can offer. Faculty should expect to be evaluated, recognized, and rewarded for their roles as university citizens because it matters to the survival and success of our institutions that they perform these roles well.

ACKNOWLEDGMENTS

This chapter was truly the result of a group effort, with different individuals contributing initial drafts of sections of this chapter. The group included Lawry Finsen (University of Redlands), Graeme Auton (University of Redlands), Janet Brown (Valparaiso University), Warren Kozman (Valparaiso University), Mike Awalt (Belmont University), Susan Traverso (North Central College), Dean Wright (Drake University), James Marshall (Quinnipiac University), Lynn Franken (Butler University), and Steve Kaplan (Butler University).

REFERENCES

AAUP Committee A on Academic Freedom and Tenure. (1999). On collegiality as a criterion for faculty evaluation. *Academe, 85* (5), 69-70.

Berberet, J. (1999). The professoriate and institutional citizenship: Toward a scholarship of service. *Liberal Education, 85,* 32-39.

Boyer, E. (1990). *Scholarship reconsidered: Priorities of the professorate.* Princeton, NJ: The Carnegie Foundation for the Advancement of Teaching.

Chait, R. (2000, August 6). Trustees and professors: So often at odds, so much alike. *The Chronicle of Higher Education,* p. B4.

Denham, R., Kramsch, C., Phelps, L., Rassias, J., Slevin, J., & Swaffar, J. (1996). Making faculty work visible: Reinterpreting professional service, teaching, and research in the fields of language and literature. [Modern Language Association Commission on Professional Service Report.] *Profession,* 161-216.

Glassick, C. E., Huber, M. T., & Maeroff, G. I. (1997). *Scholarship assessed: Evaluation of the professoriate.* San Francisco, CA: Jossey-Bass.

National Center for Postsecondary Improvement. (2000, March/April). Why is research the rule? The impact of incentive systems on faculty behavior. *Change, 32,* 53-56.

4

FACULTY WORKLOAD: DIFFERENTIATION THROUGH UNIT COLLABORATION

Workload Differentiation Working Group
Linda A. McMillin, Group Coordinator

P hase I of the Associated New American Colleges' (ANAC) Faculty Work Project uncovered significant disconnections between the existing workload structures of our institutions and the actual complex work that faculty do. This lack of correlation negatively affects how institutions use faculty time and talent to meet the needs of their students. The result is poor faculty morale, ineffective resource management, inappropriate assessment, conflicting priorities, and less agile responses to change. By consciously differentiating individual faculty workloads in the context of collaborative academic units, however, faculty and their institutions can create more satisfying and more efficient structures of planning, support, evaluation, and reward that align faculty work with institutional mission. This process will require a fresh examination of both the nature of faculty work and the relationships among individual faculty, academic units, and the institution as a whole.

THE PROBLEM

The complexity of faculty work today results from a variety of factors. Overall, faculty responsibilities have grown both in number and in kind, in each of the three traditional areas of faculty work. New

87

demands for teaching require that faculty not only create engaging lectures but also individualize curriculum, incorporate technology into courses, accommodate a variety of student learning styles, employ pedagogies that enhance active learning, and deliver classes off site and/or online. The requirements of campus citizenship—governance, strategic planning, student recruitment, grant writing, alumni relations—and local community citizenship—public service, K–12 support, collaborative business and government ventures—have grown for faculty as well. At the same time, expectations for scholarship, especially that which leads to public presentation and publication, has grown exponentially and expanded well beyond research universities to become a greater part of the workload of faculty at almost all institutions. Like a number of other schools, faculty at ANAC institutions have an additional responsibility that grows out of our commitment to interdisciplinary studies and the combination of theoretical and practical education. This commitment requires faculty to make collaborative and creative connections among subfields of a discipline, across disciplines, and between liberal arts and professional training in both their teaching and research—an exciting but time-consuming challenge. Furthermore, as faculty move through the stages of their careers and as institutions strive to be more flexible to meet the emerging needs of students and society, so do faculty responsibilities constantly change.

Faculty work is further complicated by demographic changes within the academy. As institutions increase the diversity of their workforce both to include women, people of color, and the handicapped, and to accommodate differences of age, ethnicity, and sexual orientation, new tasks for and approaches to faculty work emerge. For example, a Hispanic faculty member might be called upon to work on minority student recruitment, a wheelchair-using faculty member to help evaluate the accessibility of new building and renovation projects, and a lesbian faculty member to meet with gay alumni. This is work that often comes in addition to other responsibilities. The commutes of dual career couples, the childcare arrangements of working parents, the elder care responsibilities of many, and the universal desire for greater balance between professional and private life add additional layers of complexity to faculty work in the twenty-first century. Finally, for better or worse, changing patterns of hiring and staffing—tenure track versus adjunct versus multiyear contracts—have created hierarchies of status, contribution, support, and responsibility within institutions and departments. Thus, the "complete scholar" envisioned by Rice (1996) can seem a distant dream to faculty in the trenches who are constantly bombarded by so many competing demands. Faculty juggle priorities, douse hot spots, try to focus on what seems most important, dodge a few bullets, and hope that in the end what they have done in idiosyncratic ways will be enough to survive.

Although the increased complexity of faculty work and the multiple demands on faculty time currently result in individualized work patterns, existing structures of faculty work tend to impede rather than support this emerging differentiation. Data from the Phase I study showed both the time pressures experienced by faculty and their perception that institutional policies do not well support and reward faculty work most tied to institutional mission. Indeed, the main formal acknowledgment of differentiated work patterns is the special deal negotiated on occasion between a faculty member and administrator. Such deals bypass the formal structures in which most faculty operate and often cause considerable disruption and resentment. For the rest, the one-size-fits-all approach to workload and the evaluation of faculty work does little to encourage and support the increasingly diverse work models needed to fulfill diverse institutional missions. Current structures almost assure that a faculty member will be pulled simultaneously in many directions with no coordination and no assurance of appropriate recognition. For example, Assistant Professor Smith may teach some courses for a department program and others for the general education curriculum, may serve on an elected campus-wide committee (or two), while at the same time working with an ad hoc faculty group designing a new, interdisciplinary program. With one article in press and another under revision, Smith may be asked to serve on a dean search committee and simultaneously be offered the opportunity to edit a volume of an online journal. Smith may see the editorial work as an important scholarly endeavor for rounding out a tenure portfolio, but the consequence of taking on this additional task, without letting go of some other piece of the workload, will be an impossible juggling act. Current structures do not provide Smith with much help in prioritizing these opportunities, or guidance in determining which one or more of these tasks should be dropped. Whatever balance this faculty member strikes among these demands and opportunities, this workload will surely look different from that of other colleagues, who also face their own panoply of tasks and competing priorities. Instead of working together to meet common goals, faculty are at times not only ignorant of collaborative opportunities, but may even work in ways that are repetitive or at cross purposes. Unfortunately, at present, most institutions are providing little coherent strategy for coordinating or balancing the growing diversity of demands on faculty, taking best advantage of individual interests and expertise, and fostering collaborative efforts.

Healthy institutions need to formally acknowledge the validity of differentiated faculty work patterns and create a structure that will foster increased collaboration and interdependence among faculty so as to increase their satisfaction and enhance their effectiveness in achieving institutional goals. Therefore, we propose the academic unit as a structure that can provide faculty with a context for setting priorities in individualized work and collaborating with each other as fellow teachers, scholars, and institutional citizens. The unit might be a department, a division, a program, a professional school, or any appropriately sized group of faculty gathered around a common set of goals. It is the structure through which individual faculty most readily and concretely experience academic community, the place where the compact between institution and individual is realized on a day-to-day basis. To be most effective, the unit must be large enough to allow significant differentiation of faculty work, and small enough so that face-to-face interaction can happen on a regular basis. Units, however, should not be conceived of as discreet worlds onto themselves. Rather, such groupings of faculty must constantly interact and collaborate with each other to further the work of the entire institution. If the members of the unit have a clear enough sense of their collective work and the ways that work contributes to the mission of the institution, then they can collaboratively negotiate the individual, differentiated work plans of members in such a way that the work of the unit is accomplished while taking best advantage of the interests and opportunities of the individual members.

So, in the case described above, Assistant Professor Smith would discuss multiple work opportunities with colleagues in the unit. They might collectively decide that maintaining their contribution to the interdisciplinary program is a clear priority for the learning outcomes of their students, but that another member could take on that role for the coming year. Or they might negotiate with another unit so as to pass off their responsibility in the interdisciplinary program for a period of time. They could also consider a reduction in course preparations for the coming year that would allow Smith more comfortably to take on the task of editing the online journal. In that case, the other members of the unit would take on the responsibility of additional preparations, because having a colleague edit the journal would enhance the visibility of the unit and the academic reputation of the institution. They might discover, however, that Smith had little interest in editing the journal beyond a misperceived notion of needing to increase scholarly output. Here colleagues could reassure Smith that the serious scholarly component of designing an interdisciplinary program would be amply recognized in both unit and institutional evaluation, thus creating a choice—journal or program—rather than the impossible mandate of both. By collaborative effort and negotiation, faculty members can shape work priorities that align individual skills and needs with the goals of both the unit and the institution. Such negotiations taking place across the stages of an individual career allow faculty to chart a realistic course toward becoming a complete scholar.

Workload differentiation is already a reality, and a focus on the academic unit is an effective way to cope with the multiplicity of tasks facing faculty. Therefore, healthy institutions should strive not only to accommodate differentiated faculty workloads, but also creatively to direct differentiation toward institutional goals in ways that support a faculty of complete scholars. The compact concept we are proposing can be a mechanism through which institutions direct and support individual faculty to such ends. However, to be employed strategically, workload differentiation must take place in the context of increased collaboration and interdependence among individual faculty. Such collaboration in the creation of differentiated work plans among the members of the unit should involve regular, collective planning to ensure that all the common goals of the unit are furthered. The unit structure must be flexible enough to allow change and renegotiation both to accommodate individual faculty career stages and to meet the evolving needs of the institution. Such a structure would call for collective evaluation and reward, so that, while the contribution of the individual members to the work of the unit would differ, the unit would be evaluated on the degree to which its contribution to the work of the institution was fulfilled. Collaboration in workload differentiation should lead to collective planning, evaluation, and reward at the unit level.

Moving from one-size-fits-all toward a more differentiated and collaborative approach to faculty workload requires a high level of trust and openness among faculty, staff, and administrators. First, they must together determine which tasks need to be accomplished by faculty at the institution. Then they must jointly acknowledge and enhance the ways in which individual faculty, academic units, and the institution as a whole both add value to and are dependent on the work of each.

WHAT IS THE WORK OF FACULTY?

In current practice, faculty often view their work in terms of their individual interests and expertise so that the range of their work results from a complex negotiation between these individual considerations and the needs and demands they perceive from their students, disciplines, academic units, and institutions. But, as stated above, we propose that faculty work be regarded first in the context of both the academic unit and the larger institutional mission.

1) Institutions and their faculty must inventory and evaluate the range of faculty tasks needed to meet institutional mission.

The starting point in defining faculty work is to prioritize those tasks that are central to the mission of the institution and the needs of the students it serves. Together, faculty, administrators, and staff delineate the disciplinary demands of the curriculum, the responsibilities of institutional citizenship, and the appropriate connections to forge with local and national communities. The range of these tasks can then be aligned with the expertise and interests of both particular units and their individual faculty members. Thus, the goals and priorities of the institution, the unit, and the individual are clearly connected.

INSTITUTIONAL EXAMPLE

INVENTORYING FACULTY WORK AT HAMLINE UNIVERSITY

At Hamline University, an ad hoc faculty group from the five divisions of the College of Liberal Arts (CLA) created an inventory of faculty work outlining the range of faculty tasks and duties. After collecting data, the ad hoc group shaped its findings into a faculty work diagram that visually represents the work of the faculty. The one-page diagram places the faculty member at the center of the page with long "spokes" to four broad work categories: teaching, department service, college/university service, and scholarship/professional activity. Each of these four categories has shorter spokes to a full range of tasks and duties that Hamline faculty perform and fulfill. This work inventory represents all the possible kinds of work a faculty member can do, but not how it breaks down in actual practice individual by individual. Inventorying actual work contributions falls to the academic units. This creates a more manageable process than at the college-wide level, but it also begins moving the unit toward a collaborative understanding of work contributions, and provides institutions with insight into how academic units contribute to the overall mission of the college. The academic unit examines its unit inventory (what individuals are doing or planning to do) against the college-wide inventory (the full range of faculty work). The unit identifies for the institution how workload breaks down among its individual faculty members and where each of them is concentrating effort. The academic unit also identifies the percentages of its contributions in each of the categories. By examining inventories against the CLA mission and strategic plan, Hamline can begin the evaluation process of faculty work. Each unit can be assessed in terms of its ability to meet college-wide needs and expectations. Units can be asked to contribute more or less in certain categories, or more or less in its total contributions to the college. Units and the individuals within those units are also empowered to refuse additional work if they are already meeting college-wide needs. Units can also be flexible in reducing or increasing workloads of members in order to meet the mission of the college.

2) *Academic units and their faculty must together define the*
collective work of each unit, work for which faculty within
the unit agree to be held both individually and collectively
responsible.

Collective work is not the same as aggregate work. The work of an academic unit is more than the sum total of what its faculty do: It is a negotiated understanding of how the work of the unit as a whole fits within the larger mission of the institution. This process is not simple. Many mission statements are decidedly fuzzy and difficult to translate into clear priorities. So too, strategic plans are often ambitious but only vaguely articulate the everyday work of faculty. The better faculty, administrators, and staff can jointly articulate a compelling mission and a pragmatic institutional strategic plan that connects to the actual work that faculty do, the more successful individual units and faculty can be in bringing their own agendas into alignment. At the same time, there needs to be sufficient flexibility and openness to meet changing student needs and to take advantage of unforeseen opportunities. Perhaps the most challenging piece of this process is not deciding what work is valuable and should be done, but rather letting go of tasks that are compelling but not currently central priorities.

Much of the work that faculty do is highly individualized and idiosyncratic. Faculty operate independently in research and in the classrooms. They highly prize autonomy and academic freedom, as well they should. At the same time, faculty work becomes meaningful only in the context of a wider academic community. Discoveries and applications build on and connect to the intellectual work of others. Individual classes are a part of a larger curriculum that structures and enhances the learning of our students. The work faculty do as institutional citizens also entails a high degree of cooperation. Complete scholars are not made in isolation but require collegial association. Collaborative effort to increase work differentiation should not negate autonomy. Indeed, it could even enhance it.

After participating in and understanding the institution-wide discussions of mission and strategic planning, faculty within units identify which pieces of this larger mission and plan will shape their particular unit's goals. They articulate the ways they will collaborate, taking on collective responsibility for the outcome of their work. Thus, individual responsibility becomes intertwined with collective responsibility at the unit level.

FACULTY AND INSTITUTIONAL RELATIONSHIPS

Greater synchrony among the roles of members of an institution, that is, with fewer gaps and redundancies, will produce healthier institutions, with more satisfied members. Thus, understanding and clarifying the various roles, contributions, and relationships among institutional members is essential. We propose that the nature of these relationships should comprise a circle of adding value, such that participants (or group of participants) not only strive to find meaning, satisfaction, and efficacy in their own work but also add value to or enhance the work of others. Adding value means enabling or contributing to the work of others. Thus, individual faculty structure their particular work experiences to pursue their specific interests, skills, and talents but in the context of identifying the ways in which their work adds value to that of the academic unit to which they belong. Similarly, the work of the unit, as a collective, must add value to the work of the institution. While each discipline may have very specific requirements and concerns, the mission and goals of each unit must harmonize with those of the other units and the institution as a whole. Finally, to complete this circle, the institution must also add value to the work of the faculty. Administrators in particular have a responsibility to identify the ways in which the resources of the institution can be directed toward supporting and adding value to the work of individual faculty. Thus, it becomes the obligation of all members of the institution—faculty, staff, and administrators—to add value or contribute to the whole (Figure 4.1).

FIGURE 4.1 Circle of Value

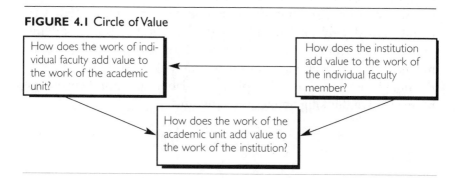

This "circle of value" should not be viewed as a closed system; there are additional relationships within the circle. For example, institutions add value to units as well as to individual faculty. Each component draws energy from outside the circle as well. Faculty collaborate with students, faculty in other units, and colleagues in their discipline at other institutions. Units interact with other units and with community-based organizations. Participation in a consortium brings new ideas to an institution. Nevertheless, this circle of value represents the core relationships that will lead to healthier institutions with faculty, administrators, and staff who find their work more meaningful, satisfying, and effective. In the next sections we describe the components essential to answer our circle of value questions: How does each add value to the other?

How does the work of the individual faculty member add value to the work of the academic unit?

1) Each faculty member should have a home academic unit, though he or she may work in more that one academic unit. The home unit serves as the primary source for feedback and advocacy for its individual faculty members.

Since differentiating faculty workloads is best accomplished in a collaborative context, individual faculty need to be part of a specific team—a group small enough to allow regular face-to-face interactions but large enough to allow the flexibility to accommodate significant differences in work duties. An individual faculty member would receive feedback and peer evaluation within a home unit and would first turn to that unit to work out problems as well. But no matter how rooted a faculty member is in a particular unit—even within a traditional department structure—the realities of interdisciplinary curricula and institutional citizenship necessitate that most faculty members will take on some roles outside of their home unit. Traditional departments immediately come to mind as a natural starting point for defining home units. But for many ANAC institutions in particular, departments are not large enough units to accommodate workload differentiation. In such cases, interdisciplinary collaboration could encourage more creative thinking about unit structures.

INSTITUTIONAL EXAMPLE

HOME UNITS AT THE UNIVERSITY OF HARTFORD

At the University of Hartford, faculty have several options for appointments that reflect the variety and complexity of their research and teaching commitments. In addition to conventional appointments within a single department in a school or college, faculty can receive appointments in departments in two different colleges. These appointments allow for the designation of one unit as primary for the purpose of faculty evaluation. Chairs and deans of the units involved consult about the evaluation of faculty; however, the Faculty Policy Manual stipulates that "unless otherwise agreed to in writing by the faculty member and the primary unit chair or dean, the requirements and expectations of the primary unit shall serve as the standard by which the faculty member is reviewed." In addition, the faculty senate of the university is currently considering a faculty teaching load proposal that would allow the dean and the faculty to collaborate in the definition of the units that would form the basis for the calculation of collective teaching loads. Such a proposal encourages faculty to see their teaching responsibilities not only in a departmental context but also in the context of a larger unit—a division, or in some cases, the whole college.

One could argue for a model in which faculty belong to and negotiate with multiple units for various percentages of their workload. Such a model could work. But too often faculty are left with percentages of responsibilities that add up to more than 100%, spotty feedback, and little direction in setting priorities among competing unit demands. The recommendation of creating a home unit recognizes the importance of having a consistent group of peers with whom to collaborate and from which to draw feedback and support. At the same time, membership in a home unit might be modified to accommodate the evolving career paths of individual faculty and the units themselves might need to be reconfigured over time to meet the changing needs of the institution.

2) The faculty of these academic units need to define their unit's work in such a way that it connects the interest and expertise of the faculty to the mission of the institution and the work of other units.

The greatest drawback of focusing on academic units as the primary site for faculty collaboration is the fear that individual departments will simply become even more introspective and engage in competitive fief building. Such is already the case in many institutions, and we are not proposing to strengthen the walls that divide disciplines. Rather, the academic unit needs to be the conduit through which individual faculty work connects to the larger work of the institution. In collaborating to identify all the work of the unit, faculty have the opportunity to match individual interest and expertise to the priorities delineated in an institution-wide discussion of faculty work. Faculty within the unit need to understand how their efforts contribute to the mission of the institution.

Part of the value that individual faculty members add to a unit is their ability to make connections to the work of other units and the institution as a whole. One faculty member's class contributes not only to a particular disciplinary major and minor but also to the curricula of general education, of related fields, of interdisciplinary programs. One unit's cocurricular planning—for speakers, workshops, field trips—joins with that of other units to create a complementary series of programs. The community outreach project of faculty in one unit collaboratively builds on the endeavors of faculty in other units. One faculty member's participation in a university-wide committee gives voice to the concerns of several related units. All units need to demonstrate how the work of their members interacts with and contributes to the work of other faculty and units.

3) Faculty members within home units collaboratively establish individual work plans for fixed lengths of time, differentiated according to how individual talents and interests best add value to the work of the unit. These plans should include clear outcomes on which the faculty member will be evaluated. Assessment, in turn, should reflect individual differential contributions to the work of the unit.

Once a unit has set its goals and defined the work it needs to accomplish, the next step is to decide collaboratively which individuals will take on specific tasks. The goal is to find the best match between individual talents and interests and the work at hand. The result should be an individualized work plan for each faculty member. Institutions will have to decide just how differentiated such work plans can be. Some parameters may be set on a campus-wide or unit-wide basis, that is, the minimum/maximum percentage of weight faculty may place on citizenship, scholarship, or teaching in evaluation. Some parameters might be set by the contract status or career stage of a particular faculty member, that is, probationary faculty might need to attend more to teaching and research than citizenship; faculty on part-time or visiting contracts might have limited student advising or service commitments. However, the greater the flexibility given to the faculty of a unit to negotiate their plans collaboratively, the more creative possibilities that can be generated. Incorporating both part-time and probationary faculty into these unit negotiations is preferable; however, units should take care to acknowledge and mitigate the differences in power and privilege among those of various status. Overall, we would encourage institutions to minimize boundaries and maximize flexibility. One size does not have to fit all units any more than all individual faculty.

INSTITUTIONAL EXAMPLE

THE USE OF WORK PLANS AT THE UNIVERSITY OF THE PACIFIC

For many years now, the School of Pharmacy and Health Sciences at the University of the Pacific has developed and used work plans as a means of building more flexibility into the structure of faculty work. These individualized work plans allow individual faculty members to focus on certain areas of expertise based on a recognition of different needs within particular phases of the faculty career. This system involves the use of a faculty development goal sheet which details the goals, indicators of goal achievement, and requirements to achieve particular goals in the areas of teaching, scholarly activity, and service. Additionally, faculty members are allowed, through negotiation at the departmental level, to decide on percentages for weighing and evaluating their academic activities in the areas of teaching, scholarly activity, and service. To illustrate, during a recent academic year, it was decided, through departmental discussion and negotiation, that a junior faculty member needed more time to focus attention on grant proposal development. Therefore, a senior and tenured faculty member in this same department agreed to take on additional teaching assignments in order to facilitate this extra time needed for research by her junior colleague. This exchange resulted in the securing of a very prestigious research grant by the junior faculty member which placed him in a much better position to meet the eligibility standards for promotion and tenure. Furthermore, the department's prestige was also enhanced by this acquisition of federal research funds. The entire unit also benefited from funding for overhead. All in all, negotiating flexible work plans brought about a win-win situation for the individual faculty member, the department, and the unit.

Work plans need to be tied to a particular time frame in order to recognize the evolving work of faculty. What is proposed is not a set of distinctive tracks for individual faculty. Rather, work plans should be the backbone of a system that allows faculty to cycle through a variety of roles throughout the course of a career. Both student needs and faculty skills change over time. Curricular, research, and service projects all have patterns of intense and less intense effort that work plans should reflect. Both career stages of individual faculty and the emerging priorities of the institution must be acknowledged. And there will always be those unit responsibilities considered onerous to all that will need to be rotated as a matter of equity.

So too, work plans need to include clear outcomes that connect to individual evaluation—otherwise these plans become just another layer of meaningless paperwork. At the same time, work plans facilitate faculty involvement in all levels of creating, evaluating, and rewarding differentiated work. Individual faculty establish and evaluate their own differentiated work plans, review other faculty work plans in their unit, and review and reward work plans as members of tenure and promotion committees. However, faculty need to recognize that a work plan does not guarantee successful evaluation. Work plans set boundaries and priorities for evaluation and indicate types of evidence that demonstrate quality work. Nevertheless, some individuals will be more successful in carrying out their work plans than others and evaluations will perforce reflect this.

How does the work of the academic unit add value to the work of the institution?

1) Units should negotiate a set of expectations relating to how the unit is to add value to the larger school and/or institutional mission, with the understanding that units will add value to that mission in different ways.

Currently in many institutions the only quantifiable measure of faculty workload is tied to student credit hours and/or courses taught. This measure has become the common coin of the realm in weighing both individual and unit productivity. However, it has a limited ability to capture the spectrum of faculty work, even in the area of teaching. As a result, complex formulas have been created to try to accommodate differences between lab and lecture, lecture and seminar, internship and practicum, independent research and private music lessons, with added variants to credit new pedagogical approaches that are writing intensive, technology intensive, and/or asynchronous. Other formulas are added on for released or assigned time in an attempt to incorporate work on research or service projects within a single metric. Unfortunately, student credit hour data, no matter how creatively crunched, reveals very little about how faculty work adds value to the missions of our institutions.

This traditional system does have certain advantages. It places teaching and students at the center of the enterprise—even if it only measures the input of "seat time" rather than the outcome of student learning. Student credit hours generated also ties nicely to accounting systems for resource allocation—even if it chronically undervalues individualized, time-intensive faculty-student interactions that many mission statements tout as a central institutional value. It also gives lip service to fairness in measuring value across units and institutions—even as it discourages innovation and diversity.

INSTITUTIONAL EXAMPLE

HOW A UNIT ADDS VALUE TO THE COMMUNITY AT ST. MARY'S COLLEGE OF CALIFORNIA

When St. Mary's began a Master of Fine Arts program in creative writing, it did so in part because of the good fortune to have an unusually strong contingent of creative writers on the faculty (one later became Poet Laureate of the United States). But another reason was the fact that almost all the college's graduate programs were outside the School of Liberal Arts, which was seen as anomalous in an institution formally dedicated to fostering the liberal arts in its mission. One goal of the MFA was to enhance the literary life of all students on campus and people in the surrounding community as one way of making our liberal arts tradition more visible. So one formally defined part of the program is sponsoring a reading series which brings well-known writers to campus (Gary Snyder, Michael Ondaatjie, Csleslav Milosz). The program also sponsors a series of student readings at which graduate and undergraduate students share their work with the campus community and students in other writing programs in the area. While this example may seem mundane—many institutions engage in similar efforts to bring speakers to campus and/or show-case student work—what is unique for St. Mary's is the inclusion of such activities in the formal identification of unit work for which the unit will be held accountable. Such contributions add value to the entire institution even if they do not generate student credit hours.

Proposed here is not a radical new system to replace the current credit hour measure. Rather, institutions are encourage to recognize the limitations of the existing system and to move toward creating other ways to recognize the diversity of value that individual units add to the mission of the institution. This imperative has become even greater as technology forces a rethinking of the temporal and spatial boundaries of the classroom. The work in class, online, and in the community of musicians, historians, biologists, and physical thera-pists within the units to which they belong add value to the institu-tion in their diversity. A public recital, a published monograph, a joint student-faculty research presentation, a successful service-learning/com-munity outreach program, a productive accrediting agency review all defy measurement in calculated student credit hours but all are out-comes that demonstrate valuable contributions to institutional mis-sion. Just as differentiation can happen among individual faculty, so too can it be recognized and encouraged among individual units. But the caveat of collaboration still holds. Unit contributions must clearly connect to the mission of the institution.

2) Units should be held responsible for engaging in self-assessment, based upon student learning, and for making constructive changes based upon these assessments. For its part, the institution is responsible for supporting, recognizing, and rewarding academic units that can demonstrate success in carrying out their work.

One way to begin to create new measures of value is for units to reflect critically on and assess their work on a regular basis. This assessment should lead to constructive change. The actual tasks examined and the measures used perforce should vary depending on the unit involved. However, one criterion that crosses all units is the imperative to enhance student learning. Another is for the assessment to lead to meaningful change and improvement. Most institutions already have some cycle of unit reviews—often connected to outside accrediting agencies. However, the impact of such reviews is often limited and not connected to institutional rewards or other review cycles.

INSTITUTIONAL EXAMPLE

UNIVERSITY OF REDLANDS ASKS: "WE REVIEWED OUR PROGRAM— NOW WHAT?"

Departments and programs of the College of Arts and Sciences at the University of Redlands complete a self-study every seven years, composed in light of guidelines created by the college's curriculum committee. Departments consider such things as the success of curricula and programming for majors and other ways the unit contributes to the college overall (e.g., through general education, interdisciplinary programs, etc.). Following input from outside reviewers, the curriculum committee reviews the self-studies and makes recommendations to the department.

In addition to the obvious benefits of periodically taking stock of programs, permission from the curriculum committee (which plays a crucial role in prioritizing position requests) to search for new tenure-track faculty is contingent on a department being up to date on its review. The assumption is that the careful thinking and planning that goes on in the review is an important element in determining whether to commit long-term to proposed positions. In some cases, failure to complete the self-study has led the curriculum committee to postpone its decision about whether to recommend a new position until the review process was completed. In other cases, the review process has helped programs find the support to expand, to redefine positions requested, and even to obtain new facilities (the self-studies of science programs in the early 1990s was one early step that lead to the building of a new center for the sciences, dedicated in fall 2000).

Meaningful unit evaluation is a key piece of directing individual faculty work differentiation toward institutional mission. Support, recognition, and reward for unit success needs to be embedded in the regular life of our institutions. It should affect allocation of resources as well as symbolic tokens of status and esteem. Moreover, cycles of planning, reporting, and evaluation for individuals and academic units should interconnect and build on each other. The interdependence of differentiated workload for individual faculty members and collaboration on the unit level necessitate that these cycles be brought into alignment.

3) Units should nurture the development of faculty leadership, particularly the ability to negotiate group values.

Working in a collaborative unit requires that everyone become more skilled in negotiation and compromise. Faculty within the unit articulate together the common mission and goals of the unit and how their individual work contributes to this larger whole. Leaders facilitate useful discussion, mediate conflict, and build consensus. They collaborate with the leaders of other units as well and connect the work of their unit to the mission and goals of the larger institution. The acquisition of such skills by all faculty, and in particular those who serve as leaders, should not be left to chance. Opportunities to learn and enhance necessary skills should be a regular part of orientation, mentoring, and faculty development.

How does the institution add value to the work of the individual faculty member?

1) Institutions must provide resources appropriate for the work expected of faculty and foster a climate of support for risk-taking and innovation that furthers institutional mission.

A healthy institution constructs a compact with faculty that recognizes its role in the circle of value. Institutions add value to faculty members by recognizing that faculty need varied forms of support, action, and reward. If faculty feel valued by the institution, they will be more invested in the institution's health, potential, and future growth. Institutional support for faculty work adds value not only to the faculty member's work but also to the academic unit and ultimately to the institution. Support is also provided through institutional infrastructures that include faculty development programs, appropriate governance structures, and even campus facilities, all of which provide an environment in which faculty work is valued. Clearly, much of the responsibility for making sure such institutional structures function well and efficiently will fall to individual staff and administrators working in concert with faculty.

To nurture this supportive environment and to encourage faculty to explore innovative work, the members of an institution must together establish accountability measures through which faculty work can be evaluated and provide appropriate professional and financial support and reward. Institutional support for faculty work is expressed by academic administrators, presidents, and governing boards who demonstrate a constancy of purpose in which consistency and commitment to act are givens. By nurturing the work of both the faculty member and the academic unit, the institution takes ownership and responsibility for the circle of value and its effectiveness. While the work of the faculty and the academic unit energizes the process of adding value, it is institutional commitment and support—made concrete by administrators and staff, presidents and governing boards, and the faculty themselves—that reinforce this effort and guarantee its success.

2) Promotion and tenure standards and other faculty reward systems should reflect institutional values and respect the diversity of faculty work.

As the first phase of the ANAC Faculty Work Project demonstrated so clearly, the espoused values of the institution are often not reflected in the ways in which faculty work is recognized and rewarded. Rhetoric is often incongruent with practice. If the one-size-fits-all culture is to change, the faculty reward system in use must change as well. Standards for the evaluation of faculty work will have to shift from a focus on individual accomplishment based on merit—work intrinsically valued by the individual—to accomplishment based on worth—the individual's contribution to the unit and to the university. While the institution may have common academic standards to which faculty in all units are expected to adhere, academic units will define and implement these standards differently. Especially challenging will be decisions about tenure. Traditionally, junior faculty are expected to show excellence in teaching, scholarship, and citizenship. Faculty and administrators will need to decide together whether and how differentiation of work should extend to tenure track assistant professors and to what extent they should be expected to demonstrate competence in all three areas before they are free to focus their energies in different ways. So too, part-time and adjunct faculty are often only evaluated on teaching. If an institution chooses to distinguish workload differentiation prerogatives by career stage or contract status, it will need to acknowledge and understand the impact such a class system might have on individual, unit, and institutional work.

INSTITUTIONAL EXAMPLE

RECOGNIZING ADJUNCT FACULTY AT NORTH CENTRAL COLLEGE

A strategy for integrating adjunct faculty into the fabric of institutional life and for finding meaningful ways to recognize the realities of their daily experience and aspirations has become a way of life at North Central. Fractional positions reflecting half-time status bring adjunct faculty into a formal, continuing relationship with the college that allows for faculty salaries commensurate with their fractional appointments, for benefits, promotion, and professional growth. With a full-time faculty workload that includes teaching 21 credit hours a year and advising, citizenship, and professional growth estimated at roughly the equivalent of another nine credit hours, half-time faculty teach 15 credit hours, about half of the composite workload of full-time faculty. While their contracts are primarily and sometimes exclusively devoted to teaching, half-time adjuncts, because of their continuing relationship with the college, often seek to take on responsibilities related to advising and, increasingly, campus citizenship.

The majority of half-time faculty either have terminal degrees which do not qualify them for full-time status or have professional or other affiliations that they do not wish to alter (among them, half-time faculty are lawyers, physicians, corporate executives, care givers, journalists, physicists, and computer scientists). Some have taught for 15 years and many have taught for five or more. A few others will teach for several years and then enter the job market seeking full-time employment.

For students, half-time faculty offer the opportunities traditionally associated with full-time faculty: campus availability, awareness of curricular connections and the network of support for student needs, as well as the professional experience or real-world practice that gives added stimulus to the classroom. In some departments, half-time faculty participate fully in the life of the department and the day-to-day experiences of traditional-age students. In others, half-time faculty become a particularly effective resource for the adult student taking weekend and evening programs. All half-time faculty have full voting privileges in the faculty governance. The faculty evaluation process is an adaptation of that used for tenure-track faculty, intensive evaluation in the first six years, afterwards slightly longer intervals and emphasis on long-term concerns.

Emerging in the 1970s and continuing through the mid-1980s as a singular solution to a unique departmental need, no more than four such positions existed. Today, 28 faculty members participate in the features of half-time status. They have enabled North Central to consolidate part-time per course positions with all of their limitations for the individuals involved and for the institution in favor of long-term professional partnerships. They have been able to do so without impacting the commitment to full-time tenure-track positions that proceed to be filled and that grow in number based upon the usual needs evaluation. The result is a mutually beneficial relationship between North Central College and faculty on fractional appointments.

One of the most important nonmonetary ways that institutions can reward faculty is to respect and act upon the results of faculty work that contribute to the health and vitality of the institution. Too often, faculty serve on committees that spend valuable faculty time defining problems and proposing solutions only to discover that their recommendations have no real input in institutional decisions. Any number of scenarios are possible: Either the decisions have already been made by the administration, the process for considering faculty input is not communicated, no resources are available to implement the new initiatives, or no one is willing to risk changes to the current institutional structure. Before faculty undertake such tasks, individually or jointly with other campus constituencies, they need to have clarification from administrators about how their input will impact the decision-making process, who is ultimately responsible for making the decision, in what time frame, and with what resource limitations. Administrators, presidents, and governing boards then have an obligation to honor those decisions made by faculty in appropriate areas, thoughtfully consider faculty recommendations, and consistently communicate and clarify the outcomes of the decision-making process.

This central obligation must also extend beyond the faculty role in traditional institutional governance. Faculty regularly contribute to their institutions through teaching and scholarship, through collaboration with their colleagues within and outside of academic units, and by serving the broader community within which the institution is situated. All too often, these vital contributions go unrecognized because they fall outside faculty committees, the traditional conduit by which faculty shape the institution. These other forms of faculty work, however, strengthen and enrich the institution by making it more externally visible and more of an integrated whole. Administrators, in particular, have an obligation to create opportunities for faculty to take on the work of institutional citizenship in these ways and then to act upon the results of faculty contributions that create a healthier, more vital institution.

3) Institutions should support faculty exploration of new career trajectories and renegotiate their work responsibilities accordingly.

Differentiating faculty workload needs to accommodate change over time. Faculty will take on different task at different stages of their careers. New opportunities for research and service projects will arise, curricular innovations and changes will be required, new institutional needs will emerge. Faculty must be given the opportunity and skills to meet these challenges and explore emerging possibilities. The impetus for such exploration might come from an individual faculty member, or through the encouragement of colleagues, administrators, or students, or from the demands of new institutional initiatives. Tenure alone should motivate institutions to invest and reinvest in individual faculty so as to assure their continued engagement and productivity in projects that further institutional mission. The shape of such explorations and support will vary considerably by discipline, experience, career stage, and individual skills and interest. But such opportunities represent the concrete ways in which the institution continually renews its compact with its faculty.

CONCLUSION

The ideas presented here may seem to be an utopian dream: individualized faculty work plans, collaborative units, institutional support all adding value to the other and directed toward fulfilling a joint mission to enhance student learning. In the real world, however, the layering on of faculty responsibilities, competition between units, and one-size-fits-all institutional policy making are impeding our ability to connect what faculty actually do with our mission to serve students. It is time, then, to reenvision the relationship between faculty and their institutions in ways that will lead to greater satisfaction, productivity, flexibility, and focus on mission. The schema outlined above allows individual faculty a greater degree of autonomy in shaping their work. At the same time it increases the collaboration of faculty within and among academics units—the primary institutional context where individual faculty connect their work with that of the larger academic community to which they belong. Finally, it enhances the institution's ability to align both individual faculty and unit work with its mission in ways that allow for ongoing change and flexibility in meeting the needs of our students. This chapter has defined faculty work in ways that are more representative of what faculty actually do. It has developed a conceptual framework and a process for identifying what faculty really do. Institutions which engage in this process will be better positioned to recognize and value faculty work in ways that are beneficial to both faculty and their institutions.

ACKNOWLEDGMENTS

The Workload Differentiation Work Group included Ed Biglin (St. Mary's College of California), Garry Brodhead (Ithaca College), Elizabeth Burt (University of Hartford), Jim Malek (Ithaca College), Heather Mayne (University of the Pacific), Linda McMillin (Susquehanna University), Robert Morrow (University of the Pacific), Pat O'Connor (The Sage Colleges), Ray Posey (University of the Pacific), Alan Silva (Hamline University), George Sims (Belmont University), Catherine Stevenson (University of Hartford), Barbara Temple-Thurston (Pacific Lutheran University), and Jon Wergin (Virginia Commonwealth University).

REFERENCE

Rice, E. (1996). *Making a place for the new American scholar.* American Association for Higher Education New Pathways Working Paper Series. Washington, DC: American Association for Higher Education.

The Compact
in Action

5

SHARED GOVERNANCE AT BUTLER UNIVERSITY

Patricia Bacon

Butler University, a small, comprehensive institution in Indianapolis, Indiana, has been operating under a new governance structure for the last three years. The model has been presented at various forums and used as a foundation for discussions and surveys to discover other views about shared governance and what the keys to continued success might be for Butler University as well as other colleges and universities. The results of the assessment of the new governance structure at Butler University have demonstrated a continued desire on the part of all constituencies to encourage and increase the positive working relationship between faculty, administration, and trustees. At the same time, all realize that these desires must be balanced with the undeniable reality of the increased demands for faculty accountability and assessment of faculty workload, for administrative productivity increases and efficiency, and for trustee understanding of these processes. It is a fine balance, but one worth continuing to improve.

The Butler University model gives everyone an opportunity to explore the most efficient ways of defining roles and responsibilities while maintaining the foundation on which the institution was built—creating the best learning environment for students. As explained in this chapter, one of the largest successes of the system is the involvement of faculty in the direct decision-making in all facets of the institution and the redefinition of the roles of the deans. The largest challenge that still faces Butler University, however, is how to continue to encourage more participation in this system, given both internal and external demands on faculty and administrators time.

WHY NEW GOVERNANCE?

The impetus for change in university governance stems from the generally held opinion that current governance structures are inadequate and dysfunctional. This argument is supported by Dionne and Kean:

> One of our strongest recommendations is that institutional restructuring . . . be made a national priority. Like the health care industry, the higher education sector must systematically address issues of cost, productivity, and effectiveness . . . We believe that colleges and universities must make major organizational changes. To do so their governance systems must be changed so that they can reallocate scarce resources and permit fundamental reform in the way they do business. (1994, p. 14)

There is a fundamental mismatch between current higher education governance systems and the collegial traditions of shared governance in the academy. This structural flaw inhibits communication and shared work processes and has produced a virtual standoff that is managed only through an uneasy exercise of extraordinary goodwill. The structure is remarkably congruent between public and independent sectors because these sectors have two important historical roots in common. The first is the powerful standardizing influence that has been contributed by widespread adherence to the postwar guidelines established by the American Association of University Professors (AAUP). The AAUP Redbook and subsequent standards have helped to define a national model for appropriate governance (Kreiser, 1990). Such standards emerged from the AAUP's early days as a purely professional association and have been influenced by its more recent role as a collective bargaining entity. Second, there has been a decades-long transition in the composition of boards of trustees to a dominance by corporate representatives (Marsden, 1996). Through these powerful forces—corporatization of administration and collectivization of faculty—the two "sides" have been backed gradually into a classic production-sector structure of labor and management, a structure that does not sit easily with the traditions, expectations, and self-images of the university community. Figure 5.1 is what a general model looks like.

FIGURE 5.1 The Simplified General Model

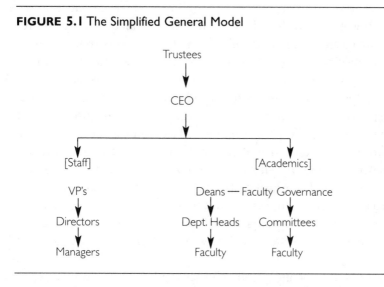

Faculty members are defined as professionals but treated as production workers; administrators are defined as managers, but constrained to mediation; and trustees are defined as policy makers, but effectively disbarred from academics (Bannister & Bacon, 1999). The most critical issue concerns the status of faculty because, in the end, change needs to occur in the classroom, not just the boardroom. Faculty status in the modern university was addressed perceptively by the Supreme Court of the United States in its ruling on NLRB versus Yeshiva University, Yeshiva University Faculty Association versus Yeshiva University, 1980. The court characterized not just department heads but all full-time faculty members as managers because of their role in such processes as admissions, retention, and graduation of students. While this may be an accurate interpretation of the system in terms of the production-sector oriented National Labor Relations Act, most faculty correctly see this ruling as perverse and inaccurate. In reality, they are buried too deeply in a mixed hierarchical, corporate model of management to be effectively described as managers. The AAUP has been forced to protect faculty interests through collective bargaining structures and processes designed for production workers, while simultaneously making the case for the shared management status of the professorate.

These trends and interpretations, together with some half-century of negotiation have produced two cultures—for faculty a flat, representative structure rooted in a collegial history of weak management, and for professional staff, a newer and more powerful hierarchical structure of corporate management. Trustees and others have sponsored the latter because their experience in the corporate sector makes them suspicious of the unfamiliar and untidy looking processes of faculty-based collegial decision-making. The result is an unfortunate and unproductive standoff that can only be resolved by concessions and structural change by all sides of the university governance system. Surrounding this uneasy standoff is a sense of urgency. It is becoming increasingly important that this issue be addressed sooner rather than later. This poses a real dilemma, because it is often thought that universities and colleges do not easily adapt to rapid change.

This may be a misconception. The strong historical cultures with traditions that exist in colleges and universities within the faculty ranks may, in fact, make them better at adapting to new organizational systems than our corporate counterparts. There is a longstanding tradition in the academy of collegial decision-making, consensus seeking, and critical self-appraisal that many corporations must create. Trustees and others with experience in the corporate sector are suspicious of the unfamiliar and untidy-looking processes of faculty decision-making, but they are learning to tolerate and even support the messiness of decision-making at the frontline level in their own organizations. In this sense, what is needed is not so much a change in faculty culture, but rather an extension of the collegial culture to include administrative staff on a professionally respected basis, with a new system of support and training to make collaborative decision-making work. With this as the backdrop, and the hopeful premise that universities, if given the proper support can make change, the trustees, faculty, and administration of Butler University set about to design a new structure. The new structure would address these urgent issues, particularly as they affected Butler, while keeping in mind the need to preserve the history and traditions of the institution.

BUTLER UNIVERSITY'S TIMELINE: AN OVERVIEW

Given the climate described above, Butler University began a discussion of how to respond to changing forms of and demands on institutional governance. As far back as 1991, trustees began to examine the effectiveness of the board and set a path for strategic planning for the university. By 1993, the new strategic plan set the stage to focus on learning and effective outcomes. The strategic plan 2005 articulated seven strategic issues: quality, price, effectiveness, reputation, technology, community, and global. Goals and objectives to be reached by 2005 were set for each of the seven issues. Effectiveness was the strategic issue associated with governance.

By 1994, a dialogue ensued among trustees, faculty, and administrators which compared the current climate, both internally and externally, to the focus outlined in the strategic plan. Facilitation for these roundtable discussions was provided by The Pew Charitable Trust. This dialogue led to some consensus on the meaning of quality education and effective pricing, the process for accomplishing this within a learning environment, and the responsibilities of the university within the greater community. Discussions focused on the challenges facing higher education in general: escalating costs, price resistance, unfunded discounting, consumer pressures, dwindling state support, erosion of public confidence, and competitive recruitment. It was important to identify the issues that faced Butler University and what role the university wanted to play in setting the agenda for the community.

In 1995, the faculty governance structure was revised to create joint faculty-administrator committees to enhance communication and facilitate more input into decision-making. At the same time, the human resource function was elevated to report directly to the president. More emphasis was being placed on costs of programming and the human resource component of all programs was continuing to be a key piece. Therefore, it was prudent to make sure the human resources were being considered in strategic decisions.

The year 1996 was full of transformation. The trustees voted to formally change the focus of the university from a teaching institution to

one founded on learning and learning outcomes. A change management consultant was hired to help guide the evolution of a cabinet
from an administrative group to team-based decision-making. The
university became a member of the Knight Collaborative to improve
access to like-minded organizations and national expertise. A team of
faculty and staff from the university was sent to the Wharton School
for a Pew-sponsored training program on managing change. During
this year, the Lilly Endowment granted the university $4.6 million to
develop the student learning initiative. It was now imperative that the
university develop a structure to support this new learning initiative.

Butler began implementing a new structure in 1997. First, there was
a flattening of the hierarchy. The decision was made to leave the current provost's vacancy unfilled, and the deans were made a part of the
cabinet. The administration was reorganized to narrow the span of
control of each vice president. The chair of the faculty assembly
replaced the provost position on the cabinet and subsequently two
more faculty positions were added (vice chair and former chair of the
faculty assembly). Finally, and one of the most important pieces of the
new structure, the budget was decentralized so that budget managers
now had control over the priorities of the area under their supervision. By 1998, the establishment of a totally redesigned structure was
in place (Figure 5.2).

HOW DOES THE NEW MODEL WORK?

The result of this structure is a flattened hierarchy that replaced the
former traditional vice presidential team with a broader cabinet that
includes deans and other administrative decision-makers. The
responsibilities are as follows.

University cabinet. This body is the institution's executive leadership team. Its charge is to review, revise, and refine institutional
strategies and to verify them with trustees. Members include the president; vice presidents for enrollment management, organizational
development, student affairs, advancement, operations, and finance;
the deans of academic affairs and various colleges; the directors of ath-
letics, information resources, and public affairs; and the chair, immediate past chair, and vice chair of the faculty assembly.

FIGURE 5.2 Team Reporting Structure

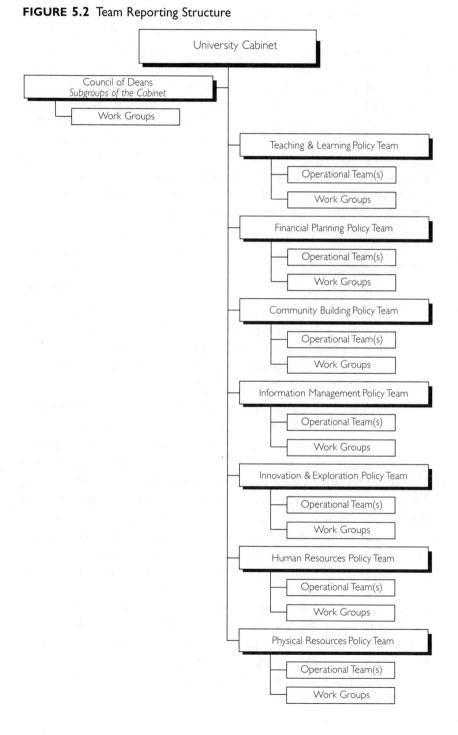

Policy teams. Each policy team has a specific charge related to a core function or process of the institution. These include teaching and learning, information management, and financial planning, among others. Among other functions, the teams propose policies or strategies and seek consensus among various groups. Each team has about seven members and a cabinet contact, with membership balanced about equally between faculty and staff. In addition, each team has a handbook that includes work pages for designing the team charter, goals and objectives, and implementation plan. The handbook also includes places for keeping meeting notes, reports, agendas, and proposals. Team conveners meet periodically with the office of organizational development to discuss support needs.

Operational teams. These teams have a wider membership that draws on needed expertise or perspective in specific areas. They may propose solutions within or across functional areas of the university. Some examples include parking, risk management, and information resources.

Work groups. These groups may be established to complete short-term assignments related to specific operational problems. The cabinet must approve their creation. Members may include faculty, staff, students, trustees, or others with interest or expertise.

Council of deans. This council is a subgroup of the cabinet. The group provides communication on academic issues across colleges.

Issues can be identified by policy teams, cabinet members, and/or individuals from any part of the university. Individuals send their concerns to the appropriate policy teams as determined by the area of emphasis for that team. To have an issue reviewed, a case statement is prepared, recommending that a work group be formed to review and make recommendations. The proposal contains a clear explanation of the problem/issue, some recommended members for the work group, suggested resources, any relevant background and/or research suggestions, and a timeline for completion. Either the policy teams or the cabinet receive the proposals for work groups. Policy teams review and prioritize requests and forward endorsed proposals on to the cabinet. The cabinet reviews all proposals, whether received directly or through policy teams. Work groups are formed, if approved, or proposals may be sent back to the policy teams for refinement or postponement. Once a work group is agreed upon, a charge is prepared. Having all proposals come through the cabinet ensures that university priorities are considered and respected and allows for careful tracking of the progress of work groups. The office of organizational development is responsible for this tracking and also provides general support, if needed (facilitation, workbooks, guidelines, and samples of final proposals).

Work groups present a final recommendation in a standard format to the cabinet or policy team (whichever is designated by the cabinet). There is a review, and a decision made whether to adopt the proposal as is, modify, or return it to the work group for further clarification. Figure 5.3 illustrates the process.

THE NEW MODEL: IS IT EFFECTIVE?

Despite the difficulties surrounding this kind of change, Butler University is particularly well positioned for a model of this kind to be effective. It is small enough that communication can be handled efficiently (this does not mean that it always is, but the capability is there). It is a community where dialogue is accepted and where people readily participate in it. It is also a community where collaboration is not a new phenomenon. The new model has been in place about three years, so it is appropriate to assess its effectiveness and use that assessment to determine the direction for the future. This section outlines the criteria and why they are important to success; how Butler University measures up to those criteria; the successes we have had; and finally, some areas for further growth.

The Criteria

Butler used six criteria for measuring the effectiveness of its new governance model.

1) The model must effectively support the academic agenda. This is first and foremost a model that must support the agenda for which the institution stands. These are not corporate entities, but organizations focused on learning. This is the core mission.

2) The model must encourage participation from all areas of the university. In this way, ideas can come from all sources, leadership can be developed at all levels, and communication is enhanced.

FIGURE 5.3 How Issues Move Through the Shared Governance System

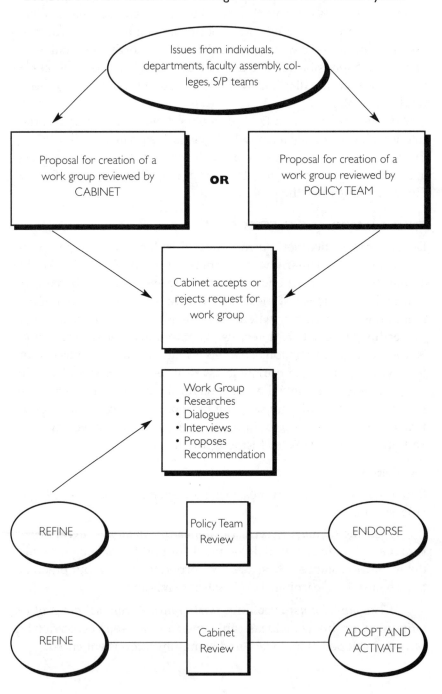

3) There must be a high degree of trust for those who are acting as champions of the change. Change is difficult even when it is desired. To institute changes that may not be understood requires trust and goodwill on all parts. Trust inspires support and a willingness to join in the process even if one is not completely sure.

4) The model must be built out of the institutional history and culture. Again, a successful model allows for the blending of the old and the new so that people can accept that there was value in what was done before.

5) The model must focus the discussion on the system rather than the people. Models often fail because the systems that are in place will allow for no change or deviation from old practices that were not successful. This makes it very easy to blame the individual.

6) There must be institutional support and resources for the model. The model will only succeed if resources are provided to support the model. This must take the form of training for participants, staff support, and financial resources.

The success of this model is contingent upon the continued agreement that the criteria above are the correct ones and that all stay vigilant in comparing progress to these criteria. It has been easy to track the participation levels and the quality and quantity of decisions made. It is less easy to track perceptions and feelings. To ascertain the progress to date a survey was completed in December 1999. Participants in the survey included all members of the policy teams and work groups as well as a random sample of other individuals throughout the university who were not actively involved. In addition, individual meetings were held with each of the conveners of the policy teams to gather more detailed information about successes and needs for the future. This survey and the meetings helped to determine the level of understanding and support of the new model. The responses indicate successes using all of the above criteria. However, the two most significant criteria that relate most directly to faculty workload are the first two: supporting the academic agenda and increasing participation.

Supporting the Academic Agenda

Focusing governance in a way that supports the academic agenda of the university is perhaps the most important and dramatic success of the model and goes most directly to the issue of faculty workload. The model supports the academic agenda in three ways. First, the deans' role has expanded so as to be much more involved in priority-setting agendas and budget control. Second, faculty make up at least half of the membership on each of the policy teams and are always included in any work group. And third, there are specific policy teams for academic agenda-setting: teaching and learning and innovation and exploration.

With the elimination of the provost's office, the deans now participate fully on the cabinet, and in that capacity are able to share actively in the decision-making and in hearing the university-wide issues first hand without interpretation. The voices of the deans are a very positive force on the cabinet, bringing to the table very timely and heartfelt academic issues. Decisions are made with full knowledge of all areas. The university budget has been distributed to each dean along with the contingency funds. The deans were challenged to be responsible for their own budgets, taking the budget and presenting the best college administration as evaluated against best practices. There were contingency mechanisms put into place.

The deans now have both responsibility and authority. They can clearly articulate their college's academic agenda. They can be much more active in allocating resources to the priorities of each individual college more quickly and effectively and they can assist with the external fundraising agenda. They can ensure that curricular models integrate with other colleges because there is much more discussion and collaboration between deans. They have a group of colleagues that can discuss issues of similar concern. Overall, there is one less level of interpretation when priorities are discussed on an institutional level, and one less layer to keep informed. All are hearing the same information so there is less likelihood of misinformation or conflicting information across colleges. Finally, deans have the advantage of being closer to their colleges than a provost could, and they are able to make better decisions and to make them more quickly than before. Since this model has been in place, four new deans have been hired. All four have said that Butler's governance structure was a major factor in their decision to accept these posts. They are supportive and anxious to see it in full force.

Participation

Participation is the second most important success of the model because it encourages the development of leadership and growth in all areas of the university, not just at the top. Leadership is as important for those performing the activities of aligning people, inspiring action, and getting results in smaller groups within the organization. More participation promotes growth for all staff and faculty involved, facilitates better understanding of the challenges that face universities, and adds strength and confidence within the organization so that decisions can be encouraged at lower levels. Participation also fosters a common understanding and more collaboration. It encourages idea sharing from all over the university. Answers to issues cannot always come from the same small group of people. Putting the right people together fosters creative and better solutions and puts the issues and decisions where they belong.

Faculty make up at least half, often more, of the members of all work groups and policy teams. This means that recommendations now come to the cabinet with faculty input, making discussions more fruitful and the cabinet decisions easier. Issues and alternative solutions have already been discussed and resolved where necessary, before reaching the cabinet. The faculty members of these teams are chosen for their interest and expertise rather than their representation. This enables the team to work toward institutional priorities rather than a personal agenda and keeps the academic priorities at the forefront. In addition, there are two policy teams designated solely for the academic agenda—the teaching and learning team and the innovation and exploration team. Each of these teams designs and considers new ideas and programs for the academic agenda.

There has been good participation for the first year of a new model. Seven policy teams have involved approximately 49 people. The work groups, as of April 1999, have involved 43 faculty, 57 staff, and six students, bringing the total participation to 155 people. (See Table 5.1 for examples of work groups.)

TABLE 5.1 Examples of Work Groups

Administrative costs work group
Benefits analysis work group
Reconciliation and planning for building projects
Marketing communications assessment
Faculty compensation incentive programs
Tuition remission analysis
University priority events and meeting space
University software
Vacation/sick leave

Other Successes

The surveys and interviews indicate other successes as well. First and foremost, this new model was able to maintain trust by the use of familiar people as champions and leaders. All the participants work together, through dialogue, toward a solution that involves looking at the system rather than pointing fingers at individuals. Decisions and priorities are made by deliberately and consciously referring to the priorities that were established through a group exercise. These priorities are well grounded in the history and culture of the institution, and were agreed upon as ones that would guide thinking as decisions were made and priorities assigned. They are (in order of priority): student learning, responsibility to the future, innovation and change, reputation (internal and external), interaction and dialogue, globalization and diversity, morale, and tradition. Finally, there has been structural support and financial resources for this effort. The office of organizational development was restructured to provide this support through handbooks, research materials, and facilitation and staff support for teams and communication mechanisms. Institutional research is also available to provide support where data is needed to evaluate systems and to support new initiatives. This built-in support encourages consistency and builds strength in the participants and in the system.

NEW CHALLENGES TO MEET

Overall, the scorecard appears positive. The model is effective. However, as with any new attempt at governance, challenges remain.

It is evident from the surveys, the conversations and observations that three areas need continued attention: participation—by even more people; communication—more of it, accurate and timely; and support/training—for time-weary people both academic and administrative.

These issues are being addressed by the continued support of the office of organizational development. This office is redefining itself and assessing the staffing and resources needed to make improvements in these areas. Organizational development and public relations, together, are developing ways for input, information, and decisions to be received and delivered through a variety of communication methods.

The survey and interviews indicate that participation is a very positive aspect of the model. Efforts must be made, however, to assure that a wider variety of people become involved. In particular, support staff would like a greater opportunity to participate in teams. Additionally, participants in the model feel they face four major challenges: a need for more time, more help, more relevance, and verification that all "walk the talk."

CONCLUSION

The model provides for more widespread participation, information sharing, and participatory decision-making. All constituencies have been assured that their feelings and opinions are heard, that they have actively participated, and their recommendations are acted upon quickly and effectively without the need to go through another layer of bureaucracy. The university is a relatively small community and should respond well to less bureaucracy. But a model like this can only survive through the dedication of the participants and the support of the trustees, administrators, faculty, and staff.

Butler University is now reaping the benefits of the successes, and feeling stronger in meeting the challenges identified. The university is in a transition period from one president to another. This model will play a lead role both during the transition and in the selection of a new leader. It will be an important place to watch.

ACKNOWLEDGMENTS

I would like to acknowledge the leadership and ideas shared by Dr. Geoffrey Bannister, former president of Butler University. It was his leadership, and his interpretation of changes happening in higher education, that led to this new governance structure.

REFERENCES

Bannister, G., & Bacon, P. A. (1999). From competitive to collaborative governance. *Trusteeship, 7,* 8-13.

Dionne, J. L., & Kean, T. (1994). *Breaking the social contract: The fiscal crisis in higher education* (online). Available: www.rand.org/publications/CAE/CAE100/

Kreiser, B. R. (Ed.). (1990). *AAUP policy documents and reports.* Washington, DC: American Association of University Professors.

Marsden, G. M. (1996). *The soul of the American university.* New York, NY: Oxford University Press.

6

WORKLOAD DIFFERENTIATION AT
ITHACA COLLEGE
Garry Brodhead

Participating in the Associated New American Colleges' (ANAC) Faculty Work Project has provided Ithaca College with an opportunity to address critical issues in the area of faculty work. Like other ANAC institutions, Ithaca has viewed workload primarily in terms of teaching load. Yet faculty stretch themselves to maintain rigorous standards as teachers and scholars/performers while also performing substantive work as campus leaders in governance and other service activities. The traditional model of faculty work based on a single professional profile, a one-size-fits-all approach, has served the college well, but efficiency and effectiveness in faculty work and student learning have reached a point of diminishing returns. Through the Faculty Work Project, a new model of faculty work has emerged, one which optimizes faculty collaboration across the range of departmental work and encourages thoughtful planning and development, while advancing the teaching and learning mission of the college. Seven departments are participating in the three-year campus Faculty Work Project: art history; organizational communication, learning, and design; physical therapy; physics; psychology; sport science; and writing. Each department has designed a project that will enable its faculty to explore a number of different and innovative teaching and learning models that will make their work more efficient and effective. Consolidating and streamlining the curriculum while expanding learning environments beyond traditional classroom activity and increasing the use of technology in learning activities are a few of the features of the departmental projects. The projects also are making more efficient use of faculty time by "banking" student credit hours, narrowing the scope of individual faculty responsibility through collective agreement, and using "non-seat time" learning activities. Faculty in participating departments will make group decisions pertaining to the assignment of certain teaching-related nonclassroom and service-related activities on the basis of faculty interest and expertise. Because teaching is the largest component of the workload, increased efficiency in that area, as well as flexibility in the assignment of nonclassroom work, will allow faculty to spend more time on scholarly and creative work.

The planning year, 1999–2000, has increased faculty awareness of alternative workload models that encourage exploration of innovative approaches to teaching and learning and more efficient use of faculty time in a collaborative departmental environment. The individual department plans establish a variety of faculty work models that can be considered and implemented by other departments at the conclusion of the project. A two-year implementation phase, 2000–2002, includes an assessment component at the end of each year. The Faculty Work Project has great potential for overhauling an inefficient and ineffective system of assigning faculty work and for developing greater collaboration among faculty within a department. By focusing on the departmental unit as the basis for determining work assignments, individual faculty interest and expertise can be identified and maximized while the full complement of the department's work is recognized and rewarded. Additionally, the project has helped forge a more productive relationship between faculty and administration while tackling one of the most perplexing problems facing comprehensive colleges today.

PROJECT PROBLEM

The issues surrounding faculty work amply demonstrate the complexities of a comprehensive college. Depending on the number and nature of professional disciplines, definitions of work vary widely and include a range of faculty responsibilities. Most, however, center on teaching load as the primary element for defining a faculty member's work. Other components of the faculty member's work, such as advising and nonclass instructional activity, scholarship/creative activity, and service, are expected but usually are not specified as part of the assigned load. The substantial differences that occur as a result of the wide range of disciplinary offerings and the unique pedagogies that are integral to each area of instruction further complicate the issue. Curricula are focused on achieving precise yet different outcomes, and the diversity of student and faculty learning and professional activity and expectations results in an institutional thrust that can be centrifugal. The variety of preprofessional programs in which instruction is often best given in the studio, the rehearsal hall, the laboratory or clinic, or in a venue other than the traditional classroom and for which credit is allocated in components other than the traditional three-credit course model makes attempts at standardizing faculty workload difficult if not impossible. (At Ithaca, only 52.5% of the courses offered during the 1999–2000 year were for three credits.) Approaches to workload standardization that employ the best of efforts at balancing teaching loads among faculty rely on weighting various teaching, scholarly/professional, and service responsibilities. Many employ formulae that measure the work in relation to that perceived to be entailed in an established model (such as the three-credit course). Curricular and staff changes make the defining of faculty work a constant and substantial challenge.

Ithaca College confronts each of these issues in a significant way. The college is a midsized comprehensive institution (Carnegie classification: Masters I) of approximately 6,000 students and approximately 400 full-time faculty organized in five schools: business, communications, health sciences and human performance, humanities and sciences, and music. Each of the four preprofessional schools devises its own curricula, has a discrete faculty whose teaching and professional activity is highly specialized, and makes its own decisions as to the structure and content of degree programs, personnel, and budget matters. The School of Humanities and Sciences comprises approximately 2,000 students and 200 faculty—a size typical of many liberal arts colleges. Ithaca in many ways is more like a small university than a college. But because the college historically has viewed itself primarily as an undergraduate institution with teaching as its first priority, it has resisted identifying with the university model. Teaching excellence is the sine qua non for tenure and promotion, although faculty continue to demonstrate increasingly higher levels of scholarly and professional accomplishment, in many cases that are associated with research university expectations. Collaborative research and creative activity between faculty and students are imbued in the educational culture of the college, which began as a music conservatory in the late nineteenth century. Teaching and research activity are a substantial part of a faculty member's day-to-day work at the college. Thus, the challenge to balance these responsibilities is often daunting even to the most seasoned faculty member.

Shared governance, a priority at Ithaca College because of its complex organizational structure, contributes to the issues relating to faculty workload. Faculty take their role in this work seriously, and a majority of them spend significant amounts of time performing governance and leadership work. They participate in departmental, school, and all-college leadership and governance activities that entail not only regular attendance at meetings but also periodic writing and revision of documents that relate to this participation.

A matter further complicating discussions of faculty work at the college is the institution-wide downsizing project implemented between 1993 and 1996. In response to a 10% enrollment decline from fall 1992 to fall 1994, substantial cuts were made in faculty, staff, and capital budget amounts in all five of the college's schools. One resulting expectation was that faculty as well as staff and administration would have to "do more with less." Following downsizing, staffing in many academic departments remains limited; thus there is not much "wiggle room" in which to be creative.

THE ANAC FACULTY WORK PROJECT

The opportunity to participate in both Phase I of the ANAC Faculty Work Project in 1997–1998 and the follow-up Phase II Project in 1999–2000, both funded by The Pew Charitable Trusts, was timely given the workload issues outlined above. Ithaca College has defined workload almost exclusively in terms of teaching load—24 load hours or the equivalent for an academic year—and faculty have continued to express strong interest in reducing the number of courses and/or load hours they teach. Expectation of significant scholarly/creative/professional accomplishment and substantial service for tenure and promotion and other institutional rewards add to the pressure they feel. Because the college is heavily tuition dependent (approximately 92% in 1999–2000), the return of faculty lines eliminated during the downsizing years has not been possible and the amount of responsibility shouldered by individual faculty has increased accordingly. Nevertheless, many felt that some approach that would allow flexibility in the standard teaching load was possible.

The fall semester of 1997 brought a new president who was interested in exploring alternative approaches to workload—teaching load, in particular—to address faculty concerns. A logical link between the president's support and faculty interest in workload relief was the ANAC Faculty Work Project. The project also became an opportunity to encourage the development of innovative approaches to teaching; to consider as yet untried uses of technology in teaching, learning, and research activity; and to "think out of the box," getting away from the view that every faculty member's work profile must adhere to a single model and encouraging faculty to "work smarter, not harder." This undertaking, though ambitious, could only result in gains, since both the president and the provost fully supported the project as an experiment bound to provide solutions rather than continued constraints.

Using data from the Carnegie/ANAC faculty survey administered during the 1997 spring semester, and the evolving ANAC discussion about faculty work, Ithaca College formulated a three-year Faculty Work Project. The objective was to completely revise the concept of faculty work, taking into account the total complement of work activity for which any given department was responsible. The Ithaca College workload project statement can be found in Appendix 6.1.

ITHACA COLLEGE WORKLOAD PROJECT OVERVIEW

The project was designed to take place over a three-year period. Radically different from any other large-scale, college-wide project, the schedule was purposely extended over a multiyear period to allow for thoughtful discussion and decision-making and deliberate implementation. From its inception, the project was viewed as a partnership between faculty and administration for the express purpose of solving complex workload issues; the project would also serve as a means of reinforcing a positive collaborative environment within departments. To underscore the importance of the project and its collaborative premise, the president and provost assured faculty that there would be no risk of penalty for participation, despite the experimental nature of the project.

A collateral project in the provost's office was to collect and analyze comprehensive data on the details of individual faculty work in each department, with consideration given to activity beyond teaching load to include departmental or project administration, supervisory activity, field work supervision (including student teaching), leadership and governance responsibilities, and course/curriculum development and management. These data will establish a base for crediting workload activity on an institution-wide basis upon completion of the work project.

The Faculty Work Project was presented to the faculty in two stages. At the opening faculty meeting for the 1998–1999 academic year, the president announced the project as a priority institutional initiative that would have both her and the provost's full support. The faculty were encouraged to attend the meeting at which project details would be discussed. Within a few weeks, a written project presentation was distributed (see Appendix 6.2).

Following the presentation of the project at the September 28 faculty meeting, the provost and associate provost met with several departments that were interested in exploring further participation in the project. The discussions were productive, though one or two faculty members in nearly every department were reluctant to participate. Most concerns pertained to a perceived lack of flexibility stemming from downsizing reductions. Many of the departmental discussions focused on ways to change institutionalized thinking about fairness and equity issues relating to work assignment and what, in fact, constituted work. Some faculty members expressed concern about the permanence of the changes that might result from the workload project effort and questioned whether their time would be well spent if there were a chance that there would be a return to the established institutional model after the conclusion of the project.

Nine departments ultimately submitted proposals: art history; music theory; organizational communication, learning, and design;

physical therapy; physics; psychology; speech communication; sport science; and writing. All of the proposals reflected to varying degrees the proposal guidelines (variations resulted from individual department goals and outcomes). Because the number of proposals was within the range originally projected, all were accepted. One of the departments (music theory) soon withdrew from the project because of incompatibility between the workload project timeline and that of a larger School of Music curriculum revision project which was formulated after the department had submitted its proposal. The Department of Speech Communication also subsequently withdrew from the project due to staffing changes within the department. The participating departments were listed in a memorandum to the faculty that restated the project goals. Summaries of the seven department projects follow.

Art History

Well established and committed equally to teaching excellence and scholarly accomplishment, the faculty in art history decided that their teaching and research time would be more productive and economical if they could design a multiyear staffing plan that would provide a teaching-free semester. Faculty then would have time to work on a project in some depth and with appropriate concentration. To support this goal, a credit "banking" approach was devised whereby each faculty member would teach an average of five additional students per class. Doing so would generate the stipulated number of student credit hours over six, rather than seven, semesters. With seven faculty in the department, the credits are amortized over three and a half years, creating the possibility of a release from teaching midway between sabbatical leaves. However, the teaching-free semester is not to be construed as a minisabbatical: All faculty agree to be available for all other responsibilities through the course of the teaching-free semester. This approach has resulted in a 14% reduction in teaching time that can be reallocated to research.

Organizational Communication, Learning, and Design (OCLD)

The faculty of OCLD have focused on curricular innovation, instructional strategy development, and the utilization of technology in both their undergraduate and graduate programs as areas for development in the workload project. The department's goal is to maximize instructional effectiveness while making more efficient use of faculty time. Building on previous experimental work in online communication, a capstone course will be taught through a combination of lecture, class discussion, and online laboratory work rather than employing lecture only, as was the case previously. Similarly, interactive technology will be implemented in certain courses in order to reduce repeated lectures and provide more individualized, self-paced instruction. A more fully developed internship program for both undergraduate and graduate students will link student projects with community groups and organizations that have communication needs. Finally, faculty will explore the possibility of forming interdisciplinary linkages with other departments so program options such as health communication and environmental communication can be created.

Physical Therapy

Physical therapy enrolls an average of 90 new students annually. Instruction in this preprofessional program is time intensive, and much of it is provided in clinical and nontraditional classroom settings. Thus, the physical therapy faculty looked to the workload project as a means of establishing benchmarks for crediting all aspects of faculty work in the department, enabling them to devise an equitable standard for the various types of work they perform. Part of the effort will be to quantify each work activity and to design formulas that will make possible more equitable and balanced loads.

Physics

Like faculty in the physical therapy department, the physics faculty seek to quantify all aspects of department work so they can establish a more efficient and equitable means of assigning it. The major enrollment in physics is very small, but the credit hour generation rate is very high due to the number of courses offered to nonphysics majors, particularly in astronomy. In addition, the range of department activities that entail administrative and supervisory responsibility, some of which is noncredited, is extensive and in need of a means of crediting.

Psychology

Historically, the psychology department has been innovative in the areas of curriculum development and instruction. Several years ago, the department redesigned its curriculum and staffing with the goals of enhancing research opportunities for its majors while maximizing its teaching efficiency. The department design became a model at the college and externally in the discipline. The number of majors has increased significantly in recent years, and the scholarly output of department faculty and students is notable. For the workload project, faculty identified its complete workload complement and allocated all of its teaching, support, and service activity on the basis of individual faculty discipline specialty, interest, and equity of assignment. Doing so enabled the faculty to reduce their teaching load by 25% while producing the required number of student credit hours and covering the entirety of its departmental work.

Sport Science

The faculty in sport science are exploring the use of Internet technology to establish consortial relationships with a number of international universities that have sport science programs, thereby expanding course offerings for Ithaca College students and enabling international students to take Ithaca College courses. Redesign of the curriculum in certain areas and reconfiguration of staffing and course enrollments will provide opportunities for greater efficiency in the teaching load of some faculty.

Writing

The writing faculty have only recently achieved department status with the major in writing approved for first offering in fall 2000. One goal for the workload project is to revamp the first-year curriculum for the general student and some aspects of the major. The main feature of the project will be the inclusion of a lab hour in the first-year writing course required of all students at the college using student apprentices as tutors. Outcomes should include more efficient faculty class time and a decrease in the amount of out-of-class time spent on remediation.

The February 22, 1999 organizational meeting for the participating departments laid out the details of the workload project, the expected outcomes, the timeline, and the work to be accomplished in preparation for the first year of the project. That work was to include finalization of the design of the individual department projects and the implementation plan for the project's first year (2000–2001).

THE PLANNING YEAR: 1999–2000

The agenda for the planning year was to have each department finalize its project plan during the fall 1999 semester and begin devising an implementation plan for the 2000–2001 academic year in the early part of the spring 2000 semester. During the planning year, the associate provost who served as the campus project coordinator for both phases of the ANAC Faculty Work Project met monthly with the campus project steering committee, comprised of a representative from each of the participating departments. Steering committee meetings were planned around the larger ANAC Faculty Work Project meetings so that ANAC planning could inform the Ithaca College project. Research and information from the literature on faculty work was shared at the steering committee meetings and members discussed the progress of their individual department projects. Initial discussions revealed that some faculty (and some steering committee members) were having difficulty shedding institutionalized thinking about what other than teaching constituted work and how to value other work activity, despite their interest in expanding the parameters of work. Some faculty continued to express concern that the project would have limited lasting effect. Reassurance from both the president and the provost allayed that concern. Disciplinary differences in the types of faculty work precluded a unified approach to the project. However, after a few meetings thinking solidified along several lines, and the individual projects began to evidence progress. While much of the thinking remained focused on ways to reduce the teaching load, scholarly and creative activity and service were considered increasingly as factors in the department plans. Areas that emerged as fruitful for exploration were curricular consolidation and streamlining; enumerating and valuing both quantitatively and qualitatively the complete range of a department's work activities; increased consideration of a range of instructional and learning formats, including a number of innovative approaches to both classroom and nonclassroom activities; using technology to facilitate individual student learning; and using individual faculty interests and expertise as factors in the assignment of nonteaching responsibilities of the department, for example, advising, leadership, and governance work. At the conclusion of the 1999–2000 year, both the provost and the president reviewed and approved the individual department project plans.

Early in the spring 2000 semester, plans for the first year of the project were established and details of scheduling and teaching assignments were finalized. During the second half of the spring 2000 semester, discussion of assessment for the first year of implementation began. Two meetings were devoted to a review of literature in this area and discussion of pertinent issues. To facilitate the assessment phase of the project, the college consulted with one of the ANAC faculty work project resource personnel, Jon Wergin. He visited the campus early in the first semester of implementation (fall 2000) and worked with the steering committee and participating departments to set up the assessment mechanism which will be used both at the end of the first year of implementation (spring 2001) and at the conclusion of the project (spring 2002).

Three campus community updates on the Faculty Work Project were provided during the spring 2000 semester. Faculty were sent a memo detailing the progress of the project as well as the planning for its implementation in academic year 2000–2001. The associate provost and three members of the project steering committee made a formal presentation to the board of trustees at its spring meeting. The larger institutional project was outlined and each of the three steering committee members talked about the details of his or her department's project. The presentation was well received, and several board members complimented the group on its work. The steering committee gave a similar presentation to the deans and department chairs. Further updates will be provided at critical points in the project.

ASSESSMENT

The assessment phase of the project has two direct benefits: it identifies both the successes of the first year of implementation and the areas for improvement. This information will be used to modify and fine-tune the individual department projects during the second year of implementation and will begin to lay the foundation for a college-wide plan for revising the institutional model of faculty work. Similarly, the final project assessment at the end of the second year will identify the strengths and weaknesses of the various department workload models. Planning for college-wide adoption of the workload project models will begin once the assessment information has been reviewed.

CONCLUSION

The Ithaca College Faculty Work Project is an experiment that will attempt to redesign the way faculty work is defined, assigned, assessed, and rewarded. Recognizing that faculty have different professional goals during the various phases of their career life, this model of faculty work accommodates those differences and capitalizes on individual faculty strengths, interests, and expertise while encouraging innovation in teaching, exploration in scholarly and creative activity, and vital participation in leadership and campus governance. A collaborative department environment that recognizes these differences will permit flexibility in work assignment with the responsibility for assessment of its effectiveness lying within the department among colleagues. Recognition of both individual and collective departmental accomplishment and productivity will establish the basis for a reward system that will reinforce the goals of the workload project and advance the mission of the college.

APPENDIX 6.1 PROJECT STATEMENT

BALANCING WORKLOAD: A FACULTY DEVELOPMENT MODEL
PROPOSED PROJECT OVERVIEW, ITHACA COLLEGE
ANAC/PEW FACULTY WORK PROJECT, PHASE II
FALL 1999–SPRING 2002

BACKGROUND

Among the results of the first phase of the ANAC/Pew Faculty Work Project (1997–1998) was an understanding that faculty work in ANAC institutions generally has increased over the past decade. Add on responsibilities have increased the professional commitment of faculty, though there has been little or no recognition of this additional work in the institutional literature which addresses faculty work and the reward system. ANAC institutions typically identify faculty work in terms of teaching load while other responsibilities, such as advising, committee work, etc., either are assigned or are taken on as a professional obligation. The vastly varying nature of faculty teaching assignments, a result in part of the wide-ranging disciplinary make-up and differing types of instruction necessarily associated with these disciplines, further complicates the situation. Most institutions use a modification of the standard three-credit model or a weighted load to compensate for these differences, resulting in a one-size-fits-all mentality. Faculty at Ithaca College, as at other ANAC institutions, have expressed concern about the apparently increasing expectations that have resulted from working to maintain excellence in teaching and related out-of-class obligations, the sense that greater levels of accomplishment are required in the area of scholarly/professional accomplishment for tenure and promotion, and increasing amounts of time required for service.

PROJECT STATEMENT

As its Phase II project, Ithaca College will undertake a three-year experiment to balance faculty workload through a faculty development model. Eight to ten departments from the college's five schools will participate. Using an individualized work plan/differential work assignment/growth contract model, each participating faculty member will design a three-year work plan which takes into account all of the professional activities in which he or she will engage during that period. Faculty members will assess their progress by means of an annual self-evaluation which will be discussed with their chair and/or dean. Full accountability of the project will be evaluated at the department level. It is hoped that a variety of successful approaches to defining full-time faculty workload will emerge, with the result that the college as a whole may adopt new workload models.

RATIONALE

Ithaca College uses teaching load as the single factor in determining workload, yet myriad other time-intensive activities are considered integral to faculty members' work and are evaluated as part of salary, tenure, and promotion decisions. These expectations are clearly considered in various performance reviews, but neither are they formalized for accountability purposes nor is there any attempt to use them to the institution's advantage. The college has essentially boxed itself and its faculty into a one-size-fits-all approach which does not reflect the reality of higher education in the twenty-first century. The proposed Phase II project will provide faculty the opportunity to explore alternatives to the current system and will thereby encourage them to consider innovative instructional approaches that will result in greater teaching efficiency and more reasoned approaches to other aspects of faculty work.

TIMELINE

The three-year project schedule is as follows.
- 1998–1999: Preliminary discussion; selection of participating departments
- Year 1 (1999–2000): Project design in departments and approval
- Year 2 (2000–2001): Implementation
- Year 3 (2001–2002): Continuation and assessment

DETAIL

Depending on the number of applications received, eight to ten departments from the college's five schools will be selected to participate in the project. Each faculty member will design an individual work plan for the three-year period. Department faculty will discuss the work plans collectively to ensure that there is balance among them and that all departmental responsibilities are accounted for. A 21- to 24-credit hour annual teaching load will form the basis of each work plan, with other duties, based on individual plans, interests, talent, and departmental needs and obligations (including a specified credit generation number), taken into account. Departments will be encouraged to explore innovative alternative approaches to traditional instruction as a means for achieving its goals. The experimental course format may be used so these new approaches to pedagogical method and course delivery can be tried. A steering committee consisting of the chairs of the participating departments will provide leadership for the project; the associate provost will serve as the project coordinator.

TERMS AND CONDITIONS

The project will be a partnership among participating faculty/departments, the deans, and the provost's office. Faculty will be free to explore options that allow creative flexibility in designing workload but within the existing faculty resources. Additional faculty lines will not be created. However, resources that will support innovative and alternative approaches to instruction—such as technology—may be requested through the annual budget process. Faculty in participating departments will be given full support in all review processes, including tenure and promotion, and will not be penalized for the experimental nature of their work in these reviews.

Appendix 6.2

PROJECT PRESENTATION TO FACULTY

Faculty at Ithaca College, as at other ANAC institutions, have registered concern about the sense of increasing expectation that has resulted from working to maintain a standard of excellence in teaching and related out-of-class activities, striving to achieve perceived greater levels of accomplishment in creative/scholarly/professional work in order to receive tenure and promotion, and contributing greater time to service work. Ithaca College will undertake a three-year experiment to balance faculty workload using a faculty development model consistent with the college's mission as a teaching institution.

PROJECT GOALS

- To explore new models of faculty work that are inclusive of all faculty roles
- To introduce innovative modes of instruction that will enhance student learning and allow faculty greater flexibility in their roles in that process (away from "seat time" approach)
- To explore alternative course and curricular models
- To provide new models of faculty work and learning that can be applied by other departments at Ithaca College
- To share the results of this work with other ANAC institutions

TIMELINE

- 1998–1999: Preliminary discussion; set up project and select participating departments
- Project Year 1 (1999–2000): Project design in departments and approval
- Project Year 2 (2000–2001): Implementation and assessment of year 1
- Project Year 3 (2001–2002): Continued implementation and final assessment; report on project; begin planning for college-wide implementation

METHODOLOGY

- Eight to ten departments representing all five schools of the college (25–30%) will participate
- Departments will identify and discuss the complete workload for which they are responsible
- All aspects of faculty workload are open for discussion and inclusion in the project
- Each faculty member in the participating departments will design an individual two-year work plan reflecting the full complement of departmental responsibilities
- The departmental plan will be balanced against a student credit hour generation figure (average of most recent three years)
- Departments will be encouraged to explore innovative approaches to instruction and other aspects of workload
- All members of each participating department must agree to the plan
- The appropriate dean and the provost must approve the plan
- Chairs of selected departments (or a designate) will serve as the steering committee for the project

AREAS FOR CONSIDERATION

- Interdisciplinary initiatives that would consolidate course and teaching load
- Experiential learning (credit bearing, "non-seat time") options: required internships, independent studies, service-learning and community service activity
- Integration of technology into courses and programs
  - Use of specially designed software
  - Use of Internet/CD-ROM technologies to complement classroom instruction
  - Use of laptop (Internet access) in daily classroom instruction
  - Customized learning modules that provide individual instruction and thereby allow the professor to serve as mentor/consultant
  - Distance learning options

- Incorporation of outcomes as a basis for assessment—demonstrated knowledge beyond traditional examination methods; Lee Shulman's "making public" through presentation and discussion
- Realign course/section enrollments based on use of different methodologies (e.g., rather than teaching two sections of 30 students each at six load credits, teach one section of 60 using a combination of lecture, integrated technology, group work, and consultation. Result: less "seat time" for students; more independent learning; greater flexibility and control of workload)
- Specialize nonteaching responsibilities among faculty on the basis of interest, experience, and expertise—e.g., service/governance/advisement—and build into each faculty member's load. Give load credit for creative/scholarly/professional projects
- Allow for flexibility among faculty year by year: for example, one year a faculty member may want more time to finish a book, but in another year, may wish to focus on teaching; another faculty member may enjoy significant participation in governance work, etc.
- Recognize that faculty have different needs and can make differing contributions during the various phases of their career (e.g., young faculty will need more mentoring and supervision during their early years while more senior faculty may desire to "give back" in the years prior to their retirement)

PROJECT GUIDELINES

- Workload accountability based on department model rather than traditional institutional model
- Partnership between faculty and administration: faculty-dean-provost
- Annual student credit-hour generation amount, normally average of the last three years (1996–1998)
- Total departmental workload package basis for the plan (full academic year)
- Individual faculty work plans for two years
- Balance among all department faculty, allowing for differences in assignment on an annual basis
- Departments will discuss parameters for change, taking into

account
- in-class load hours
- out-of-class mentoring hours
- preparation time (paper grading; exam preparation and grading; technology development)
- course and curriculum development
- creative/scholarly/professional activity
- advising responsibilities
- service/community service responsibilities—quantity and participation profile
- governance responsibilities—quantity and participation profile

The Faculty Work Project will allow faculty from selected departments to engage in a three-year process to examine their work and establish more efficient and effective ways to organize it. The desired outcome is to provide a variety of models for other departments on campus to emulate. A second goal is to explore innovative models of instruction that focus on student-centered learning.

The project is an institutional challenge to change in forward-looking ways; to think differently about what we do; and above all, to "work smarter, not harder." We need to change the institutional culture from one that is insular, inward-looking, and dependent to one that is integrative, outward-looking, and independent. This must be done not from the top down nor from the bottom up, but from the inside out.

TERMS AND CONDITIONS OF PARTICIPATION

- Faculty and departments are free to explore options that allow creative flexibility in designing workload, but within existing faculty resources
- Additional faculty lines will not be created
- Resources that will support innovative and alternative approaches to instruction (such as technology) may be requested through the annual budget process
- Faculty in participating departments will be given full support in all review processes, including tenure and promotion, and will not be penalized for the experimental nature of their work

DEPARTMENT PROPOSAL GUIDELINES

- Two to three pages written in narrative form, to include
  - a statement outlining the department's interest in the project and expected outcomes
  - recent curricular/workload initiatives that indicate potential for success with the project
  - possible areas/directions/approach(es) for exploration
- Sign-off by all full-time faculty of the department indicating support for participation in the project.

PREPROJECT YEAR SCHEDULE: 1998–1999

- August 24: Announcement of project by president at opening faculty meeting
- September 28: Project defined at open faculty meeting
- February 1: Department proposal submission deadline
- February 15: Participating departments identified
- February 22: Project organizational meeting for selected departments

SUMMARY

The Ithaca College Faculty Work Project recognizes
- The need to address faculty concern over increasing workload
- The need to develop alternative instructional models that account for greater emphasis on student-centered learning
- Changes in the nature and definition of institutions of higher learning, scholarship, the scholar, and teaching and learning
- The need to address rapid change in higher education vis-à-vis expectations for the next century
- The need to develop faculty work models that account for individual strengths, interests, and career stage needs

7

WORKLOAD REBALANCING AT ST. MARY'S COLLEGE OF CALIFORNIA

Ed Biglin

Anew academic compact calls for a self-conscious renewal of the faculty-institutional compact in American higher education. At the heart of this compact is a vision of the college as an academic community where institution and faculty alike nurture the effectiveness of the other in a collaborative effort to enhance the quality of academic life and advance the mission of the institution. The academic community envisioned in this compact is organized around certain core values—chief among them is the emphasis on a highly personalized teacher-student relationship which is an expression of the student-centered missions of the Associated New American Colleges (ANAC).

The Saint Mary's Workload Rebalancing Plan was the result of just the sort of faculty/administrative collaboration which the compact envisions, save only that students and staff from key areas were included in Saint Mary's planning process. The plan acknowledged faculty frustration with the increasing demands on their time which they felt were limiting their effectiveness. In return for a direct and tangible investment in faculty time, the plan commits faculty to invest part of that time in an area central to the Lasallian mission of the college, forming academic mentoring relationships with students outside the classroom. That kind of mutual investment in the mission of the institution is central to the vision of academic community.

In addition, the Saint Mary's plan paid particular attention from the outset to the issues of cost, accountability, and effectiveness which have been central to discussions of higher education in the past decade. The ability to find ways to reduce the costs of the plan, share the costs among the various constituencies, and find additional revenues to offset part of the cost contributed greatly to its viability. Departments were asked to demonstrate how they could maintain their curricula and their contributions of faculty time to important campus-wide programs after rebalancing, which was a small but important step toward unit assessment. Faculty members were asked to produce a work plan for the year, demonstrating how they would use the time to enhance their work in ways that would contribute to the goals of the plan and the mission of the college. At the end of the year, those contributions will be compiled and assessed in a report to the president and trustees. Students are being surveyed as well to determine their satisfaction with the college's academic life.

Saint Mary's plan also formally recognizes the differentiation of faculty work patterns. All faculty are asked to emphasize the informal academic mentoring of students outside the classroom. But that is not the only goal of the plan, and faculty members must assess their work in all areas to determine and justify their use of the time to enhance their work. Faculty who already spend a great deal of time with students outside of class will spend all of the rebalanced time on other areas.

Saint Mary's Workload Rebalancing Plan took shape very much within the framework envisioned by the new academic compact. It may well be that, in the long run, the most important effect of the plan will come from the mutual commitment to a collaborative approach to governance which shaped it and the focus on enhancing the academic community it embodies.

WORKLOAD REBALANCING

In the spring of 1999, the Board of Trustees of St. Mary's College of California approved a plan to change the teaching load of all tenure track and tenured faculty from seven to six courses per year. The plan acknowledged that the growing complexity of academic life had placed increasing demands on faculty time over the past two decades. At the same time, the goal of the plan was greater than simply adjusting faculty work to meet those demands. The plan specifically sought to enhance the college's ability to fulfill its mission by supporting the work of faculty, in particular the often invisible part of faculty work that creates an academic community characterized by close interaction between faculty and students outside the classroom. The following excerpt from the president's letter to the board of trustees makes that focus clear:

> This plan is not about faculty workload, but rather about how the College can invest in its future by affirming the place of students at the center of its mission. Both the proposed general and specific recommendations herein are designed that the student learning experience at Saint Mary's is of the highest possible caliber considering the resources available to the community. During the past two years in which I have been involved with the faculty in drafting the current proposal, I have been impressed with the breadth and depth of their analysis of the ways they can better serve our students. They have endeavored to develop creative and innovative programs which will make our students more satisfied with their learning experience here at Saint Mary's and have offered activities which will help to build a Lasallian community where the intellectual endeavors of students and faculty can be nourished in a mutually supportive atmosphere.
>
> Contemporary educational literature is replete with a single admonition: one of the best ways to enable student learning to permeate the campus is to associate students with teachers in both formal and informal activities. While many of our students have had the rich opportunity to interface with our talented faculty within the classroom, because of demands placed upon them, these faculty have had limited opportunities for informal interactions. The proposal . . . endeavors to change this—to allow our faculty to better serve students by dedicating additional efforts to advising, counseling, collaborative student research, collective activities, etc. Our hope is that enduring, nurturing partnerships can be formed between stu-

dents and their faculty as a result of this kind of activity. It is further hoped that this proposal will enable the community of Saint Mary's to build itself up through collaborative and mutually supportive activities.

BACKGROUND

St. Mary's College of California is a Catholic, midsized comprehensive institution located in the San Francisco Bay Area. It was founded in 1863 by the Christian Brothers, a worldwide Catholic order devoted exclusively to teaching, and was exclusively male until 1970. It became coeducational and placed greater emphasis on graduate and extended education programs as a response, in part, to the enrollment crisis that affected many single-sex, religiously affiliated colleges in the early 1970s. Since that time, the college has grown steadily to its current size—approximately 2,300 on-campus undergraduate students and 2,000 on- and off-campus graduate and extended education students enrolled in 31 undergraduate programs and 16 graduate programs. They are taught by about 180 full-time faculty and faculty from numerous professions who serve as adjunct faculty in graduate and professional programs. In undergraduate programs, the student-faculty ratio is approximately 14:1 and average class size is under 21.

As the college has grown, its reputation for academic quality, its location in the San Francisco Bay area, and its proximity to major research libraries have allowed it to attract an excellent faculty from top-ranked graduate programs across the country. As the college has become more complex, the demands on faculty time have increased dramatically. Though excellent teaching is the primary criterion for tenure and promotion, expectations for faculty to be actively engaged in scholarship, particularly scholarship related to their teaching, have increased significantly in the past two decades. The size of the college means that faculty usually do not teach multiple sections of the same course, and it is common for faculty to have three different preparations each long semester, as well as a separate preparation for the January term (the college uses a 4-1-4 calendar). The interdisciplinary approach of the college means that faculty, unlike those at many institutions, often teach in two, three, or even four separate programs (e.g., Collegiate Seminar great books program, women's studies, freshman composition, graduate liberal studies, in the case of one senior faculty member). Each program entails distinct preparations, additional staff meetings, faculty development programs, and cocurricular events.

In addition to teaching and scholarship, the growth and complexity of the college has created a great deal of add-on work for faculty. Developing the college's many new courses and programs has required much research and effort. A larger faculty means that more time is spent visiting colleagues' classes, mentoring new faculty, and writing extensive rank and tenure reviews. National searches for new faculty are much more labor intensive than the previous local searches. Increased external demands, such as those for assessment, have grown, as well as internal demands for faculty to serve on numerous governing boards (e.g., women's studies, Collegiate Seminar, diversity task force) and bodies seeking to enhance community life (e.g., women's resource center, presidential commission on student retention, presidential commission on building community, technology coordinating committee). The size and complexity of the college also means that traditional committees on curriculum, academic policies, and faculty affairs have grown and their work has become more complicated (e.g., the college currently has five academic calendars in simultaneous operation in various programs). Teaching students to write effectively has become a goal in many more disciplines, which involves the assignment of multiple drafts, frequent conferences to review drafts, and so on.

In addition to the increased quantity and complexity of faculty work, the growth of college facilities has lagged behind the growth of the student body and faculty, so most faculty have had to share offices, which can make it difficult for them to come to campus on days when they do not teach. Housing prices near the college, and in the Bay Area generally, have meant that faculty tend to live farther and farther from the college at a time when increased traffic has significantly lengthened commute times. Those factors, together with the declining number of Christian Brothers teaching at the college, have tended to weaken the vibrant academic community which has traditionally been a hallmark of Saint Mary's. In focus groups, ANAC and Carnegie surveys, and discussions of this topic, faculty overwhelmingly reported that these and related demands on their time have stretched their work very thin. What had suffered, in their minds, was not their preparation and work in the classroom, but everything else, most particularly the amount and kinds of time they could spend on campus in informal mentoring activities with students outside the classroom.

THE WORKLOAD REBALANCING PLAN

The Workload Rebalancing Plan is intended to enhance the quality of the academic community at Saint Mary's by allowing faculty to put more energy into the areas of their work where they have felt the increased demands on their time have created the greatest need. The plan is directly related to the mission of the college in its emphasis on informal academic mentoring of students outside the classroom. The guiding educational philosophy of the college is that of the founder of the Christian Brothers, St. John Baptiste de la Salle, who called the brothers and their educational partners to attend directly to the needs of each student as an individual, helping to form the whole person by example and by constant contact. Since small classes and the Lasallian character of education are what distinguishes Saint Mary's from the many less expensive options available to students, the plan also seeks to enhance our position in an increasingly competitive marketplace.

The plan reduces the teaching load of all tenure-track faculty from seven courses per year to six. The plan envisions a rebalancing rather than a reduction of faculty work, because faculty are asked to commit the time they would have spent teaching the seventh course to enhance other areas of their work, with special emphasis on informal mentoring and contact with students outside the classroom. The plan is not based on a one-size-fits-all model of faculty work—each faculty member is asked to carefully assess the areas of his or her work to determine where the increased demands over the years have created the greatest need, and to create an individual work plan for enhancing those specific areas of their work.

By the end of the fifth year of implementation, all courses which will no longer be taught by existing tenure-track faculty after rebalancing will be taught by new, tenure-track faculty hired during implementation phase of the plan. The plan calls for all such courses taught by adjunct faculty in the second year of implementation, with the number taught by adjuncts diminishing to zero by the fifth year, as new tenure-track faculty are hired.

The plan calls for an ongoing process of assessment. At the beginning of each year, faculty will create a work plan detailing specific ways that they intend to use the rebalanced time to enhance various areas of their work, with some special attention paid to informal mentoring and contact with students outside the classroom. Then, at the end of the year, faculty will be asked to provide a review of the year which addresses the activities detailed in their work plans, as well as any other activities that were undertaken. The work plans and annual reports will be retained in the academic vice president's office. A faculty workload implementation committee will compile an assessment report for the academic vice president to use as part of her report to the president and board of trustees.

The first draft of the plan, which was devised by a subcommittee of the academic senate and the campus chapter of the American Association of University Professors (AAUP), was the result of many years of discussion by faculty and administrators in various venues. That draft then was revised through a process of ever-wider collaboration among the various constituencies of the college. The first revision was produced by a faculty/administration committee chaired by the academic vice president. The second and final revision was produced by a faculty/administration committee chaired by the president, which sought formal input from vice presidents responsible for all areas of college operation (student affairs, enrollment management, development, finance and administration). That committee also held open meetings for faculty, students, and staff to discuss the implications of various elements of the plan. Those meetings caused a number of changes to the final plan, and were crucial in allaying fears and allowing various groups to buy in to the final version. For example, a part of the original plan called for changing the current January term graduation requirement from four courses to three, to achieve some cost savings by offering fewer January term courses. That element troubled the students, who value the range of choices in January term. It also caused difficulties for residence life because students not currently enrolled in courses are not allowed to live on campus, and the fact that students are not billed separately for January term made tracking students not enrolled and refunding housing fees difficult.

A number of principles remained unchanged through the various iterations of the plan.

A cost-sharing approach. Obviously, the teaching load of faculty could be reduced by simply eliminating one course per faculty member from the curriculum, or it could be reduced by increasing the budget to hire full-time tenure-track replacements to teach the courses that would be removed from the teaching load of current faculty. The plan consistently emphasized that various cost savings would pay for part of the implementation, with the remainder supplied by budget increases.

Focus on the mission and goals of the college. One of the main goals of the plan was always to enhance the ability of the college to fulfill its mission and remain competitive.

Enhance academic quality. The plan should enhance academic quality and not weaken the curriculum by eliminating essential courses or narrowing student choices.

Maintain the current ratio of full-time to part-time faculty. Obviously, cost savings could be achieved by increasing the number of part-time faculty. While that will happen briefly during the implementation phase of the plan, by the time of full implementation in four years, the ratio should be unchanged or shifted slightly toward full-time.

Neutrality about existing perceived inequities. The plan was not intended to rectify existing differences in workload among schools or departments.

IMPLEMENTATION AND COSTS

Full implementation of the plan is spread over a five-year period beginning in 1999–2000, in order to spread both the financial and intangible costs (Table 7.1). The need to hire 16 new tenure-track faculty to staff the courses no longer taught by existing faculty would cause stress in many areas if done too quickly—conducting simultaneous national searches, finding office space and mentors for new faculty, and having that many faculty come up for promotion and tenure reviews all at once for the next six years. Additionally, the college needed time to conduct a thorough staffing survey to determine where to allocate the new positions, which meant that a planning year was a significant part of the implementation.

Table 7.1 Implementation Schedule

Year 1 (1999–2000)
- Survey all chairs and program directors to determine adequacy of current staffing levels, and to determine exact number of courses needing to be staffed by adjunct faculty in each year of implementation
- Determine which departments will be understaffed/overstaffed after rebalancing and allocate new positions among various departments and programs. Determine which new faculty will be hired in which years
- Develop assessment plan and conduct baseline assessment survey of faculty work allocation, with particular emphasis on informal academic mentoring outside classroom
- Interview and hire adjunct faculty needed to staff courses in 2000–2001 academic year

Year 2 (2000–2001)
- Teaching load of all eligible faculty reduced to six courses
- Begin and complete searches for approximately four new tenure-track positions
- Implement first-year assessment—obtain from faculty individual work plans and end-of-year work review. Workload implementation committee compiles and analyzes data and prepares report for associate vice president, who reports to president and trustees

Year 3 (2001–2002)
- Begin and complete searches for approximately four new tenure-track positions
- Ongoing assessment continues

Year 4 (2002–2003)
- Begin and complete searches for approximately four new tenure-track positions
- Ongoing assessment continues

Year 5 (2003–2004)
- Begin and complete searches for approximately four new tenure-track positions
- Ongoing assessment continues

Year 6 (2004–2005)
- Ongoing assessment continues
- First "steady-state" year—all adjunct faculty hired to staff workload rebalancing courses now replaced by tenure-track faculty

The costs of the plan are almost entirely composed of the cost of hiring new tenure-track faculty to teach the courses formerly taught by existing faculty. Some modest, one-time costs for planning and searching for new faculty will also be incurred. Because the new faculty will be hired over a five-year period, the cost of implementation increases each year for the five years of implementation.

The cost-sharing approach used in designing the program reduces the full cost borne by the college's annual budget by finding some cost savings and additional revenues which can be used to support the program. Some schools proposed to use part of the faculty time freed up by rebalancing to design or implement new revenue-generating programs or make other revenue-generating adjustments to existing programs. Some of those adjustments were made—for example the School of Education made minor modifications to the summer tuition schedule. But those revenue sources were not used in the initial funding scheme because the amount of new net revenues could not be known.

Other cost savings were used to minimize the dollar cost of the program. For example, the college used to annually award 12 reassigned times to faculty (called FDOs or Faculty Development Opportunities) to help them meet publication deadlines, further research projects, and so on. These were eliminated because, in effect, the entire tenure-track faculty gets a reassigned time under the new plan. Some departments were able to eliminate small courses by consolidating sections of other courses. Major savings were achieved by defining the class of faculty eligible for rebalancing—full-time nontenure-track faculty were not included in the plan, and department chairs and program directors were not included, on grounds that they already had a reduced teaching load as compensation, in part, for providing direct services to students.

The college has approximately 180 full-time faculty. Eliminating nontenure-track faculty and department chairs/program directors brings the number of eligible faculty down to around 124. Other cost savings mean that the number of courses which will need to be staffed, because of workload rebalancing, by newly hired tenure-track faculty will be about 100—that will require an estimated 16.5 new faculty. The annual operating budget of the college is approximately $70 million. The cost for the first year of implementation will be only some modest planning costs and the costs of searches—about $25,000. The cost for the second year, when all eligible faculty will have their teaching load reduced and those courses will all be staffed by adjunct faculty will be in the vicinity of $500,000. The full direct cost of the program when fully implemented in year six will be just under $1 million per year. Full cost including indirect costs (sabbaticals for new faculty, office space and supplies, increased benefits, etc.) are estimated at $1.5 million per year.

BENEFITS

As a part of the ANAC Faculty Work Project, Saint Mary's faculty were surveyed to determine the areas where they felt that their work could be enhanced by some additional time. Table 7.2 briefly summarizes some of the most common responses.

Since the Workload Rebalancing Plan is just being implemented as of the time of this writing, we do not yet have much information on the actual activities of the faculty beyond their plans. The single most important effect thus far has been the institution of a freshman cohort advising plan which takes advantage of the rebalanced time of faculty. Saint Mary's requires four semesters of Collegiate Seminar, a great books program at the core of our undergraduate general education requirements. Beginning in the fall 2000 semester, every incoming freshman will have as his or her academic advisor the instructor in his or her freshman Greek Thought Seminar. The plan will increase the contact between freshmen and their advisors, a large majority of whom will be full-time, tenure-track faculty, during the crucial first months of their college careers. Faculty advisors will not only teach the class and offer academic advice to freshmen, but they will engage in many other activities to enhance the academic community life—host dinners for freshmen and their parents at the beginning of the year, take their advisees to on-campus and off-campus cultural events, introduce students to the resources of the Bay Area for outdoor and other recreation, host group discussions of the problems of college life and possible solutions, and host social events for their students. The goals of the program are to enhance advising of freshmen, enhance the sense of academic community on campus, and to reduce freshmen attrition rates.

A number of the other proposals are being implemented in various departments, though most are in their early stages. Faculty in anthropology/sociology and psychology have begun shaping student research projects. Individual meetings with students to discuss papers are now strongly encouraged for all instructors in the Collegiate Seminar program and a number of departments. Faculty in communications, economics, business, and politics have begun to incorporate web-based technology in their courses.

TABLE 7.2 Faculty Responses

Informal Academic Mentoring of Students

- Institute freshman cohort advising program (designed to have the instructors of freshman Collegiate Seminar classes (Greek Thought) also serve as freshman advisors for students in their classes, to create small cohorts of freshmen who explore college life and the Bay Area together. Instructor/advisors will meet students' families, take students on cultural excursions in the Bay Area, etc.)
- Foster internships and experiential learning experiences and mentor students closely while they are engaged in those activities
- Additional office hours for small group tutorial sessions (math, science, accounting)
- Enhance the informal curriculum (sponsor guest speakers, panel discussions, film series, associated with course materials)
- More time working in labs with student researchers and foster more student research projects
- Use individual meetings to return students' essays
- Host informal gatherings of students (e.g., dinners in homes, pizza dinners on campus before cocurricular events)
- Meet with student groups (e.g., departmental clubs) as a way of discussing with students the realities of graduate education, future career possibilities for those in the field, etc.

Enhanced Teaching Effectiveness

- Devise new courses in specific areas
- Revise and update courses which have not been recently taught, or which have not been updated recently
- Integration of technology into courses (posting course materials on the web, use of computers/multimedia materials in the classroom)
- Assign essays in courses that often don't require them and essay tests instead of machine scored tests
- Incorporate full capabilities of lab equipment in courses
- Integrate more specific case study material in courses
- Research materials tailored to the direction of interest and discussion in particular classes and incorporate them during the class
- Institute senior thesis requirement in major
- Participate in faculty development workshops (e.g., currently offered workshop on "Becoming a Critically Reflective Teacher")
- Make greater use of community resources in classes (e.g., sociology of homelessness)
- Write grant proposals for more specific lab equipment related to course materials

Active Scholarly Engagement

- Devise research projects in humanities similar to those sponsored in the School of Science which involve students in summer research and expand program of student summer research in sciences
- Attendance/presentation at scholarly conferences more frequently
- Continue work on research projects through the academic year as well as summer
- Review journals to keep current in field
- Turn chapters in scholarly books and scholarly articles into more popular format for wider public audience
- Write and produce original materials and videos for classes
- Research and publish in academic disciplines and for general public

GRADUATE PROGRAMS

Many, though not all, students in Saint Mary's graduate programs are older, working adults. When graduate faculty were asked how the Workload Rebalancing Plan could enhance the quality of what they do in their programs, they a saw many opportunities to enhance student/faculty contact in ways that would be particularly appropriate in their programs.

Typically, students in these programs meet less frequently than those in undergraduate programs, primarily in the evenings and on weekends. Students are usually on campus only for classes or they attend class at off-campus sites; therefore, these students can contact faculty only in the brief times before or after class. Faculty look to technology to provide more time for conversation and questions, and for ways to remain in contact with their students in the long intervals between classes. Thus, a number of faculty want time to create web sites for their courses, and to incorporate into them a forum for virtual class discussions where both instructors and students can post questions and responses. Some faculty have experimented with this approach and found it both extraordinarily valuable and extraordinarily time-consuming.

Many graduate faculty felt that a formal academic mentoring system would put students in closer contact with the college's faculty and provide an avenue for programmatic questions to be answered. Working adults, with family and employment obligations, need faculty to be available at unconventional hours and in unconventional ways. Faculty also valued greater involvement in the recruitment and orientation of adult students, both as part of a marketing program and because doing so would foster a more collegial atmosphere.

Faculty in some graduate programs noted that increased competition means that they now serve students who need greater support in some areas, particularly in writing, where additional classes and off-campus tutorial sessions would be particularly valuable. Faculty in some programs with a relatively large number of adjunct faculty felt that greater service on college committees by the small number of tenure-track faculty is particularly important if the needs of their students are to be fully understood by the campus community.

CONCLUSION

Saint Mary's Faculty Workload Rebalancing Plan is now beginning its second year of implementation, when the course load of tenure-track faculty has been changed from seven per year to six. Perhaps the most important element that allowed our planning to succeed was the genuinely collaborative approach we took, even with nonacademic constituencies.

At the beginning of the process, the issues were seen as almost entirely academic, primarily concerning academic quality. Faculty tended to see quality as largely defined by their ability to produce good scholarship and teach up-to-date courses informed by that scholarly work. As the discussions progressed, those elements remained central but the operative definition expanded to include areas of faculty work which directly enhanced the sense of academic community on campus. Many faculty came to recognize that, as their workload had increased over the past decade, academic advising and informal, out-of-class academic mentoring of students were the areas that had slipped the most, and were parts of their work which they saw as among the most satisfying. Expanding the conversations to include trustees, administrators, and students reinforced that vision and created the climate of support for the proposal among all constituencies. Additionally, open and frank discussions of the costs of the plan and their impact on the college's budget tended, in the end, to reduce students' anxieties about tuition and the fears of nonacademic departments that the plan would starve all other areas of the budget. Collaboration was vital, both politically and intellectually, and the plan's emphasis on a collaborative academic community is exactly the vision at the heart of a new academic compact.

The willingness of faculty to address issues of cost and budget impact directly in the plan was crucial to its successful adoption. However, reliance on programs to generate new revenues proved problematic. The programs that were started (a new MBA in an off-campus location, summer tuition adjustments in graduate education, larger cohorts of students in some extended education programs) did generate the revenues promised, but fluctuations in enrollments in other areas of those schools meant that they did not generate new net revenues. Our decision not to rely on such new revenues in funding the plan meant that we avoided an unpleasant surprise in the budget for 2000–2001.

In retrospect, our decision that workload rebalancing would not include two segments of the faculty proved problematic. The plan did not include nontenure-track faculty and it also excluded chairs and program directors who were already compensated for their work with two or more reassigned times. Some of the nontenure-track faculty are full-time, longstanding members of the faculty (seven, ten, 18, and even in one case, 25 years). Their work is widely respected by other members of the faculty and valued by chairs, and often they are the faculty who spend the most time working with student clubs, mentoring students in internships, and otherwise engaging students outside the classroom. Chairs and program directors often see themselves as the most overworked members of the faculty, reassigned times notwithstanding. They teach up to five courses per year and try to maintain a scholarly life, while their jobs require many additional office hours and meetings, as well as work on evenings and weekends. Many faculty felt that leaving out those two groups did not enhance the sense of academic community among faculty.

The individual, annual faculty work plans are a new idea at Saint Mary's, and they have caused some anxiety among faculty, as have the plans for assessment. Two elements of the plan are designed to address those anxieties. Assessment will be conducted by a faculty committee which will report to the academic vice president on the aggregate effects of the plan rather than the extent to which individual faculty fulfilled their work plans. Additionally, the plan recognizes that different faculty will have different work patterns so that those who already spend considerable out-of-class time with students will feel free to enhance other areas of their work.

Some of the proposed cost sharing elements did not work because they are inherently hard to explain to students and not enough time was taken with students and others to help them understand. Proposals by some departments to consolidate sections of multiple section courses, to change the schedule on which required courses are offered, and to reduce the number of required January term courses aroused anxieties of students and some other campus constituencies.

On balance, however, all segments of the college look forward to the benefits of the plan outweighing the compromises. And the greatest benefits might well come from recognition of the possibilities of collaboration and the renewed emphasis on community.

The Compact in Context

8

A PANEL OF EXPERTS RESPONDS

In June 2000, the Associated New American Colleges (ANAC) held their annual Summer Institute at Ithaca College in Ithaca, New York. The focus of the institute was the preliminary report of the Faculty Work Project II. Joining in the discussion were invited leaders from across the spectrum of higher education who had some stake and expertise in issues of faculty work. Below are the comments of six such leaders.

FORGING A NEW RELATIONSHIP—BROADENING THE COVENANT: A RESPONSE

Christine M. Licata

Marcel Proust reminds us that the real art of discovery consists not in finding new lands but in seeing with new eyes. The Associated New American Colleges Faculty Work Project report succeeds in generating such new vision because it offers an innovative lens for viewing the relationship between faculty and their institution in the twenty-first century. What the report's recommendations propose more

vividly and more boldly than most other recent change mandates is a
well-connected and integrated framework for considering faculty
careers and academic work within the context of institutional mission
and environmental forces. What strikes me about the recommendations is that they center on faculty-institutional mutuality and in so
doing reach the conclusion that changes in faculty work models and
institutional policies are necessary in order to better fulfill the shared
mission of enhancing student learning.

Using adult development theory as the organizing framework, the
authors of Chapter Two provide a solid base for describing faculty
career stages and stress the importance of adopting a proactive professional development model. The model proffered anchors the work
relationship by recognizing shifting faculty interests and talents as the
pathway to effectively satisfying institution and unit needs. The idea
of an individualized work plan requires that the specific contribution
of an academic unit to the mission of the larger institution be clearly
articulated. Individual contributions over one's career can then be
negotiated within this paradigm. In essence, this only works if institutional mission and strategic direction are clear, constantly
reassessed, and consistently articulated. It can only succeed if broader definitions of teaching, scholarship, and service are accepted, valued, and rewarded.

The second and the fourth chapter are closely tied together and
grounded in redefining the constructs of faculty work. Chapter Four,
"Faculty Workload: Differentiation Through Unit Evaluation," calls
for moving from the notion of individual, aggregate achievement to
collective responsibility for unit outcomes. A "circle of value" is
intended—an open system where the work of individuals adds value
to the whole and the collective achievements of the whole add value
to the individual. This proposition is exciting (and frightening)
because it takes the theory of professional development across the faculty career to its logical resting place: implementation within a unit
where goals are collectively set and where individual contributions
do not follow a one-size-fits-all formula. This type of workload envi-
sioning requires radical changes in how performance standards and
reward systems are established. It seems to me that affecting this type
of change in the system will be the most challenging task to making
recommendations implementable, but also the most essential, if

differentiation in faculty work effort is to be realized. The authors contend that faculty work is already differentiated but just not formalized. I agree. Given what we know about changing interests and priorities over a professional lifetime, placing individualized work plans within this circle of value context strongly and bravely roots faculty work in an environment of collective trust and compromise. Quite different from the current departmental silo mentality.

The third chapter on "Faculty as Institutional Citizens: Reconceiving Service and Governance Work" dovetails well with the belief that faculty work should include meaningful and valued opportunities to serve the local and broader community. However, the salient point here is that desired service opportunities also change in scope, intensity, and nature over a career and are influenced significantly by life stages and institutional needs. Theodore Roosevelt cautioned that "the good citizen is not a good citizen unless he is an efficient citizen." The responsibilities and paradigms offered in this chapter for how institutional service and governance might be exercised and rewarded can definitely lead to efficiency and effectiveness. Realistically, I think the service recommendations might be more easily accomplished than the change imperatives called for in the area of faculty governance. While the collegial governance piece is critically important if an overall sense of teamwork and mutual investment are to be achieved, this will require widespread perspective transformation about the specific roles of stakeholders and how each voice contributes directly to institutional decisions. This is a daunting prospect and not easily or quickly endorsed. In fact, of all the recommendations advocated, I believe the notion of expanding faculty involvement and voice in institutional decision-making will be a hard sell and will require exemplars to lead the way. It is too amorphous to fly in the abstract.

In our work at the American Association for Higher Education (AAHE) New Pathways II Project, we have directed considerable energy toward gaining a better understanding about recent policies established for the evaluation and development of tenured faculty— referred to commonly as post-tenure review. While this movement has primarily picked up steam within the public domain, private institutions are also beginning to put policies in place that focus on either accountability demands, career development needs, or both.

On the surface, these two objectives appear to be antithetical. Yet, most tenured faculty review policies today seem to combine both formative and summative objectives within the same policy framework. In so doing, faculty and administrators recognize that these goals need not be mutually exclusive and try to find ways to make such practices effective and practical for mid- and late-career faculty. In essence, enlightened recognition of the changing professional and reinforcement of professional renewal are important goals of developmental post-tenure review as we see it practiced today.

ANAC's report fits squarely with this developmental post-tenure review orientation and provides a strategic and interesting intersection. Institutions with a periodic approach (all tenured faculty are reviewed at a five- to seven-year interval) or a triggered approach (only tenured faculty who receive a substandard rating on the annual review are evaluated further) should study this text carefully because ideas advanced in it can be the springboard for leading post-tenure review follow-up conversations into the beginning steps for negotiating elements of the new academic compact. Institutions only in discussion stages about issues related to tenured faculty review and development should seize this text's provocative ideas to help frame the possibilities that might flow from linking elements of this new compact to the overall design of faculty work, evaluation, development, and reward.

From my perspective, the goodness of fit between ANAC's recommendations and formative post-tenure review is very strong. Post-tenure review may actually be a means and a formal opportunity to convert such propositions about individualized work plans, faculty development, differentiated workloads/unit evaluation, and expanded constructs for service into meaningful action. The tie that binds both initiatives is the same: maintaining institutional and individual vitality and viability.

The theory and ideas presented in this text are elegantly and thoughtfully constructed. How one turns the espoused theory into practice, particularly within the variety of higher education settings, is less well articulated. Nevertheless, with over 3,600 institutions in this country, a bit of ambiguity about application is desirable so that contextual modification and refinement can occur in an unencumbered fashion. These recommendations may, in fact, be better suited for teaching institutions—the liberal arts and the comprehensives—where mission drift does not pervade and where strategic planning prevails. While intended to represent an integrated approach, the recommendations could actually be separated and implemented independently. This, in fact, may be attractive in certain settings.

Regardless of institutional setting, if this new academic compact is to take hold, the academic community must be ready and willing to accept changes in the culture: There will be more career opportunities but less job guarantees; individual autonomy will be kept constantly in check by institutional mission; traditional faculty productivity metrics will be replaced by reasonable accommodation for career interests, talents, and changing priorities; strategic planning will be a continuous iterative process, not a one-time event; trust between faculty, administration, and boards will be crucial; collaboration within and across units will be the operative condition; and communication will become seamless. Sounds a bit like Camelot, doesn't it?

In this new world design, what must be understood and embraced is that every stakeholder gives up something but in return gains synergy, mutuality, and integration. How this new arrangement will affect or should affect part-time nontenure track and probationary faculty is unclear. For the time being, this omission seems appropriate because the journey must start one step at a time, and these first steps are definitely not for the faint of foot.

What inspires me about the ANAC Faculty Work Project is that it has been conceived by faculty for faculty. What delights me the most about the approach these faculty have taken is that they recognize that a new relationship is warranted but at the same time respect and keep alive cherished academic traditions. What energizes me most about this call to action is the riveting nature of the ideas about how to negotiate faculty work over the duration of an academic career in order to maximize interests and talents and strengthen institutional mission. What gives me considerable pause, though, is that these ideas complicate rather than simplify policy formulation; alter rather than sustain current role expectations and skill requirements of chairs, deans, and departmental peers; depend critically on mutual abilities to collaborate, compromise, and negotiate. A tall order by any measure. Even so, this text deserves serious consideration and spirited debate because invitations to adjust one's worldview of faculty work life don't come along very often, and when they do, they are usually spawned in corporate waters or high-powered institutes. Some will reject the invitation as unneeded; some will rebuff it as unrealistic. But those that accept it have a good chance to actually use this text as an occasion to see with new eyes, reshape the relationship between faculty and their institution, and transform faculty work into business not as usual.

FACULTY AND INSTITUTIONAL PRIORITIES: A MATTER OF SURVIVAL

Robert M. Diamond

How colleges and universities use their greatest resource, their faculty, will determine not only how they will meet the challenges they face, but whether or not they will survive and prosper in the twenty-first century. While this statement may appear to many as an exaggeration, it is for a growing number of public and private institutions far more accurate than their boards, presidents, and faculties are willing to admit. Parents, employers, and community leaders are expressing their increasing concern about the quality of the postsecondary education offered students. Students and their parents worry about an ever-rising cost of education that far outpaces inflation. College and university decision makers, for their part, view with alarm—but with little comprehension of the implications—the rapidly growing for-profit sector that promises students a college education at substantially less cost and at a time and place convenient to them. Thoughtful critics of American higher education point out that few colleges and universities are even attempting to define what it means to be educated let alone accurately assessing whether their graduates meet the institution's intended learning goals.

How well colleges and universities respond to these and other challenges—including especially the matriculation of more and more students who are part-time, adult, or underprepared—will be determined largely by how actively their faculty participate in the process of revitalization and change and how the individual priorities of faculty members mesh with those of the institution. As this outstanding text from the Associated New American Colleges concludes, it is no easy task to bring the institution's policies and practices and the actual work patterns of faculty into optimal alignment with institutional mission. It will require that administrators, faculty members, and trustees recognize that faculty knowledge, skills, and attitudes need to be fully engaged to help institutions find creative and implementable solutions to the challenges facing higher education.

Unfortunately, we enter this century with faculty that are often frustrated and disillusioned. Faculty members often see little relation between what they do and think must be done and how their institution makes decisions and distributes resources. Many perceive the governance and management of their institution as out of touch with their needs and often inefficient. On many campuses they believe the primary goal of the institution—students' learning—is supported by lip service and little else.

The contributors to this volume have provided an invaluable service. They have not only identified key problems that must be addressed in a successful change process, but have provided specific recommendations that are not only direct but doable: an increased cooperative and supportive relationship among administrators, faculty members, and trustees; clear priorities, and a reward system that supports and reinforces these priorities; a faculty development program that functions throughout an individual's career; and greater focus on the academic department as the key operational unit. The volume also provides an excellent bibliography.

Major, sustainable institutional change occurs only when the administration, the faculty, the support staff, and the governing board work collaboratively and with a collective sense of urgency, a clarity of purpose, and a sense of community. Using this volume can be a key first step in getting the essential conversation underway.

VALUING FACULTY WORK: RESEARCH

Mary Burgan

In discussing efforts to reward the faculty work of teaching and service, it is important to imagine significant alternatives to the transitory and sometimes divisive measures that have been established in the past. These take the form of special prizes for teaching and service—medals, names cast in bronze on a plaque in the Union Building, and one-time monetary awards in the range of a thousand dollars or so.

For an hour, or a day, or a week, these can seem beneficial, but in the long run, they may be window dressing only. Faculty members tend to be leery of such rewards, and rightly so, because they rarely compare favorably with the rewards for research. After all, research rewards come in the form of higher salaries—benefits that go into the base and grow over time. Rewards for teaching and service tend to be one-time only; when that time passes the salary settles down to its habitual modesty.

The other problem with special rewards for teaching and service is that they are special; what we want to insist upon, however, is that these activities should form part of the norm for faculty work. Further, there is the suspicion that special, one-time rewards can be subject to the kind of benign manipulation that often occurs in colleges and universities: friends and colleagues of a deserving faculty member can summon extraordinary reserves of rhetoric, pressure, and tradesmanship to win a prize in any one year. It is thus essential to make the rewards for teaching and service general, continuing, and determined by the faculty itself through ordinary measures of review within their departmental units. Otherwise, they can make losers out of everybody else. And their value can be undermined by accusations of cronyism.

The final point I would make about reforming the academic value system is that we must not engage in an unacknowledged animus against research itself. General faculty engagement in independent inquiry has been, and should be, a continuing mark of higher education in America. Teaching that is not based upon a freshness of encounter with recent thinking and discovery will be as stale when it is processed in small discussions as it is when delivered from the lecture podium. There are some further truths about research that should be acknowledged.

First, research is glamorous, and it ought to be. It offers us an investment in the larger enterprises of the mind, links us to the world outside our colleges, brings us into the fellowship of like-minded and smart people, and entices us with the surprise and excitement of the new. Even as we engage in balancing teaching and service with research, let us admit that these are worthy as well as enduring attractions. And they should be considered as aspects of all the work of faculty across our institutions, even when those institutions are not large enough to offer the critical mass of technology and the number of researchers to yield specialized experimentation and discovery.

We know the problems that the glamour of research can present to institutions like those in the Associated New American Colleges. First, there is the urgency among presidents and members of the board to compete in national rankings, which frequently draw upon the fame generated by research. More significantly, there is the tendency of faculty themselves to try to replicate the research environment of their graduate training, no matter how inappropriate that may be. One distortion caused by this academic myopia is to refuse to teach introductory students, always gravitating toward the majors and leaving the others to increasingly exploited adjuncts and part-time faculty. Graduate programs can be at fault here if they hold up landing a job in a research institution as the only respectable achievement of the training they give. A student from such a program may end up spending a whole career dreaming of being called back to Harvard or Duke or Berkeley—missing, in the interim, the fulfillment in the balancing of talents and aims that can be achieved on a variety of campuses. The worst feature of such an internalization of the values of the research university is the increasing enforcement of research as the only currency in tenure and promotion decisions at every level. The resulting irrationality of decisions, and the burnout suffered by junior faculty who try to best them, have become too well known as the major negatives in academic careers.

But let us not mistake the misperceptions about the value and uses of research for the realities of study and discovery that have brought all of us into the professorate in the first place. We are attracted to research, and we give it special status because we know how difficult it is to amass evidence, to master a skill, to control a project, to understand a problem, and to formulate a new understanding. To achieve any one of these feats in research is to engage in work that is risky, esoteric, selfish, and obsessive. But faculty members also know that the excitement and pleasure of such engagements are also at the center of our vocations. It is true that if we cannot do them, we can teach them. That is the balance that our reward system must maintain, after all.

A NEW ACADEMIC COMPACT

Charles E. Glassick

The Carnegie Foundation surveys have, since 1968, described faculty loyalty to be first to the discipline, second to the department, and third to the institution. A survey of faculty attitudes in 14 countries confirmed that this same sequence is the predominant faculty response in every nation surveyed. Recently there have been influential voices calling for a closer tie between the professional scholar and the institution. And now the Associated New American Colleges propose a compact that would be designed to strengthen the relationship between faculty, administration, and institution.

My particular orientation to this proposal is that the expanded definition of scholarship stated in Boyer's *Scholarship Reconsidered* (1990) can aid and abet the process of forming such a compact. As Boyer suggested, this expansion of the definition of scholarship provides an opportunity for an expanded mission and purpose of the college. Now colleges can state a mission which would include aiding in solution of problems in their city, region, or state. They can assist local scholarly agencies such as historical societies. The options are virtually endless. Institutions can commit to enriching learning through the scholarship of teaching. Of course, the traditional mission including research will continue. But the point is that because of the expanded definition of scholarship, individual faculty can choose among several scholarly thrusts and at the same time be promoting the mission of their institution. Colleges will now be able to select new faculty on the basis of the fit between the scholarly interests of the candidate and the institution's needs.

Senior faculty will be able to move to new scholarly challenges as their interests change and they will still be supporting the mission and purpose of their institution. In short, an expanded definition of scholarship will enfranchise faculty who previously were on the fringe (clinical staff), bring learning to the center, and align faculty scholarly interests with college purposes. All of this sounds to me like a solid basis for a new, vigorous compact between faculty and administration.

SCHOLARSHIP UNBOUND FOR THE 21ST CENTURY

C. J. Weiser

The Associated New American Colleges have made an important contribution in rethinking faculty work and relationships between faculty and their home institution. ANAC's proposals explore the full scope of faculty work, how it should be evaluated and rewarded, and the obligations of institutions to support career-long faculty vitality and service to institutional mission. ANAC addresses issues similar to those involved in the development at my institution, Oregon State University (OSU), of what we call a faculty "living job description," a mechanism that enables the university and individual faculty members to negotiate and articulate individual work plans and expectations in their tenure unit.

The living job description identifies the percent of a faculty member's time allocated to assigned duties, to scholarly work, and to service in order to better achieve university missions and individual faculty work objectives. These time allocations and descriptions of assigned duties, scholarship plans, and service are developed jointly by the faculty member and department chair, and are reviewed and updated each year at the time of the annual performance review. The job description becomes a covenant between the faculty member and the institution and serves as the basis for the evaluation of the faculty member's performance in annual reviews and during the tenure and promotion process. This enhances the fairness of evaluation and reward processes and increases faculty effectiveness and satisfaction.

ANAC's project and our efforts at Oregon State suggest that there may be commonalities about faculty work that cut across institutional types and sectors in American higher education. At least two questions come to mind in thinking about the fundamental nature of faculty work wherever it is performed.

> 1) What do we mean by scholarship, the defining feature of what faculty do? In answering this question my institution used Ernest Boyer's *Scholarship Reconsidered* (1990) as a starting point, but ended at a somewhat different place in defining scholarship simply as creative intellectual work that is validated by peers and communicated.

2) Do we believe that we can actually engender the spirit of collaboration and trust that will be necessary for successful implementation of ANAC's recommendations and the long-term
well being of OSU's living job description system?

What follows is a description of development at OSU of our new
definition of scholarship and its implementation in our promotion
and tenure guidelines, a process we have labeled "Scholarship
Unbound for the 21st Century." Our rethinking of faculty scholarship
for a land grant research university parallels in many ways what
ANAC has accomplished in rethinking faculty work for private midsize comprehensive colleges and universities.

To provide a conceptual base for reviewing and revising tenure and
promotion guidelines a faculty senate task force at Oregon State
University undertook the challenge of defining and articulating the
core characteristics of scholarship that apply across academic disciplines and university missions. The end result is the following:
Scholarship is creative intellectual work that is validated by peers and
communicated—including creative artistry and the discovery, integration, and development of knowledge.

Scholarly achievement and excellence in performing other assigned
responsibilities are the primary categories for evaluating faculty performance, but OSU's new promotion and tenure guidelines describe
other aspects of faculty performance that the university values,
including collaborative effort, international perspective, and service.
Revised tenure and promotion guidelines reflecting these values, and
basing faculty evaluation on a position description, were adopted by
the university in 1995 with unanimous faculty senate support.
Numerous universities are considering such changes, but few have
progressed this far. Oregon State University hosted a national workshop October 1–3, 1998, to provide a forum for exchanging ideas on
the nature of scholarship and the reframing of faculty evaluations and
rewards that is taking place in American universities.

OSU's guidelines eliminated the need for separate supplemental
promotion and tenure guidelines which were previously used to
describe scholarship in programs such as extension, international
development, veterinary medicine, and library and information services where scholarship sometimes does not fit the traditional research
model of results published in peer reviewed journals (Table 8.1).

TABLE 8.1 Oregon State University's Promotion and Tenure Guidelines

- Reaffirm that scholarship is required of all professional faculty, and articulate a definition of scholarship that applies across the arts and sciences.
- Require that an annually updated position description serves as the basis for evaluating a faculty member's performance. The position description explicitly describes assigned duties, relevant areas of scholarship, and the relative balance of effort among assigned duties, scholarship, service for each faculty position.
- Identify performance of assigned duties and scholarly achievement as the two primary areas of faculty evaluation.
- Recognize service performed by faculty members which is not part of their assigned duties as a secondary area of performance evaluation. Assigned duties such as administration, extension, outreach, and student advising are not viewed as service when they are assigned to a faculty member. By the same token such activities are considered service when they are performed by a faculty member whose assigned duties lie in another area, such as research or teaching.
- Recognize teaching, research, and outreach as vital university missions and faculty activities that are not scholarship in themselves but which can each involve creative, communicated, peer-validated intellectual work (scholarship) in any of its several forms (discovery, development, integration, artistry). This is a significant departure from Ernest Boyer's view per se as scholarship.
- Recognize that peer validation and communication are separate processes that can occur in a variety of ways including, but not limited to, peer-refereed publications. When peer validation and communication are accomplished in nontraditional ways it is the faculty members' responsibility to clearly describe and document how peer validation and communication were accomplished.
- Recognize that teachers and extension educators can do scholarly work in developing improved education materials, methods, or programs or in conducting research in their subject-matter discipline.
- Recognize that the audiences for scholarship in research are disciplinary peers worldwide, but that audiences for scholarship in teaching, extension, and site-specific field research are often more localized. The promotion and tenure guidelines language was changed to reflect this reality—from "professors must achieve a national or international reputation for their scholarship" to "professors must achieve distinction in scholarship as evident in the candidate's wide recognition and significant contributions to the field or profession."
- Emphasize that the university values and encourages collaborative work, and asks faculty members to report contributions to significant team efforts in documenting their accomplishments.
- Recommend that documentation of achievements focus whenever possible on what was accomplished rather than how it was accomplished; on substance rather than form; on accomplishments rather than activities. In short, on describing what changed or improved as a result of a faculty member's efforts.

The OSU promotion and tenure guidelines acknowledge that the faculty of a university performs essential and valuable activities that are not scholarship. The guidelines explicitly describe scholarship as creative intellectual work that is validated by peers and communicated, including discovery of new knowledge; development of new technologies, methods, materials, or uses; integration of knowledge leading to new understandings; and artistry that creates new insights and understandings. This view acknowledges that scholarship can be carried out by knowledgeable, creative people throughout society—not just at universities. It emphasizes the importance of ensuring validity and of communicating to broader audiences to ensure that results of scholarship will be accessible and useful to others, and articulates the fundamental nature of scholarly achievement that applies across all disciplines.

Citizen advisors value OSU's new guidelines which they feel will recognize and reward faculty efforts that benefit students and citizens in Oregon. Several universities are finding that the Oregon State University definition of scholarship provides a useful starting point for their institution's deliberations about faculty evaluation, promotion, and tenure and post-tenure review. University faculties, and the broader public, seem ready to improve faculty evaluation and the reward process.

EXTENDING THE COMPACT: THE FUTURE OF THE PROFESSORIATE

Ric Weibl

Preparing Future Faculty (PFF) programs endeavor to restore respect for the fullness of college professor's work, precisely because it has at its heart, not teaching, not research nor service, but the integration of teaching, research, and service. Effective faculty are central to any conception of effective education or effective institutions (Gaff, Pruitt-Logan, & Weibl, 2000).

Ernest Boyer, in the preface to *Scholarship Reconsidered,* wrote that at the heart of the debate in the 1990s about the undergraduate curriculum and quality of campus life was the issue of faculty time. He asked "What activities of the professoriate are most highly prized" (1990, p. xi)? Competing values and confusing goals were creating a reality on too many campuses that resulted in a campus climate that restricted creativity, revealing social separations and divisions that eroded campus life for students and faculty alike. At the same time, Boyer wrote, "we need a climate in which colleges and universities are less imitative, taking pride in their uniqueness" (p. xiii). Members of the Associated New American Colleges have taken this charge to heart in their Faculty Work Projects.

The ANAC Faculty Work Projects have engaged in rethinking the relationships between faculty members and their institutions. The projects developed principles to provide a strong foundation of self-conscious renewal of the faculty-institutional compact in these student-centered institutions. This compact, ANAC concludes, is the basis of a healthy institution where personalized teaching and learning and academic community are core values. To affirm the centrality of faculty vitality to institutional health, the projects advocated bringing institutional policies into alignment with actual work practices and institutional missions. The assumption was made that core academic values, such as open inquiry, academic freedom, and professional community, are central to an academic profession engaged in institutional planning and decision-making. The resulting organizational structure, serving the core mission and values, reflects a high degree of interdependence. And yet, as Burton Clark (1987) made so evident, the predominant paradigm in institutional location, mission, and disciplinary affiliation is the radically decentralized academic profession. The higher education system as a whole struggles with the advantages and disadvantages of competitive disorder and unplanned hierarchy. The most critical fault line, in Clark's view, was that of the differentiated work arrangements, tasks that drive apart the communal identification of academics and fracture any shared professional ideologies. ANAC campuses, in asserting a new compact between faculty and their institutions, have identified professional and institutional foundations from which to logically articulate their own faculty work policies and practices. In doing so, their faculty have cast their lot in a common, yet differentiated, future. The compact highlights components of faculty expertise and institutional need—affirming mutual interdependence. This emphasis on the institutional context and a holistic vision of faculty work in a professional career is also central to the Preparing Future Faculty program.

The Preparing Future Faculty program, like the ANAC Faculty Work Projects, grew out of a period of intense study and reflection by academic leaders. Waning public confidence in college and university faculty, slowly eroding faculty authority in the shared governance of their institutions, and increasing use of part-time instructors forecast fundamental changes that demanded action. This "movement," as Clark called it (1987, p. 258), was threatening to destroy the academy and the profession as so many had come to know it. The ANAC and PFF initiatives began at a critical time as large numbers of faculty and their institutions seemed to be making moves that effectively unbundled fundamental relationships. PFF programs assert that the academic profession as a whole, and not simply graduate faculty, has an obligation to assist in the professional development of future generations of faculty. PFF is based on the principle that the academic profession has a responsibility to acquaint students aspiring to academic careers with the broad and complex realities of faculty life. Similarly, the ANAC Faculty Work Projects have gone far to delineate the many relationships and often understated responsibilities of faculty and their institutions—realities PFF programs wish to share with future faculty.

PFF transforms the way aspiring faculty members are prepared for their careers. One hundred universities—primarily research universities—award 80% of all doctorates (Gaff & Lambert, 1996). Aspiring faculty are routinely socialized to the values of academic life in these universities. And yet we know that those who go on to faculty careers work mostly at institutions reflected in the ANAC membership. PFF programs urge doctoral faculty to create future faculty development programs informed by the kinds of responsibilities faculty members actually have, roles subsumed by the terms teaching, research, and service. Further, PFF focuses attention on the way these roles differ in a variety of institutional settings.

Since 1993, PFF programs have created new partnerships of college and university faculty working to design new approaches for the professional development of new faculty. In a process very similar to that of the ANAC work projects, teams of faculty and academic administrators meet to explore the mismatch between institutional expectations and the educational experiences of doctoral students. Graduate faculty conduct assessments and follow-up studies with recent alumni, undergraduate institutions clarify and articulate expectations of new faculty. Working together, they create new opportunities for future faculty to understand those new professional standards and to begin the lifelong practice of learning to be an academic professional (Table 8.2).

TABLE 8.2 The PFF Ideas

- Faculty should provide apprenticeship teaching, research, and service experiences that are appropriate to the doctoral student's stage of personal development and progress toward the degree. Future faculty should be given progressively more complex assignments, more responsibility, and recognition associated with increased professional capacities.
- Through direct and extended experiences in the field, faculty should provide doctoral students opportunities to learn about the academic profession. By exposing them to the full range of professional responsibilities in the variety of institutions that may become their professional homes enables them to find a better fit between their own interests and competencies and the needs of institutions.
- Doctoral programs should include formalized systems for mentoring students in all aspects of their professional development, beyond program and dissertation advisors. Graduate students benefit from multiple mentors providing them guidance as they develop their teaching, research, and service repertoire.
- Doctoral experiences should equip students for the changes taking place in today's colleges and universities. Future faculty members need to be competent in the use of instructional technologies and multiple approaches to teaching and learning, working with increasing heterogeneity among their students and colleagues, and participating in the leadership of their departments and institutions. These skills complement research competency in one's selected field.

The configuration of ideas underlying PFF programs can be easily described. None of these ideas is new or radical, but collectively they add up to a very different kind of doctoral experience from conventional graduate education. Furthermore, they connect directly to outcomes of the ANAC Faculty Work Projects. The PFF program is dependent upon a compact very similar to that proposed by ANAC. PFF programs assert that the entire profession should play a role in the preparation and renewal of its members. It is unfortunate that higher education has restricted its professional preparation of novices to the classrooms and laboratories of research universities, just as we have assumed faculty development was to assist junior faculty achieve tenure and to improve teaching. ANAC and PFF share a belief that a more inclusive and comprehensive model of professional development is preferable, if not essential, to the health of the profession and the institutions it serves.

The importance of PFF and the ANAC Faculty Work Projects cannot be understated at a time when so much is at stake. The trends and changes that threaten to further isolate faculty are detrimental to institutional quality. Academic leaders must affirm and act on the conviction that a committed, full-time faculty who can teach effectively, maintain active scholarly minds, and play positive roles in the leadership of their institutions are essential to strong institutions. Programs like PFF can only do part of what is required. New faculty must find an institutional climate that welcomes them into an academic community that has dedicated itself to a compact between faculty and their institutions, much like the ANAC Faculty Work Projects campuses that have achieved a great deal in their alignment of roles, responsibilities, and expectations.

REFERENCES

Boyer, E. L. (1990). *Scholarship reconsidered: Priorities of the professoriate.* Princeton, NJ: The Carnegie Foundation for the Advancement of Teaching.

Clark, B. R. (1987). *The academic life: Small worlds, different worlds.* Princeton, NJ: The Carnegie Foundation for the Advancement of Teaching.

Gaff, J. G., & Lambert, L. M. (1996, July/August). Socializing future faculty to the values of undergraduate education. *Change,* 38-45.

Gaff, J. G., Pruitt-Logan, A. S., & Weibl, R. A. (2000). *Building the faculty we need: Colleges and universities working together.* Washington, DC: Association of American Colleges and Universities.

9

REFLECTIONS ON THE FACULTY
WORK PROJECT
Jon Wergin

I well remember my first contact with the Associated New American Colleges' (ANAC) Faculty Work Project in June 1999, at St. Mary's College in California. The assembled campus representatives were a disgruntled lot: They had only recently been told that reduced foundation support would require them to lower their sights from an action project to a think tank that would generate principles for future action. This was seen by many in the group as little more than a plan for marking time and, quite honestly, they had been there before.

I had been there before, as well: As a consultant I knew the feeling of being thrust into the DMZ between competing agendas—and I had this feeling now. I felt sympathy for Jerry Berberet as he struggled to reenergize the group, and with project manager Linda McMillin as she put on a brave front while undoubtedly asking herself, "How did I get myself into this?" I tried to do what good consultants are supposed to do: listen carefully, offer a perspective, then get out of the way. Because of my previous work in departmental collaboration and assessment, I was asked to speak with conferees about this work and to consult with a subgroup (Group 3) charged to develop differentiated faculty workload policies and unit planning and evaluation models. I did so, giving a fairly stock speech about forces affecting faculty work and the press for differentiation, then helping the subgroup conduct a force-field analysis on the supports and barriers for change at their own institutions. I found the discussion unremarkable, even a little desultory, and while I had been invited to the next work group meeting in November, I left St. Mary's thinking that the project would likely not accomplish very much.

I did not give the Faculty Work Project much thought during the next few months. I went to the November meeting at Belmont University in Nashville because I had promised I would. But something happened at this conference, something ineffable. I wish now that I had kept a journal of those days, because I'd like to bottle what happened there. I gave another talk, this one focusing on my work on departmental assessment, and the discussion was lively. But the real change was in Group 3: It morphed into a real team, with all of the characteristics implied by the term. Looking back, most of the credit for this goes to Linda McMillin, who not only served as project manager but also chair of this group. Her indefatigable energy and friendly task orientation kept the group going. I was a catalyst as well, although not at all in the way I had intended. As I talked with them about what other institutions were doing with unit differentiation and rewards, the response, more often than not, was "wait a minute, ANAC institutions are not necessarily like those other places." For example, I spoke with them about the traditional one-size-fits-all model of faculty work, and someone said, "That doesn't really capture what we do. We may be small but we're also complex. We have to differentiate our work and collaborate across departmental lines. There is no other choice." I learned something about making generalizations, and Group 3 learned something as well: It began to see itself not just as a group of representative faculty from institutions with similar missions, but as a team with a real identity and a common purpose. And when the team began to develop a set of principles for faculty work specific to ANAC institutions, it really began to cook. We had so much energy we did not want to stop for breaks or plenary sessions. People felt as if the team were creating something new rather than rehashing ideas laid out by others in other contexts. I was energized as well. I remember thinking to myself, this stuff is different. They may really be on to something. I told them so, and I think this may have strengthened their resolve to produce something powerful and useful.

Whenever a team coalesces like this there has to be more than just a common purpose and a sense of group uniqueness. People also have to learn to work together, and our team had an excellent mix of styles. I have already mentioned Linda's skill at mixing attention to the task with attention to the process. Some in the group—Heather, Catherine, Barbara, and Susan—were principally idea-generators, putting items on the table for the group to consider. Garry and George (perhaps because they're both administrators) were the reality testers, cross-examining ideas for their feasibility. Alan, as one of only two junior faculty members in the group, made sure that his constituent interests were not left out. And Ed and Pat served the crucial roles of reframers: Each had the gift of being able to engineer a jumble of ideas into a coherent whole. I continued in my role as the external reflector, contrasting the team's work with others' and helping them define what was common and what was unique.

The sense of momentum generated by the Belmont sessions carried over to the next project meeting in February, at the American Association for Higher Education (AAHE) Roles and Rewards conference in New Orleans. Here, Group 3 reached what I think was a pivotal insight. I had suggested that any sort of planning at the unit level, including discussions of differentiated faculty roles, had to begin with some consensus as to the work of the department as a whole—and that this sense of the unit's collective work should transcend the simple accretion of individual faculty work. I suggested further that, paradoxically, the best way to do this is to begin with what individual faculty members do, then see what all of this work adds up to and whether the whole is both coherent and contributes significantly to the institution. At this point, Garry, administrator and music professor, raised the question that dogs all of the humanities: "But how can a department like music demonstrate its contribution? We do not have many students, we do not get many grants, and we do not publish much research." As I remember it, Garry then proceeded to answer his own question. "We show our value in other ways, by enriching the culture of the institution and the community." Someone—I do not remember who—then suggested that academic units ought to be accountable for adding value to the institution, and that different units would, because of their diverse missions, do this in diverse ways. For some, such traditional markers as credit hours generated and articles published would be valid criteria, but other units should be held to different standards. One-size-fits-all does not work for faculty members in a department, and it does not work for departments in a university either.

The notion of adding value proved to be a galvanizing concept for the group. How does a faculty member add value to a department? How does a department add value to an institution? How does an institution add value to faculty? By the penultimate meeting of the project, in April 2000 at Pacific Lutheran in Tacoma, this "circle of value" had become the central focus of Group 3's work. It is a concept unlike anything I had seen before, powerful and elegant in its simplicity. The group fought off the natural impulse to complicate the model by showing all possible relationships among the elements (representing them with bi-directional arrows, broken lines, and the like), and kept the circle of value simple: from the faculty member to the department, from the department to the institution, and from the institution back to the faculty member. (I suppose the geometrically correct term would have been "triangle of value" but somehow "circle of value" sounds better.) I loved it.

By the Tacoma meeting, teamwork was evident in all three project groups as pairs and triads huddled around laptops generating or editing text. In less than a year, project teams had managed to do precisely what the grant had intended: produce a report with real meat in it, one that was not only true to the culture of ANAC schools but also transferable to the broader higher education community.

REFLECTING ON THE OUTCOME

Institutions (and here I'm speaking of institutions as collectives of faculty, students, and administrators) want to be special; they want to have a niche that is theirs and no one else's. They also, unfortunately in my view, want to move up the Carnegie ladder, as if institutional quality were somehow one-dimensional. There is a real conflict here, and faculty, especially junior faculty, feel it. I recall some research the late Bob Menges (1999) did a few years ago on junior faculty members and stress. He found that faculty experiencing the greatest stress reside in comprehensive universities, not in research universities or community colleges. He inferred that the stress is due to role conflict, between satisfying the purported teaching mission on one hand, and research expectations on the other. I would take that one step further and suggest that faculty—especially junior faculty—are uncomfortable with the Janus face of their institutions, finding it difficult to feel loyalty to an institution that cannot figure out who it is or what it wants to be.

ANAC institutions are "private comprehensives," and so should share many of the same woes which plague their public counterparts. Not so, if the results of Phase I of the Faculty Work Project are to be believed. The vast majority of ANAC faculty say they understand and support their institution's mission; where they experience conflict is with the lack of reciprocity they feel between their commitment to the institution and the institution's commitment to them. Further, despite their professed institutional loyalty, fewer than half of ANAC faculty surveyed believe they share this with their faculty colleagues. And so what emerges for these faculty is not a lack of institutional connection but rather a lack of individual recognition, on one hand, and weak engagement with their academic community, on the other. I would like to assess the three facets of the compact from the perspective of these two key issues.

Faculty Development

The title of the Faculty Development (FD) Group's Chapter Two, "Professional Development Across the Faculty Career," captures nicely the vastly changed notions of what faculty development should mean in a new academic compact. When the term first became prominent about 30 years ago, faculty development was quickly tarred with two unfortunate connotations. First, it was seen principally as a way to remediate poor teaching, either because young faculty were entering the academy in large numbers and possessed weak pedagogical skills, or because older faculty were getting blasted by the new-fangled student ratings forms quickly taking hold on campus. A faculty development office was therefore a place where you were sent rather than a place you sought. (Unless, of course, you happened to be one of the fringe who were already good teachers and wanted to get better.) Second, paradoxically, faculty development did not have much of a truly developmental quality. Little attention was paid to anything beyond fixing the problems of the present: leading better discussions, making up better tests, becoming more sensitive to student diversity. The circle of value idea did not apply much to faculty development in those days; the institution's role was not about adding value to faculty members, it was about removing deficiencies. Further, because faculty development programs had a largely skill-development focus, they were often disconnected from the disciplinary context of faculty work. Teaching history was not supposed to be all that different from teaching physics. I used to run one of these offices myself, and I have to shake my head at my own myopia! How far we have come since those days is clear in the FD Group's new definition:

> We conceive of faculty development as a career-long process undertaken in the context of the institutional circle of value and where the needs and responsibilities of faculty as individuals are recognized and addressed within academic units and institutionally faculty roles are aligned with institutional mission and strategic plans.

This definition is remarkable for its recognition of two key ideas: that faculty development is a career-long process, and that faculty development must take place within the context of an academic community. I'd like to comment on each of these.

First, the FD Group's suggestion that compacts be negotiated according to career stages is a good one. Much work is yet to be done on how to weave adult development theory into the model, but I am pleased to see it the mention of it here. Erickson's seminal work on identity and generativity, Levinson's notions about mentoring and growth through discourse, and Loevinger's ideas about the development of autonomy and the conscientious self, as well as Bandura's social learning theory in a broader context, all have potentially rich applications to faculty life, but have been largely ignored in the faculty development literature. One of my favorite findings from adult development research, remarkable for its consistency across cultures, is the concept of "sex role crossover." Men and women in middle age tend to move toward more androgynous roles: Men become more caring and nurturing, women more independent and assertive. Consider for a moment the implications of this for our aging, mostly male, faculty. The most powerful source of energy for revitalizing our academic communities may well lie with the cohort least associated with change!

Second, an earlier version of this report used the Mayflower Compact and its notions of how to achieve both freedom and community responsibility as a model for the development of faculty members in an academic community. That model is not far off, in my view. John Winthrop, first governor of the Massachusetts Bay Company, envisioned Puritan community life as adhering to three interlocking themes: difference, cooperation, and justice. Winthrop believed that God had made people different from one another because they needed one another, and that communities would not survive simply by mutual agreement to live by a judicial code. Winthrop's colony was to work together so as to achieve communal well being. Freedom was to be interpreted as the freedom to contribute to the common good in ways most befitting a person's individuality, and equality was to be interpreted as respect for these differences. As the FD Group noted, academic culture in the United States has been rooted in a deeper tradition of community based on collaboration, shared work, and a collegial ethic; this tradition has eroded during the past 50 years, so that freedom has been made synonymous with autonomy, and equality synonymous with sameness. The FD Group's definition of faculty development is remarkable for how it re-centers the individual within the academic community.

The problem with this new definition, however, is that it might be interpreted by faculty as serving the interests of the institution alone. While the FD Group emphasizes in its principles the need for forward-looking thinking and flexible and ontological faculty roles, there is not quite enough emphasis, in my view, on how respect for the development of the individual is key to the development of the institution—that it is not just a matter of developing people for the purpose of contributing to institutional goals. Institutional vitality comes from within, from the health of its members. Participating in this project has caused me to reflect on why we faculty do what we do, and what it is that keeps us going. It turns out that a half-century of research on faculty motivation has given us some remarkably consistent findings, which I have described in a recent article (Wergin, 2001). In it, I discuss how faculty are driven by four powerful motives.

Autonomy. This is the reason given most often when faculty are asked why they chose the academic life. Professional autonomy is the freedom to experiment, to follow one's own leads wherever they may go, and to do so without fear of the consequences. Autonomy under-girds the principles of academic freedom. Most faculty would agree, however, that autonomy is not unrestricted: Faculty are not free to do whatever they wish, answerable only to themselves. The responsible use of autonomy is what professionalizes faculty work.

Community. The second most common reason given for choosing faculty life is the desire to join a community of scholars, a notion that seems depressingly quaint to new faculty as they face an academic culture of isolation and competitive advantage. The desire to belong, to feel part of a nurturing community, never goes away, however. Anything that eases the "pain of disconnection," as Parker Palmer (1998, p. 35) calls it, is a powerful motivator, indeed.

Recognition. People everywhere want to feel valued, to know that others see their work as worthwhile. Faculty members are no dif-ferent. We need evidence that someone's paying attention. That is why so many salary disputes in higher education seem so symbolic: Money, even in minuscule increments, symbolizes recognition.

Efficacy. Quite simply, efficacy is a sense of having had a tangible impact on our environment. We feel efficacious when we see our stu-dents grasp a difficult concept, when we have made an important dis-covery, or when we have contributed to the quality of life in our com-munities. Efficacy is what gives our work meaning.

It is interesting to speculate how attention to these four intrinsic motivators would address the two key themes—recognition and engagement—running through the ANAC research. Several years ago my colleagues and I conducted a study of career satisfaction among senior faculty, and we found that the single factor which most reliably predicted satisfaction at this stage was what we called a "sense of niche": a perception that individual faculty had a place in their aca-demic community which was theirs and no one else's. Two character-istics define a niche: It is connected (that is, it is part of an organic whole), and it is constantly evolving. Helping faculty develop a niche communicates autonomy, requires a community context, provides a subtle but unmistakable recognition of worth, and, because the facul-ty are the architects, creates and reinforces efficacy.

Service

There is much to like in the Service/Governance (SG) Group's chapter, "Faculty as Institutional Citizens." Such trenchant observations, made by faculty themselves, are long overdue. The chapter begins, quite rightly in my view, with the vexing conflicts many faculty have with their service roles. Expectations are unclear, efficacy is low, and feedback is minimal. In short, some faculty wonder to what extent service really matters—to them personally as well as to their university. The group's suggestion that service be reconceived as citizenship makes a lot of sense to me, as the two terms have vastly different connotations. Service has an obligatory, almost noblesse oblige sense about it, while citizenship implies responsibility for building and maintaining community, which is much more positive and powerful. The authors build an elegant and compelling case for change. I do have mixed feelings about their adoption of the Modern Language Association (MLA) Commission's rubric, however, in particular the dichotomy the MLA proposes between intellectual work and academic and professional citizenship. I understand the MLA's position on this: We should recognize differently work for which faculty have been specifically prepared, such as reviewing manuscripts, from the more generic maintenance activities important to any organization. In every family someone has to take out the trash. But I also agree with the SG Group's view that in a university it is impossible to separate intellectual work from the context which supports it. I would go a step further: In its very attempt to elevate the importance of citizenship as a vital part of faculty work, the MLA model produces exactly the opposite effect. Do we conclude that citizenship is therefore not intellectual work, worthy of significant faculty investment? Or that faculty who do make that investment must not have the intellectual firepower to do the real work of the faculty? I sense some academic snobbery here, which is too bad, because otherwise the model makes a lot of sense. It is not clear whether it is endorsed by the SG Group, or what the implications for ANAC colleges might be. I would like to see a stronger affirmation that the organizational learning which results from active and reflective citizenship is every bit as challenging intellectually, and every bit as useful to the academic community, as teaching and more traditional scholarship.

The SG Group's comments on the responsibilities of institutional citizenship are a refreshing change from the usual railing against the increased corporatization of the academy, an unfortunate trend for which faculty share at least some of the blame. As the group notes, faculty members are the ones principally responsible for academic integrity; what it does not say is that faculty have largely abrogated that responsibility and thus have opened the door to the bureaucracy and regulation they so disdain. If faculty do not take collective responsibility for the quality of their teaching, the coherence of their curricula, and the usefulness of the learning asked of students, then others will fill the breach. Already we are seeing evidence that college curricula are being driven by the standards of the institutional economy and of the marketplace, and faculty everywhere would do well to heed the SG Group's call for strengthened academic oversight.

I like very much the way the SG Group focuses on governance as a particularly critical aspect of faculty citizenship. They have nailed perfectly the maddening paradoxes which often paralyze relationships between faculty and administrators, and I think that their solutions are right on the money. In particular, their first recommendation for a more open organization characterized by a freer flow of information fits with my own research on institutional effectiveness. I also endorse their second and third recommendations for more collaborative governance and trust-building through the rejection of unhealthy stereotypes. Examples given from ANAC institutions reveal quite clearly how diverse collaborative models can work effectively. The key is congruence with organizational culture.

Finally, I was impressed with the work the SG Group did on evaluation and reward of faculty citizenship. This is a tough one, and while they tiptoed around it a little, the group has largely avoided the trap of making the usual ineffectual calls for more thorough evaluation and clearer and more public rewards. Instead, they suggest that while the key to better citizenship involves changing the reward system (and their suggestion that evaluation should center on reflective self-evaluation is excellent), an institution also needs to design work environments which will make citizenship more intrinsically rewarding. In Chapter One, Jerry Berberet referred to work I have done elsewhere with the concept of organizational motivation: the idea that people will work for the common good to the extent that they have a strong sense of identity with the organization and feel efficacious in working within it. Organizational motivation applies most strongly to institutional citizenship, and I would like to see more institutions take it seriously.

Faculty Role Differentiation

The Workload Differentiation (WD) Group was the group I worked with most closely, and I became so invested in its chapter ("Faculty Workload: Differentiation Through Unit Collaboration") that I am probably not able to comment on it objectively. And so instead of offering a commentary I will simply add a couple of additional thoughts. Because this group addressed the structure and organization of faculty work, its proposals underpin both faculty development and institutional citizenship. As I noted earlier, the circle of value idea has wonderful simplicity and powerful implications, as it provides a standard against which relationships between faculty and their institution might be judged. Faculty should add value to their academic units, units should add value to their institution, and institutions should add value to their faculty. The first two of these suggest standards for citizenship, the third a standard for faculty development. For example, how does the faculty's investment in academic oversight add value to academic units and to the institution as a whole? How does attention to faculty career stages add value to faculty and, in essence, create more intellectual capital for the institution?

The notion of faculty role differentiation is attractive to many in the academy, especially those in comprehensive universities: They are caught in the middle between research and teaching institutions, and thus the faculty in them are expected to do everything well. What seems to hang people up is their view of true differentiation as idealistic, even naive. There are simply too many barriers. In a workshop at the 2001 AAHE conference, Linda McMillin and I asked attendees to inventory institutional barriers to differentiated faculty work, and they generated a long list.

- Lack of commitment to differentiation at all levels, including faculty promotion and tenure committees
- Faculty autonomy and independence
- Lack of applicability to pretenure faculty
- Risk of differentiation evolving into a caste system

- Lack of pay incentives
- Resistance by faculty unions
- Less cross-fertilization among faculty roles
- Difficulty of administration
- Challenges in evaluating teaching and service
- Demands of the discipline
- Reduction in faculty mobility
- Damage to the "shared culture" of a department

It is interesting to see how many of these barriers would weaken if not disappear entirely if the recommendations made in the Faculty Work Project were implemented. Embracing the recommendations of the Faculty Development Group, particularly its recommendations on faculty development through the career span, would address the autonomy, caste, and mobility issues; and adopting the recommendations of the Service/Governance Group would address most of the others. All evidence suggests that these will be difficult changes, however. Many faculty do not see the difference between differentiation and the current pressures for greater specialization, while in fact the two are distinctly different. Differentiation is contextual to the work unit, and assumes an understanding of how individual work contributes to the collective good, while specialization does not. In the few instances where faculty role differentiation has been promulgated as an official institutional policy, these kinds of misinterpretations have been common at the departmental level—so that at one university, for example, while some departments have taken differentiation to heart first by defining the work of the department then negotiating how individual faculty members might contribute differentially to that work, others simply see the policy as a way of allowing faculty members to make individual deals with the chair, or as a way of allowing senior faculty who no longer have an interest in contributing to the scholarly literature to do more teaching or service instead. Neither of the latter interpretations pay any attention to the collective work of the department and the negotiation of faculty work plans accordingly.

These experiences suggest that in order for the circle of value concept to work as more than a rhetorical device we need to think more carefully about what happens beyond the circle. In other words, we need to link role differentiation with role integration: both the integration of individual faculty work within the department and the integration of the department and institution with the constituencies they exist to serve. What this in turn suggests to me is that we have to find ways of protecting faculty autonomy without continuing to reinforce faculty free-agency. We need, in short, to redefine academic culture in a new way, as a sort of new democracy, wherein individual freedoms are protected, but also defined more contextually, in ways laid out in this volume.

These ideas are not new, just newly framed. Many of the proposals contained in the report of the WD Group—and in the Faculty Work Project as a whole—share an intellectual home with the writings of the great American philosopher John Dewey (who, by the way, helped found the American Association of University Professors in 1915). Dewey's thoughts on democracy and education nearly 100 years ago have startling relevance to the organization of faculty work in the twenty-first century. Democracy, said Dewey, "is more than a form of government . . . [It is] fundamentally a mode of associated living, of conjoint communicated experience"(Qtd. in Boisvert, p. 56). In a later work, *The Public and its Problems* (1922), Dewey said this:

> From the standpoint of the individual, [effective democracy consists] in having a responsible share according to capacity in forming and directing the activities of the groups to which one belongs and in participating according to need in the values which the groups sustain. From the standpoint of the groups, [effective democracy] demands liberation of the potentialities of members of a group in harmony with the interests and goods which are common . . . This specification cannot be fulfilled except when different groups interact flexibly and fully in connection with other groups. (Qtd. in Boisvert, p. 56)

CONCLUSION

Herein lies what I believe to be the core issue of faculty work. Universities should aspire to be more than organized anarchies, as that cynical appellation goes. They should instead aspire to be models of Deweyian democracy, where there is wide participation in formulating policy, where faculty members and others are able to develop their individual talents to the fullest, and where relationships among academic units are fluid and mutually reinforcing. If Dewey were alive today he would happily endorse the Faculty Work Project and what it has produced, and that is a high compliment in my book.

REFERENCES

Boisvert, R. D. (1998). *John Dewey: Rethinking our time.* Albany, NY: State University of New York Press.

Menges, R. J., & Associates. (Ed.). (1999). *Faculty in new jobs: A guide to settling in, becoming established, and building institutional support.* San Francisco, CA: Jossey-Bass.

Palmer, P. (1998). *The courage to teach: Exploring the inner landscape of a teacher's life.* San Francisco, CA: Jossey-Bass.

Wergin, J. F. (2001, Winter). Beyond carrots and sticks: What really motivates faculty. *Liberal Education*, 50-53.

10

A HOLISTIC MODEL FOR FACULTY AND INSTITUTIONAL DEVELOPMENT

Jacqueline A. Mintz

Faculty development is a relatively new field. In fact, the professional association in North America, the Professional and Organizational Development (POD) Network in Higher Education, observed only its 25th anniversary in the fall of 2000. Some faculty balk at the term faculty development because, unlike the positive connotations ascribed to child development, they ascribe negative connotations to the term and see themselves as mature adults that do not need to be developed. In a piece published in *Liberal Education*, I argued that "Faculty development cannot be something *done to us* but something that we and the institution undertake together, something that forms the fabric and shapes the identity of faculty life" (1999, p. 35). For others of us, children of the sixties and seventies, the word development conjures up a less pejorative association in favor of a belief in personal growth, a commitment to continued learning, and the potential to integrate formal learning with life experience in order to pursue new challenges, better our society, and perhaps, acquire a modicum of wisdom along the way.

Most schools today have made at least nominal efforts toward faculty development. Some have embraced the idea, undergirding their mission—to realize student potential—with a concomitant commitment to develop faculty, while others, in view of the groundswell around them, have given at least lip service to the idea. Judging from what was learned from over 500 respondents to a survey published by POD five years ago (Graf & Wheeler, 1996), faculty development efforts cover a very wide continuum corresponding to the variables and needs of different institutions.

FACULTY DEVELOPMENT DEFINED

In preparation for a jointly sponsored conference on faculty development at Rollins College in March 2000, representatives from the attending colleges came up with a multifaceted definition of faculty development and their own roles in it. Among the list of descriptors of faculty development were the need to understand and shape learning and teaching cultures, to connect to resources, to advocate for newcomers and veterans, to legitimize conversations about learning and teaching problems, to integrate faculty to learning and teaching norms without squashing creativity, and to communicate expectations on teaching. As I reviewed the list, I was struck by the operative verbs: understand, connect, advocate, legitimize, integrate, and communicate. They seemed to me to describe our roles not only as citizens within a democracy but also in community. Indeed, if these things describe what it means to be human and to be realized in our communal roles as faculty, faculty developers, and administrators, then what happens to us when these are absent from our lives?

Whether or not we have encountered it ourselves, surely we have heard and read about experiencing feelings of isolation in higher education. Jane Tompkins, a senior faculty member, has written and spoken about it on a personal level (1992), and researchers have found that, despite being busy with myriad departmental and other matters, and despite the welcoming norms of the department or institution, new faculty find that "professorial life—although outwardly crowded with people, especially students—is often an essentially solitary pursuit" (Dinham, 1999b, p. 5). New Faculty Project interviews and surveys, the subject of a book by Robert Menges and Associates, *Faculty in New Jobs: A Guide to Settling In, Becoming Established, and Building Institutional Support* (1999), found that, regardless of the institutional differences, new faculty stress arises from feeling alone, misunderstood, a lack of advocacy and power, the many and competing demands, and a life out of balance (Dinham, 1999b, p. 5). What is more, women reported experiencing more stress than their male peers due to "high levels of conflict between personal, home, and professional duties" (Dey, Ramirez, Korn, & Astin, 1993, p. 17). When we read these findings and review the list of needs indicated by the operative verbs understand, connect, advocate, legitimize, integrate, and communicate, we realize that the lack of these necessary, humanizing conditions exacts a considerable toll on our lives.

As I have suggested in my articles, "Challenging Values: Conflict, Contradiction and Pedagogy" (1994) and "Recruiting Students and Telling the Whole Story about Teaching" (1997), higher education is rife with contradictory values and practices that have an impact on us as educators in our institutions, in the ways we relate to our students, and in virtually every facet of our professional, and even our private, lives. In a study of new faculty, the group freshly and most fully inculcated with the values of their mentors, Whitt (1991) discovered they had conflicting feelings that they kept strongly guarded. The fact is that we are a culture operating at cross-purposes.

TEACHING VERSUS RESEARCH

Over the course of the twentieth century, and in particular the last 50 years, status within American higher education has shifted from teachers and teaching to researchers and discovery. A star system among faculty has arisen from within our ranks bringing to institutions recognition and sustainability through external grants, major donors, corporate partners, cyberspace alliances, and other tangible resources. This spiraling process has set individuals apart from, and above, their colleagues in multiple ways. In many renowned research institutions, professors are so specialized in their fields that they are often both unwilling and incapable of teaching introductory courses.

Liberal arts colleges are not immune to this syndrome. In a trend similar to that in the social sciences, and even humanities in the second half of the twentieth century to look more like the sciences, many liberal arts colleges today imitate top research universities. As Donald Kennedy writes in *Academic Duty*, "it is clear that a single issue, division of labor between teaching and research, is affecting the quality of life for many in the professoriate . . . Increasingly it has become an issue even in liberal arts colleges of the second or third rank" (1997,

p. 25). Robin Wilson, in a January 2001 article in *The Chronicle of Higher Education*, quotes University of Richmond President William E. Cooper as saying that Richmond is "on the fast track to the top of the quality ladder" (p. A13). She writes that "Although Richmond traditionally has emphasized undergraduate education, Mr. Cooper speaks enthusiastically about putting it on a par with Princeton University, which he says is a model for an institution that puts equal emphasis on teaching and research" (p. A13). The academic version of the ubiquitous "wannabe syndrome" often makes an uneasy peace in liberal arts colleges with the attempts to retain their own distinct identities, especially with regard to the importance placed upon teaching undergraduates. This gestalt within the academy, sometimes even without our realizing it, permeates the whole system, including our interactions with our students.

For example, in his article, "The Good Teacher, the Good Student: Identifications of a Student Teacher," Chris Amirault (1995) describes how he was jolted into the awareness that he was re-creating the cycle with his student by ignoring who she really was. Through self-reflection, he discovered himself in the act of confirming the findings of Bourdieu and Passeron in *Reproduction in Education, Society and Culture*, when they write,

> As former model pupils who would like to have no pupils except future teachers, teachers are predisposed by their whole training and all their educational experience to play the game of the institution. In addressing himself to the student such as he ought to be, the teacher infallibly discourages the student's temptation to demand the right to be only what he is: the teacher respects, by the credit he gives him, the fictitious student whom a few "gifted pupils," objects of all his care and attention, authorize him to regard as real. (Bourdieu & Passeron, 1970, p. 132n7, qtd. in Amirault, p. 71)

For many academics, internalized contradictions between institutionally inherited and ingrained practices and our own values and desires lie at the heart of the faculty development dilemma. It is only when we take the time to analyze the discrepancy between our beliefs and our behaviors or, on that rare occasion when a child, our student, or some chance, often life and death, circumstance flips the "aha" emotional switch, that we realize how complex, inconsistent, and even contradictory we are.

Raised in a fiercely competitive system, where recognition is afforded both by merit and concerns for the bottom line, we should not be surprised when we confound our qualitative values regarding what is good with the quantitative realities of what is rewarded. Limits on time combined with the drive to succeed often repress or destroy youthful idealism. Animal science Professor Sandra G. Velleman describes the pragmatism of many junior faculty members when she says, "You are less likely to take a high risk if you don't think you can get a big return" (Wilson, 2001, A14). Many of our students are similarly programmed. Urged by their parents to be happy and succeed (as if these were one and the same), they often feel pressured to commit to majors and careers they dislike.

It has long been custom—not exclusive to the academy—to blame others for what is wrong or lacking. We blame our students for everything from being insufficiently prepared, to their demands on our time and wrong-headedness in choosing to major in business instead of philosophy or literature; we blame the administration or the system for failing to adequately recognize our work through what Sharon Baiocco and Jamie DeWaters (1998) call "a perverted academic reward system"; we blame the trustees for meddling in academic affairs; and we blame our colleagues for a multitude of things, including taking advantage of us when they allow us to carry too much of the load for our civic lives.

While there may be some truth in these accusations, my purpose is neither to muster our resources to fight the enemy nor to chastise, but to bring home to all of us in the academy the cost to our happiness and well being—not to mention to our productivity and relationships—of not assessing our own contradictions and inconsistencies in order to gain a new level of understanding of ourselves and our colleagues and to better the system we have created.

AN ALTERNATIVE MODEL

Not surprisingly, focusing on beliefs and feelings—the powerful and often elusive qualities that define our complexity as humans—is hardly the coin of the realm throughout much of the academic world of intellectual discovery and scientific advancement. Yet Parker Palmer, a speaker and educator, writes about the centrality of feelings to the enterprise of contemporary higher education. In *To Know As We Are Known: Education as a Spiritual Journey,* Palmer (1993) focuses on the spiritual and affective needs in each of us and wants for us and for our students to reach what Thomas Merton calls a "'hidden wholeness' on which all life depends" (p. xix). Tempting though the prospect of wholeness is, I want to suggest a conceptual model that takes into account both who we are and what we aspire to be. This alternate model acknowledges our inconsistent and complex natures, the very natures of which Palmer writes when he says, "I am frequently defeated by forces within and outside of myself, forces that lead me to objectify and manipulate life even as I yearn for mutuality and troth" (p. 17). What I submit is that, unlike the goal of wholeness that we in the Western tradition are accustomed to symbolize as an ultimate stasis or perfection—in Platonic terms—the state of being, wholeness also can be an ongoing, dynamic state of becoming that is never intended to be completely realized. Though we have been taught to think in terms of realizing our full potential, it is rather the movement toward our fulfillment that is the goal in itself.

However subtle this may sound, the difference is enormous in the way we think about ourselves and the way we interact with others. In this reoriented worldview, inconsistent behavior is not a break with our perfect natures but recognition of them for what they are. It is a welcome opportunity to examine our beliefs and feelings in their myriad contexts, mindful of the cultural and historical forces that have helped to shape them. Harmony, however pleasing to the ear, is no longer the single standard. In this new orientation, tension is not necessarily synonymous with anxiety or a harbinger of disease; it is rather a sign of a healthy, engaged intellect, informed by emotions and spurred on to a greater and deeper understanding of ourselves and of others. As Meg Wheatley writes in *Leadership and the New Science: Learning About Organization from an Orderly Universe,* "The things we fear most in organizations—fluctuations, disturbances, imbalances—need not be signs of an impending disorder that will destroy us. Instead, fluctuations are the primary source of creativity" (1992, p. 20).

What does this have to do with holistic faculty development? It seems to me that it is no coincidence that the advent itself of faculty development has overlapped with one of the most tumultuous periods in the history of American higher education. The pushing and pulling, expanding and shrinking, bombardment from the outside and both tremors and earthquakes from within have heaved us into a new century and onto the threshold of new challenges. In the traditional order, in a positivist view of reality, our questions confronted what we took to be an objective and singular reality. We believed in truth that we could all learn and share. Today, most of us no longer believe that there is a single reality; we speak of learning as a mediation or negotiation between a posited reality and our subjective histories and experiences. Holistic faculty development describes a supple and integrated system of support that takes into account our multiple, and often conflicting, realities and enables us once again to take the risks necessary to pursue creativity in our professional lives. The challenge facing us on our campuses is to acknowledge the productive tension both within and among us and, through dialogue and ongoing reflection, to create the components of a support system that fosters our individual, communal, and even institutional needs and realities. Holistic faculty development describes a process rather than an outcome—a constant becoming rather than an achieved end.

In the past, many leaders have attempted to play it safe by avoiding the hard questions. Faculty development has been relegated to a benign or custodial role, located in a peripheral site, poorly supported, and low in profile. However, in the light of numerous studies, such as the American Association for Higher Education's *Heeding New Voices: Academic Careers for a New Generation* (Rice, Sorcinelli, & Austin, 2000), we now know, by virtue of more than our personal experiences, that the future of the profession requires new commitments and new pathways if we are to continue to develop as teachers, scholars, and administrators.

What could such a faculty development look like? From an organizational point of view, faculty development could become the rubric under which all academic needs are accessed. Faculty could come to a central place on campus for support in grant writing, for teaching consultations, and to discuss the appropriate pedagogical role that technology might play in a new course under consideration. Faculty could meet both formally for workshops and consultation, and informally, to review library, media, portfolio, or other materials, and to brainstorm with colleagues about all facets of their work.

On an ideological and substantive level, faculty development could be just that. It could engage all willing faculty from the beginning of their careers in self-conscious acts of personal and professional development—not, as I said in *Liberal Education* (1999), as faculty development that is done to us but one that we do for ourselves. Faculty could organize retreats, orientations, workshops, book groups, and multi-purposed sessions in which we take up and examine the challenges of our everyday lives as teachers and scholars on our particular campuses. With the awareness of our intellectual and affective natures, we could devise programs and opportunities that plumb not only our knowledge but our values and those of our institutions. When we explore our and others' belief systems and the demands made upon them, we gain better understanding of our own and others' decisions and actions. By finding time and making opportunities together for reflection and change, we might recover some of the idealism and gratification that have been lost as our earlier dreams have succumbed to the realities of our current professional lives.

It is a commonplace of educational developers today to recommend that faculty members organize and construct our courses by setting goals. We are told to ask ourselves, "What do we want our students to take away from our classes?" We are advised to work backwards from desired outcomes in order to create diverse and appropriate assignments to engage the interests and promote the success of all kinds of learners. A holistic understanding of faculty development asks of us what we ask of our students. How many of us have asked ourselves what we want to take away from this enterprise we call our faculty lives? What are the objectives that we can pursue over time to achieve our goals? How do we construct diverse and fruitful assignments that engage our intellects and our passions at the different stages of our lives while enabling us to move toward our goals? By asking and re-asking the hard questions, faculty development metaphorically can become the framework for our own personal portfolios. This is not solely the portfolio for promotion and tenure but the integrated portfolio, extending over a career, that reveals and describes the trajectory of our faculty lives: our evolving philosophies of teaching and education; our risks, failures, and accomplishments; our reflections on lessons learned; and most of all, the evidence of our impact on other people's lives.

A truly holistic faculty development could provide the blueprint for building a new community of higher education. This time, with our 20/20 hindsight, we can engineer our "building" on a solid but flexible foundation to enable the inevitable rocking to and fro. By careful planning, our structure can be deeper, more resilient, and more responsive to the forces that challenge it. This new approach seems to be underway among the members of the Associated New American Colleges (ANAC). These campuses, guided by principles of holism and integration, are creating new structures to stand in lieu of the traditional ones. Following a study of faculty perceptions and a year-long think tank involving faculty, deans, and provosts at 19 member institutions, they are taking into account the changing stages and needs of faculty lives by recommending a faculty professional model that integrates teaching, research, and service responsibilities in complementary ways.

We in the academy have been taught to criticize and break down—to find the cracks, the holes in other people's arguments, and only too often, in other people. Our hour in the sun, like graduate students' vying to direct their insights back to the professor in a seminar, often comes from our inculcated habit to compete rather than to learn from others. It is time for us, like our undergraduate students whom we teach to work in collaborative, interdependent groups, and like this new ANAC project shows, to come together in new mutually edifying ways.

In my article in *Liberal Education* (1999), I referred to much of what goes on in the academy as the behaviors of a dysfunctional family. Nevertheless, there is a clear difference. Unlike family affiliations, we have chosen to be here and we can choose to become accountable to one another in self- and mutually affirming ways. Rather than see ourselves in traditional familial roles (faculty squeezed between administration and students, and other equally uncomfortable sand-wiched combinations that we can all recount), through holistic facul-ty development we can create new models for abiding together. We can come together as adults, accepting that we are no longer the "kids," and that we, all of us, are the system. Disbelieving and pow-erless though we may initially feel, it is time to take up the responsi-bility we ask our students to assume. By examining and questioning our own and our institutional values on a regular basis, we can work to change what undermines collegiality on our campuses. It is always easy to stand on the outside and complain. As academics and critics, it is what we often do best. What is more, it has become fashionable to be on the margin. However, this is no longer sufficient. Coming inside and building community together does not preclude having our own voices heard. By listening to others—the plurality of voices, and their silences—we earn the right, and we stand a better chance, of having our voices deeply heard and counted.

CONCLUSION

What I have been arguing is a fuller explication of what I wrote in my piece in *Liberal Education:*

> A holistic approach to faculty development requires not solely attention to quality teaching or the individual teacher, but a focus on teaching within the greater context of values espoused and demonstrated in the institution. Faculty devel-opment then becomes not necessarily or solely a place, a cen-ter for gathering over teaching issues, but an attitude and infrastructure undergirding the whole venture of higher edu-cation. (1999, p. 35)

The tension of "becoming" means dedicating ourselves, our insti-tutions, and our students to constant introspection and reevaluation. This heightened awareness energizes us and enables us to reach the emotional highs we feel when we can encourage ourselves and others to do our best. We, like our students, remain works in progress, living in the present but ever mindful of our futures. The challenge then—for all of us—is not to squelch the healthy tension, that dynamic dise-quilibrium, but to constantly use it to work toward the understand-ing, connecting, advocating, legitimizing, integrating, and communi-cating that defines our humanity and which is at the core of our fac-ulty lives.

REFERENCES

Amirault, C. (1995). The good teacher, the good student: Identifications of a student teacher. In J. Gallop (Ed.), *Pedagogy: The question of impersonation* (pp. 64-78). Bloomington, IN: Indiana University Press.

Baiocco, S. A., & DeWaters, J. N. (1998). A perverted academic reward system. In *Successful college teaching: Problem-solving strategies of distinguished professors* (pp. 44-48). Boston, MA: Allyn & Bacon.

Bourdieu, P., & Passeron, J-C. (1970). *Reproduction in education, society, and culture.* (R. Nice, Trans.). Newbury Park, CA: Sage.

Dey, E. L., Ramirez, C. E., Korn, W. S., & Astin, A. W. (1993). *The American college teacher: National norms for the 1992-1993 HERI faculty survey.* Los Angeles, CA: University of California, Graduate School of Education, Higher Education Research Institute.

Dinham, S. M. (1999a). Being a newcomer. In R. J. Menges & Associates (Ed.), *Faculty in new jobs: A guide to settling in, becoming established, and building institutional support* (pp. 1-15). San Francisco, CA: Jossey-Bass.

Dinham, S. M. (1999b). New faculty talk about stress. In R. J. Menges & Associates (Ed.), *Faculty in new jobs: A guide to settling in, becoming established, and building institutional support* (pp. 39-58). San Francisco, CA: Jossey-Bass.

Graf, D. L., & Wheeler, D. W. (1996). *Defining the field: The POD membership survey.* Ames, IA: Iowa State University, POD Network.

Kennedy, D. (1997). *Academic duty.* Cambridge, MA: Harvard University Press.

Menges, R. J., & Associates. (Ed.). (1999). *Faculty in new jobs: A guide to settling in, becoming established, and building institutional support.* San Francisco, CA: Jossey-Bass.

Mintz, J. (1994). Challenging values: Conflict, contradiction, and pedagogy. *To Improve the Academy, 13,* 177-190.

Mintz, J. (1997, Fall). Recruiting students and telling the whole story about teaching. *The College Board Review, 182.*

Mintz, J. (1999, Spring). Faculty development and teaching: A holistic approach. *Liberal Education, 32-37.*

Palmer, P. J. (1993). *To know as we are known: Education as a spiritual journey.* San Francisco, CA: Harper.

Rice, R. E., Sorcinelli, M. D., & Austin, A. E. (2000). *Heeding new voices: Academic careers for a new generation.* New Pathways Working Paper Series. Washington, DC: American Association for Higher Education.

Tompkins, J. (1992, November/December). The way we live now. *Change,* 12-19.

Wheatley, M. J. (1992). *Leadership and the new science: Learning about organization from an orderly universe.* San Francisco, CA: Herrett-Koehler.

Whitt, E. J. (1991). Hit the ground running: Experiences of new faculty in a school of education. *Review of Higher Education, 14* (2), 177-197.

Wilson, R. (2001, January 5). A higher bar for earning tenure. *The Chronicle of Higher Education,* pp. A12-14.

11

INSTITUTIONAL GOVERNANCE: A CALL FOR COLLABORATIVE DECISION-MAKING IN AMERICAN HIGHER EDUCATION

Thomas C. Longin

In an era of rapid and widespread change in nearly all areas of human experience, especially in American society, the once vaunted status of American higher education is being seriously questioned, even doubted. Indeed, the future of this "precious treasure" is often described of late in cataclysmic terms. The doubts expressed about the future of higher education, especially the inadequacies attributed to its current decision-making processes, have led me, in my work with governing boards, presidents, and faculty, to approach the issue with a set of questions intended not only to spark attention but also to heighten a sense of urgency. Let me, then, begin here with those same questions.

- In these challenging times, have governing boards become obsolete?
- Does the rapidly changing social and educational environment make shared governance obsolete?
- Are contemporary president and chancellors sufficiently savvy, skilled, bold, and visionary to lead institutions beset with so many challenges? If so, whose support do they most need if they are to be highly effective?
- Do presidents and chancellors really want effective boards?

- Do governing boards and presidents really want faculty to be effective participants in institutional governance? If so, what steps are they willing to take to ensure faculty effectiveness?
- Can informed, skilled, and committed governing boards, presidents, and faculty be effective collaborators in institutional governance? If so, then how might such collaboration best be achieved?

HIGHER EDUCATION AND A RAPIDLY CHANGING ENVIRONMENT

The drivers of change that we have all committed to memory—and about which many people tire of hearing—have and will continue to modify significantly, maybe even change radically, the environment in which we live and work and the ways in which faculty and the institution to which they are dedicated will carry out their educational goals and missions. Let me briefly list these powerful forces.

- Changing student profile and changing demographics
- Constrained resources
- Shifting and changing public expectations of higher education
- Significant paradigm shift from a teacher-oriented to a learner-centered education
- Intensifying, even destructive, competition from within and without higher education
- Sweeping changes in information technology the likes and impact of which we have not known in higher education in the last 50 years—technology with the power to enhance higher education's effectiveness extensively, but also with the capacity to make many of higher education's practices, and possibly its institutions, obsolete
- A pace and range of change that has markedly increased in the last quarter century, and consequences of change that appear awesome even as we struggle to assess them.

Somewhat surprisingly, from all quarters come various criticisms of nearly every aspect of higher education: access and availability; cost and price; failure to take seriously the new learning imperative; lack of effective integration of technology; lavish patterns of faculty work and lack of faculty productivity; misguided allocation of valuable resources; poor student performance and the lack of basic competency; "bloated" administrative staffing; embattled, constricted, or ineffectual leadership; and a cumbersome, archaic governance structure. And then comes the punch line.

> The main reason why institutions have not taken more effective action is their outmoded governance structure—i.e., the decision-making units, policies, and practices that control resource allocation have remained largely unchanged since the structure's establishment in the 19th century . . . One of our strongest recommendations is that institutional restructuring, including mission differentiation, be made a national priority . . . We believe that colleges and universities must make major organizational changes. To do so, their governance systems must be changed so that they can reallocate scarce resources and permit fundamental reform in the way they do business. (Commission on National Investment in Higher Education, 1997, p. 12)

To be sure, the American people in general consistently pay tribute to the value of a college education and to the institutions that provide it. Yet, specific criticisms abound, and many people—even many friends—question higher education's will to serve more effectively, and then doubt its capacity to change, even if the will exists.

THE GOVERNANCE PROBLEM

While most critics agree that restructuring higher education is essential, they caution that it is neither a short-term nor a simple process. They then conclude that neither presidents nor boards have the expertise or inclination to take on leadership challenges of the duration, intensity, and complexity required for restructuring efforts to be successful. Critics also argue that shared governance is doomed to failure because it requires informed and institutionally oriented faculty participation. Simply stated, many observers contend that faculty lack the necessary information, training and/or education, and professional disposition to be effective, efficient participants in a governance process which must focus on fundamental issues of mission, structure, programs, people, and resource allocation with a sense of urgency and decisiveness.

Good governance involves collectively making authoritative decisions about how to allocate scarce resources among competing interests and ensuring that these decisions are legitimate because they have been reached through participation and consultation rather than coercion (Greer, 1997). Drawing on extensive experience with current institutional governance practices and the problems that need solution, Roger Benjamin and Steve Carroll have evolved a credible and appealing list of attributes for effective governance in the twenty-first century (1998).

- Mission-driven
- Grounded in strategic planning and budgeting, a focus on priorities
- Contextual
- Open
- Participatory
- Shared, or better yet collaborative
- Decisive: Compels or facilitates implementation
- Iterative
- Based on comparative, institution-wide criteria and information

However, current governance structures and processes lack these attributes. They were set up to effect decision-making about the distribution of resources during a time of growth. They were developed to protect the status quo, especially traditional faculty values and authority (see especially the American Association for University Professor's (AAUP) *Statement on Government of Colleges and Universities* (Kreiser, 1990)). They were built incrementally on top of a higher education enterprise that was largely private and highly autonomous. They emphasize centralized authority and regulation, a command and response administrative style, and management of constituents—all of which inhibit rather than enhance constituent accountability.

Commentators on governance issues consistently suggest that boards, administrators, and faculty have too little time to focus on major institutional issues. Many of these same critics observe that boards and faculty have too little knowledge and understanding of the essential relationship between the nature, range, and quality of academic programs, the allocation of scarce resources, and sustaining institutional vitality to play effective roles in institutional planning and decision-making.

Other critics simply lay the problem at the feet of presidents. They argue that too few presidents or chancellors see themselves as agents of change, then contend that fewer still are inclined toward the level of risk-taking necessary to be effective leaders in a rapidly changing economic and educational environment.

No matter how one views the problem, the conclusion is essentially the same: The time has come to call the three major governance constituents to a more informed, sensitive, and substantive engagement with their institutions through the governance process, especially its planning and institutional decision-making components.

No longer is it appropriate to say that boards best serve institutions by limiting their focus to fiscal matters or to say that faculty should only focus on academic affairs. No longer is it acceptable, either, for anxious boards, fearful presidents, or untrusting faculty to urge other governance players to keep a respectful distance from the critical strategic activities of the institution. Governing boards, administrators, and faculty simply must play an active and collaborative leadership role in institutional planning and decision-making.

In issuing this challenge to increase board and faculty engagement with institutional governance, it is important, at the same time, to offer an essential caveat. The magnitude and complexity of the problems faced by higher education in no way justify board micromanagement of institutional operations or faculty veto of action through interminable procedural delays; rather, they require a new, more informed level of board involvement with the institution's people, programs, and processes and faculty participation in the strategic aspects of institutional decision-making. Indeed, the threats from within and without call for a more open, participatory, and timely decision-making process—a truly collaborative process—in which major stakeholders participate in the planning and decision-making process to an extent consistent with their articulated responsibilities for the welfare of the institution.

Significant reform—or, as the field has come to know it, transformation—of nearly all aspects of higher education is essential if it is to meet the learning needs of an increasingly diverse and often underprepared student population. Such intentional change must respond to a world where learning has replaced teaching as the measure of educational quality, where the consumer (the learner), rather than the producer (the institution, the faculty), drives the educational process, and where survival in the face of a raft of new competitors and in the context of a challenging global economy will require Herculean efforts.

Recognizing the necessity of change, institutional governance on each campus or for each system must be rethought and redefined to ensure informed, effective, and timely decision-making on the major issues confronting the institution. All governance activity must be focused on decision-making related to pressing issues faced by the institution and to priorities established for the institution through a participatory planning process. The roles and responsibilities of the major participants in the planning process, whether they are internal or external constituents, must be clarified.

Major constituent groups must be oriented and educated to become informed and effective participants in a collaborative governance process that is institutionally and strategically focused, broadly participatory, and sensitively responsive and efficient. All participants in institutional governance must understand and be committed to widespread sharing of information, open communication, appropriate consultation, clear delineation of the locus of decision-making on various strategic issues, mutually agreed-upon methods for resolving conflicts and deadlocks, and specified accountability for decision-making, operational/administrative activities, and institutional change.

REEMPOWERING THE MAJOR CONSTITUENTS

Despite hearing constantly from faculty and board members that they feel powerless in their respective governance roles, as well as from presidents concerning their frustrations with trustee, faculty, and administration involvement and inaction in governance, I am convinced that this apparent gridlock can be resolved if the leading players really want to make governance work. If governance is to be a meaningful and consequential activity for trustees, faculty, and administrations, all parties need to recognize that some serious dysfunctions and malfunctions will need to be overcome. Indeed, these flaws must be recognized, examined, and fixed or all the best efforts of the major constituents will only lead to greater frustration and increased dysfunctionality in the face of the powerful forces of change that are evident all around us.

The new academic compact proposed here by the Associated New

American Colleges (ANAC) has from my perspective, in both its reasoned analysis and its persuasive recommendations, the capacity to serve as the foundation and an impetus for breaking the chains of the old governance model—a model built on a separation of powers and an unworkable system of checks and balances—and moving the major constituents forward together into a new era of collaborative, effective, timely, and productive decision-making.

The faculty do and will continue to play a central role in the institutional quest for mission fulfillment. They do so first and foremost through the creation and dissemination of the knowledge students need to perform well in their work and to live as responsible citizens in a rapidly changing society. They also carry out this essential role through the development of higher order learning, communication, and interactive skills that are critical to living and working effectively in this challenging information age.

If faculty are central to the learning enterprise and if the faculty role in this changing endeavor is likely to change even more radically, then faculty, administrators, and governing boards ought to be striving to find ways for faculty to play more purposeful, meaningful, and consequential roles in defining their professional careers, shaping the components of their work, and participating in institutional decision-making related not only to curriculum, programs, and pedagogy, but also to institutional mission, vision, fiscal integrity, and academic quality.

FROM GRIDLOCK TO COLLABORATION: IMPORTANT FIRST STEPS

Clearly, the new compact proposed by the Associated New American Colleges—or something very much like it—is essential for American higher education's success in fulfilling its mission in the society of the early twenty-first century. It is not only a compelling assessment of the need for significant change, but also an enlightened formulation of the need to reconnect faculty life, work, and spirit to the mission, programs, and cultural dynamic of the institutions they serve. Based on my own work with faculty governance across some 25 years, and my more recent work with governing boards, presidents, and institutional governance, I would highlight three essential themes in the proposal.

Given that faculty are central to the achievement of higher education's mission and given that responsible engagement by faculty members in a myriad of instructional and learning support activities, as well as in institutional decision-making is essential, then boards, administrations, and faculty must move quickly beyond lip service in recognizing, nurturing, and rewarding these activities. Indeed, they must quickly move to purposeful, constructive, and systematic allocation of resources to support such faculty activity.

How might they do this? Simply stated, by mutually—that is, in a collaborative manner—identifying essential faculty responsibilities and activities, setting clear expectations for the fulfillment of these responsibilities, ensuring faculty development opportunities and services to support these efforts, rigorously and supportively assessing progress toward accomplishing goals and fulfilling expectations, and finally, substantively recognizing and rewarding these contributions to the attainment of institutional missions.

It is time to rethink and reshape the structures and processes by which institutions of higher education make critical institutional decisions. If such a transformation does not occur, the major constituents are destined to go on being frustrated with efforts to make what now passes for shared governance work, and worse yet, to fail in those important efforts to bring a sense of ownership to important resource allocation decisions upon which the quality of education and the future of institutions depend.

PERSONAL OBSERVATIONS

Before concluding, let me briefly share several insights about governance gleaned from four years of intense involvement with governing boards and their responsibilities for institutional governance.

The process that we have traditionally called shared governance, though sound in principle, has been seriously flawed in practice. The flaw should be obvious to any close observer. We speak of shared or collaborative decision-making, but we too often practice a rigorous separation of powers, a system of checks and balances, and a sometimes hostile defense of turf in our daily institutional lives. It should not take a Montesquieu, Jefferson, or contemporary scholar of political systems to tell us that, well-intentioned as we might have been, we have created governance or decision-making silos that stand as obstacles to information sharing, to understanding different perspectives, and to a truly collaborative process of decision-making.

Only when trustees, administrators, and faculty face a crisis—usually of the fiscal variety—and find that they must work together (now under the most stressful of conditions), or now and again when together they engage in strategic or institutional planning, do these major constituents clearly focus attention on first-order institutional priorities, that is, mission, vision, quality of academic programs, and the integrity of financial or resource allocation systems. Think for a moment about how operational rather than strategic are some of the best efforts of dedicated governance participants: The governing board spending most of its valuable time replicating the organization and work of the administration in its committee structure and use of meeting time—and only sporadically focusing its attention on mission, vision, and the institutional priorities that arise from a well-conceived planning process. Faculty members enthusiastically developing programs or refining existing curricula based primarily on their disciplinary interests and commitments but with little attention to the institution's precarious position in a volatile and competitive academic marketplace or to the reality of the institution's constrained fiscal circumstances.

I could go on with numerous such sad examples. The fact is higher education speaks the language of shared institutional decision-making, but too often the major players revert to sacred silos of influence when making decisions or acting on them. Such archaic behavior simply will not keep America's institutions of higher education attractive, exciting, agile, responsive, responsible, and, ultimately, viable. Indeed, it will likely lead to their demise.

CONCLUSION

In the final analysis, when it comes to providing first-rate higher education in a rapidly changing socioeconomic environment, current governance structures and processes are obstacles to informed, thoughtful, effective, and timely decision-making about issues and priorities critical to the future of the institution and the larger enterprise. Yes, the time has come to identify and develop new governance structures and processes—ones consistent with institutional mission, culture, and traditions, but not rigidly limited by past assumptions and antiquated practice.

And, if higher education believes that it should model what it teaches and if it is serious about making institutional governance the platform for informed, effective, and timely decision-making, then the process of change cannot simply be left to chance. Indeed, as educators, the leaders of higher education—boards, presidents, and faculty—must attend to this learning challenge with no less intelligence, rigor, and sense of responsibility than would be committed to the creation of a new course, the development of an exciting program, or the execution of a $100 million comprehensive campaign.

Make no mistake, the future of each institution of higher education depends on the capacity of its constituents—that is, their collaborative ability and shared commitment—to transform the way in which they relate to each other as professionals and members of the community, their capacity to transform the way in which they organize themselves to make those decisions critical to institutional vitality and viability, and their capacity to transform the ways in which they recognize and reward individual and unit contributions to fulfillment of institutional mission. Yes, the time has come when the major constituents of America's institutions of higher education can no longer let self-interest, organizational silos, or an adversarial spirit drive them to the defense of turf. They must, instead, join in respectful, collaborative efforts directed toward defining the essence of their work, and then making crucial program quality and resource allocation decisions that will successfully impel their institutions into a challenging but exciting future.

REFERENCES

Association of Governing Boards of Universities and Colleges. (1996). *Renewing the academic presidency: Stronger leadership for tougher times.* Washington, DC: Association of Governing Boards.

Association of Governing Boards of Universities and Colleges. (1998). *AGB statement on institutional governance.* Washington, DC: Association of Governing Boards.

Benjamin, R., & Carroll, S. (1998). The implications of the changed environment for governance in higher education. In W. G. Tierney (Ed.), *The responsive university* (pp. 92-114). Baltimore, MD: The Johns Hopkins University Press.

Commission on National Investment in Higher Education. (1997). *Breaking the social contract.* New York, NY: Council for Aid to Education.

Greer, D. G. (1997). *Prospective governance.* AGB Occasional Paper, No. 31. Washington, DC: Association of Governing Boards.

Kreiser, B. R. (Ed.). (1990). *AAUP policy documents and reports.* Washington, DC: American Association of University Professors.

Bibliography

General

Astin, A. W. (1994). Higher education reform and citizenship: A question of values. *Perspectives: The New American College, 24* (2), 79-91.

Barr, R. B., & Tagg, J. (1995). From teaching to learning: A new paradigm for undergraduate education. *Change, 27,* 13-25.

Bennett, J. B. (1998). *Collegial professionalism: The academy, individualism, and the common good.* Phoenix, AZ: American Council on Education/Oryx Press.

Berberet, J. (1999). The professorate and institutional citizenship: Toward a scholarship of service. *Liberal Education, 85,* 32-39.

Bergquist, W. H. (1992). *The four cultures of the academy.* San Francisco, CA: Jossey-Bass.

Boyer, E. (1990). *Scholarship reconsidered: Priorities of the professorate.* Princeton, NJ: The Carnegie Foundation for the Advancement of Teaching.

Denham, R., Kramsch, C., Phelps, L., Rassias, J., Slevin, J., & Swaffar, J. (1996). Making faculty work visible: Reinterpreting professional service, teaching, and research in the fields of language and literature. [Modern Language Association Commission on Professional Service Report.] *Profession,* 161-216.

Diamond, R. M., & Adam, B. E. (1993). Recognizing faculty work: Reward systems for the year 2000. *New Directions for Higher Education, No. 81.* San Francisco, CA: Jossey-Bass.

Diamond, R. M., & Adam, B. E. (1995). *The disciplines speak: Rewarding the scholarly, professional, and creative work of faculty.* Washington, DC: American Association for Higher Education.

Edgerton, R. (1997). *Higher education white paper.* Philadelphia, PA: The Pew Charitable Trusts.

Ewell, P. T. (1999). Imitation as art: Borrowed management techniques in higher education. *Change, 31,* 10-15.

Fairweather, J. S. (1993). *Teaching, research, and faculty rewards: A summary of the research findings of the faculty profile project.* State College, PA: The National Center of Postsecondary Teaching, Learning, and Assessment.

Gappa, J. M., & Leslie, D. W. (1993). *The invisible faculty: Improving the status of part-timers in higher education.* San Francisco, CA: Jossey-Bass.

Gillilannd, M. W. (1997). Organizational change and tenure: We can learn from the corporate experience. *Change, 29,* 30-34.

Glassick, C. E., Huber, M. T., & Maeroff, G. I. (1997). *Scholarship assessed: Evaluation of the professorate.* San Francisco, CA: Jossey-Bass.

Holt, M., & Anderson, L. (1998). The way we work now. *Profession,* 131-42.

Kotter, J. P. (1995, March/April). Leading change: Why transformation efforts fail. *Harvard Business Review,* 59-67.

Massy, W. F., & Wilger, A. K. (1995). Improving productivity: What faculty think about it—and it's effect on quality. *Change, 27,* 11-20.

Menzel, P. (1999, Spring). Liberal education and the new American college. *Prism,* 9-11.

O'Banion, T. (1997). *A learning college for the twenty-first century.* Annapolis Junction, MD: Community College Press.

Park, S. M. (1996). Research, teaching, and service: Why shouldn't women's work count? *Journal of Higher Education, 67* (1), 46-84.

Plater, W. M. (1995). Future work: Faculty and time in the 21st century. *Change, 27,* 2-33.

Reed, C. (1999). *Facing change: Building the faculty of the future.* Washington, DC: American Association of State Colleges and Universities.

Rice, E. (1996). *Making a place for the new American scholar.* American Association for Higher Education New Pathways Working Paper Series. Washington, DC: American Association for Higher Education.

Schuster, J. H. (1995, Fall). Whither the faculty? The changing academic labor market. *Educational Record*, 28-33.

Shulman, L. (1997). Professing the liberal arts. In R. Orrill (Ed.), *Education and democracy: Re-imagining liberal learning in America* (pp. 151-175). New York, NY: The College Board.

Tierney, W. G. (1997). Organizational socialization in higher education. *Journal of Higher Education, 68,* 1-16.

Tierney, W. G. (Ed.). (1998). *The responsive university: Restructuring for high performance.* Baltimore, MD: The John Hopkins University Press.

Tierney, W. G. (1999). *Building the responsive campus: Creating high performance colleges and universities.* Thousand Oaks, CA: Sage.

Tierney, W. G., & Bensimon, E. M. (1996). *Promotion and tenure: Community and socialization in academe.* New York, NY: State University of New York Press.

Wong, F. (1994). Primary care education: A new American college model. *Perspectives: The New American College, 24* (2), 13-26.

Differentiating Faculty Workload

Abdelal, A. T., Blumenfeld, D. C., Crimmins, T. J., & Dresse, P. L. (1997). Integrating accountability systems and reward structures: Workload policy, post-tenure evaluations, and salary compensation. *Metropolitan Universities, 7,* 61-73.

Allison, R. D., & Scott, D. C. (1998). Faculty compensation and obligation: The necessity of a new approach triggered by technology integration. *New Directions for Community Colleges, 101,* 69-78.

Braskamp, L. A. & Ory, J. C. (1994). *Assessing faculty work: Enhancing individual and institutional performance.* San Francisco, CA: Jossey-Bass.

Chait, R. (1998). *Ideas in incubation: Three possible modifications to the traditional tenure policies.* Washington, DC: American Association for Higher Education.

Diamond, R. M. (1999). *Aligning faculty rewards with institutional mission: Statements, policies, and guidelines.* Bolton, MA: Anker.

Krahenbuhl, G. S. (1997). *The integration of faculty responsibilities and institutional needs* (online). Available:
http:// clasdean.la.asu.edu/dean/ Krahenbuhl/

Krahenbuhl, G. S. (1998). Faculty work: Integrating responsibility and institutional needs. *Change, 30,* 18-25.

McMahon, J. D., & Caret, R. L. (1997). Redesigning the faculty roles and rewards structure. *Metropolitan Universities, 7,* 11-22.

Meyer, K. (1998). *Faculty workload studies: Perspectives, needs, and future directions.* (ASHE-ERIC Higher Education Report, Vol. 26, No. 1). Washington, DC: ERIC Clearinghouse on Higher Education.

Wergin, J. F. (1994a). *The collaborative department: How five campuses are inching toward cultures of collective responsibility.* Washington, DC: American Association for Higher Education.

Wergin, J. F. (Ed.). (1994b). Analyzing faculty workload. New *Directions for Institutional Research, No. 83.* San Francisco, CA: Jossey-Bass.

Wergin, J. F. (1999, December). Evaluating department achievements: Consequences for the work of the faculty. *American Association for Higher Education Bulletin,* 3-6.

Governance and Institutional Service

AAUP Committee A on Academic Freedom and Tenure. (1999). On collegiality as a criterion for faculty evaluation. *Academe, 85* (5), 69-70.

Association of Governing Boards. (1996). *Renewing the academic presidency: Stronger leadership for tougher times.* Report of the Commission on the Academic Presidency. Washington, DC: Association of Governing Boards.

Association of Governing Boards. (1998). *AGB statement on institutional governance.* Washington, DC: Association of Governing Boards.

Bannister, G., & Bacon, P. A. (1999). From competitive to collaborative governance. *Trusteeship, 7,* 8-13.

Bogue, E. G. (1998). The goodness guerrilla. *Trusteeship, 6,* 25-28.

Carlisle, B. A., & Miller, M. T. (1998). *Current trends and practices of faculty involvement in governance.* Washington, DC: ERIC Clearinghouse on Higher Education.

Elman, S. E. & Smock, S. M. (1985). *Professional service and faculty rewards: Toward an integrated structure.* Washington, DC: National Association of State Universities and Land-Grant Colleges.

Gerber, L. G. (1997). Reaffirming the value of shared governance. *Academe, 83,* 14-18.

Greer, D. G. (1997). *Prospective governance.* Association of Governing Boards Occasional Paper, No. 31. Washington, DC: Association of Governing Boards.

Guffey, J. S., & Ramp, L. C. (1997). *Shared governance: Balancing the euphoria.* State University, AR: Arkansas State University. (ERIC Document Reproduction Service No. ED 418 617)

Johnstone, D. B., Dye, N. S., & Johnson, R. (1998). Collaborative leadership for institutional change. *Liberal Education, 84,* 12-19.

Lynton, E. (1995). *Making the case for professional service.* Washington, DC: American Association for Higher Education.

Miller, M. A. (1998). Let's not grind the works to a halt. *Trusteeship, 6,* 20-24.

Ramo, K. (1997). Reforming shared governance: Do the arguments hold up? *Academe, 83,* 38-43.

Twale, D. J., & Shannon, D. M. (1996). Gender differences among faculty in campus governance: Nature of involvement, satisfaction, and power. *Initiatives, 57,* 11-19.

Faculty Development and Career Stages

Angelo, T. A. (1994a, June). From faculty development to academic development. *American Association for Higher Education Bulletin,* 3-7.

Angelo, T. A. (1994b). Transformative faculty development. In T. O'Banion & Associates (Ed.), *Teaching and learning in the community college* (pp. 115-142). Washington, DC: American Association of Community Colleges.

Austin, A., Rice, E., Splete, A., & Associates. (1991). *A good place to work: Sourcebook for the academic workplace.* Washington, DC: Council of Independent Colleges.

Baiocco, S. A, & DeWaters, J. N. (1998). Futuristic faculty development: Toward a comprehensive program. In *Successful college teaching: Problem solving strategies of distinguished professors* (pp. 248-277). Boston, MA: Allyn & Bacon.

Bland, C. J., & Bergquist, W. H. (1997). *The vitality of senior faculty members: Snow on the roof—fire in the furnace.* (ASHE-ERIC Higher Education Report, Vol. 25, No. 7). Washington, DC: ERIC Clearinghouse on Higher Education.

Edgerton, R. (1998, Winter). Universities, schools, and the story of education. *On Common Ground,* 13-15.

Lacey, P. A. (1988). Faculty development and the future of college teaching. *New Directions for Teaching and Learning, No. 33.* San Francisco, CA: Jossey-Bass.

Licklider, B. L., Schnelker, D. L., & Fulton, C. (1997-1998). Revisioning faculty development for changing times: The foundation and framework. *Journal of Staff, Program and Organizational Development, 15,* 121-133.

Liedtka, J. M., Askins, M. E., Rosenblum, J. W., & Weber, J. (1997, Fall). The generative cycle: Linking knowledge and relationships. *Sloan Management Review,* 47-58.

Millis, B. J. (1994). Faculty development in the 1990s: What it is and why we can't wait. *Journal of Counseling and Development, 72,* 454-464.

Mintz, J. A. (1999, Spring). Faculty development and teaching: A holistic approach. *Liberal Education, 32-37.*

Sorcinelli, M. D. (1994). Effective approaches to new faculty development. *Journal of Counseling and Development, 72,* 474-478.

Tierney, W. G. (1998). Improving life on the tenure track: An organizational framework. *The Department Chair, 8* (1), 18-19.

Zahorski, K. J. (1993). Taking the lead: Faculty development as institutional change agent. *To Improve the Academy, 12,* 227-245.

Sources on the Web

American Association for Higher Education (AAHE)
Includes links to the Faculty Roles and Reward Project. (http://www.aahe.org/)

American Association of Colleges and Universities
Describes projects and publications. Also includes The Knowledge Network, a start on a metapage for web sources on undergraduate education. (http://www.aacu-edu.org/home.html)

American Association of State Colleges and Universities
This organization has also sponsored a study of faculty work. The report of their project, *Facing Change: Building the Faculty of the Future,* can be downloaded here. (http://www.aascu.org/)

American Association of University Professors (AAUP)
Descriptions of programs and publications. Includes index of policy statements on faculty work, workload, tenure, and so on. (http://www.aaup.org/index.htm).

Associated New American Colleges (ANAC)
Includes a link to this project's web site. (http://anac.vir.org/)
Council of Independent Colleges
Describes projects and publications. At this site one can download a copy of the report *Reconsidering Faculty Roles and Rewards* which summarizes results of a three-year CAPHE program in which 22 colleges and universities received grants to explore ways to clarify emerging new relationships between institutional mission and priorities and faculty roles and rewards. (http://www.cic.edu/)
Educational Resources Information Center (ERIC)
Comprehensive database/clearinghouse for educational-related literature. Includes links to indices, publications, and other relevant web sites. ASH-ERIC publication series has produced several volumes on faculty work. (http://eriche.org/)
Harvard Project on Faculty Appointments
A web site for one of the American Association for Higher Education (AAHE) New Pathways Projects run by Richard Chait and focused on tenure. (http://gseweb.harvard.edu/~hpfa/)
New England Resource Center for Higher Education
More links to publications and resources. Emphasis on faculty service. Includes an online newsletter, *The Academic Workplace.*
(http://www.nerche.org/index.html)
Re-Envisioning the PhD
A project at the University of Washington sponsored by the Pew Charitable Trusts to foster a national dialogue on graduate education reform for the twenty-first century. (http://depts.washington.edu/envision/)

Index